What people are saying...

"The key to success is building long-term, mutually beneficial relationships with your customers. Selling must be done at every level of the organization—not just in the sales department. *State of the Art Selling* provides an excellent road map to make this happen."

J.W. Marriott, Jr., Marriott Hotels

"A terrific book on the importance of partnership selling in today's competitive environment."

Bob Puette, president, Apple U.S.A., Apple Computer, Inc.

"*State of the Art Selling* is terrific. I was amazed at how chock full of information this book is, and at its depth and insight. I learned an enormous amount about the qualities that set apart successful sales people and their companies."

Success magazine

"It's a knockout! *State of the Art Selling* will help anyone improve their business and selling skills with hundreds of real-world ideas and techniques from the best in the business."

Bob Arum, chairman of the board, Top Rank, Inc.

"*State of the Art Selling* is truly a joy to read. It is filled with true life stories that are sure to be invaluable to all who read and apply a small portion of what they learned."

Michael T. Stramaglio, vice president—sales and marketing Minolta Corporation

"*State of the Art Selling* contains a rare collection of ideas that you wish you had thought of yourself first. Reading this book gives you the distinct feeling of stepping into a mental gym where you are challenged to achieve your own sales breakthrough."

Personal Selling Power magazine

"To read the thoughts and stories of some of the best salespeople was very enlightening and interesting. I highly recommend for anyone in sales to read this book."

Franco Harris, former Pittsburgh Steeler and 1990 Hall of Famer, and now with Super Bakery, Inc.

"Peak performance is more critical than ever to top sales professionals in the tumultuous 1990s. Men and women in sales must be mentally, physically and emotionally prepared to meet the requirements of an extraordinarily demanding profession. *State of the Art Selling* provides dozens of valuable ideas and strategies for developing and maintaining peak performance."

Charles A. Garfield, author of *Peak Performance: The New Heroes of American Business*

"*State of the Art Selling* tells it like it is—all meat, no bones."

Sales and Marketing Management magazine

"It's finally happened! Someone has captured the true selling process of today's business environment. The book zeroes in on establishing and building the relationship in a consultative selling situation. It's the best collection of selling strategies I've ever seen. I'm glad it's finally here!"

John P. Burns, vice president of advertising, marketing service and sales training, Tarkett, Inc.

"The book is solid proof that the giants in sales are master people pleasers. Don't miss learning the secrets of those who are passionate about the art of selling."

Danielle Kennedy, author of *Selling—The Danielle Kennedy Way*

"A really useful book that will put money in the pockets of salespeople who follow its guidelines."

Reseller Management Magazine

State
of the
Art
Selling

By
Barry J. Farber

CAREER PRESS
180 Fifth Avenue
P.O. Box 34
Hawthorne, NJ 07507
1-800-CAREER-1
201-427-0229 (outside U.S.)
FAX: 201-427-2037

If you don't get at least one idea from this book that is worth more to you than what you paid, we'll be happy to refund the full purchase price. Just return the book and your sales slip to:

Career Press, 180 Fifth Avenue, P.O. Box 34, Hawthorne, NJ 07507

STATE OF THE ART SELLING

ISBN 1-56414-131-4, $16.95

Cover design by A Good Thing, Inc.

Printed in the U.S.A. by Book-mart Press

To order this title by mail, please include price as noted above, $2.50 handling per order, and $1.00 for each book ordered. Send to: Career Press, Inc., 180 Fifth Ave., P.O. Box 34, Hawthorne, NJ 07507

Or call toll-free 1-800-CAREER-1 (Canada: 201-427-0229) to order using VISA or MasterCard, or for further information on books from Career Press.

Library of Congress Cataloging-in-Publication Data

Farber, Barry J.
    State of the art selling / by Barry J. Farber.
      p. cm.
    Includes bibliographical references (p. 229) and index.
    ISBN 1-56414-131-4 : $16.95
    1. Selling. 2. Sales management--United States. I. Title.
HF5438.25.F373   1994
  658.85--dc20   94-27494
                                                                          CIP

Dedication

To Allison

Special thanks

Special thanks to Joyce Wycoff for her long hours of hard work and creative ideas that made *State of the Art Selling* a reality.

Producing a book is an interesting project—once it's finished and the author's name goes on the cover, it looks like the work of just that author. However, that's almost never the case. There are almost always dozens of people who have spent endless hours listening to the author talk, reading countless drafts and providing untold ideas that wind up in the finished product. The help authors get from their families and friends cannot be overemphasized.

I am extremely grateful to all the people who helped arrange the logistics of the interviews: Sandra Munoz at Federal Express, Dwight Weber, Dave Lane, and Bruce Bunch at GE, Michele Szynac at Gillette, Judy Knipper at Northwestern Mutual, Charlie Lewis at Oracle, Lynne Snead at Franklin International Institute, Kaye Bennett at Upjohn Pharmaceuticals, and Holiday Vaill and Laura Roberts at Pecos River Learning Center.

I am in debt to Richard Farano, Frank Levine, Dave Crestin, David Lubetkin, Sheryl Siegel, Richard Tapp, Lawrence Cohen, Bob Siegel and David Ironson for their tremendous support.

Special thanks to Sy Farber for his creative input and direction and to the people who spent hours reading early manuscripts and helped shape the book—Allison Farber, Amy Metzger, Ruth Gardner, Jeff Herman and Sy Farber.

Contents

Section II

Section III

Section IV

The sales process

"Everybody sells."
—*Bill Razzouk, senior vice president of sales, Federal Express*

Sales is the last profession where the American Dream still prevails. The Bureau of Labor Statistics estimates a total sales force of more than 13 million nationally. Lured by "no-limit" incomes, self-determined hours, the glamour of travel and endless company-paid lunches, many would-be salespeople are mashed down, chewed up and spit-out long before their commissions cover minimum wage.

But the lure remains. Some experts estimate that as many as 100,000 new salespeople enter the labor force each year—replacing others who have been promoted or redirected to different pastures. Like most frontiers, sales is beginning to be tamed and civilized. Although the fringes will always be wild and woolly with bright-eyed youngsters and calloused old-timers, the mainstream of sales is passing into a real profession demanding dedication, education, integrity and abundant amounts of perseverance.

Selling is the backbone of our society. Nothing happens until someone sells something. And, each of us is a salesperson, daily selling our ideas, our beliefs, our capabilities, our services and our products. At Federal Express, the philosophy that everybody sells is actually written into the manager's guide: Every employee must be sales-oriented and each manager must be an outstanding individual salesperson. Federal Express backs this philosophy throughout the organization. Every senior manager, even when she has no direct sales responsibilities, spends time in an assigned sales territory, meeting with customers and developing a better understanding of the customer's needs.

Everybody sells...but not everybody sells well. The purpose of this book is to help you become a state-of-the-art salesperson and break through to a higher level of sales success. Whether you have been selling for 20 years or are just contemplating a career in sales, this book can help you develop the customer-building strategies that it takes to succeed in today's environment. Many of the creative techniques included here can be instantly implemented to help you become more successful. Some of the techniques and philosophies will have to grow on you for a while—you will find yourself developing them slowly, implementing them as you recognize their value and find ways to adapt them to your sales environment.

To help you understand how to make the strategies, tools and tips part of your repertoire, I have interviewed hundreds of salespeople from different industries and from big companies and small—people from each part of the sales process. You will hear stories, techniques, ideas and tips that you can use to build your sales business. Included is a broad spectrum of styles and situations to give you a wide range of choices to fit your needs. *State of the Art Selling* is meant to be a workbook. Activities at the end of each chapter will help you incorporate the techniques into your sales process. I encourage you to underline, highlight, make notes and generally treat this book as a success text.

In the following pages you will meet stars from all parts of the sales process—from sales masters to CEOs; sales training directors to customer service specialists; sales managers to top rookies—you will even hear from customers. Each person brings a slightly different perspective to the sales process and, together, they constitute an enormous wealth of ideas, stories, and experiences.

Associating with successful people is an important part of developing our own success. We not only learn how they achieve success but we also absorb their attitudes and philosophies. The stars you will meet in *State of the Art Selling* are all successful people. For the time it takes you to read this book, you will be associating with some of the most powerful sales stars in the country. You will hear their stories and learn about their successes—and their failures. They will share invaluable insights and techniques learned in their combined hundreds of years of experience. They will tell you about the attitudes and philosophies that have maintained them through their ups and downs. If there was ever a graduate course in selling, it's here in these pages brought to you by the masters of selling.

The profession of selling requires a complex set of talents and skills. It also requires the ability, and the willingness, to continue learning new information and skills. The talents required are so diverse that the salesperson is described by a multitude of terms including coach, counselor, detective, friend, consultant, expert, partner, orchestra conductor, problem-solver, orator, adviser, persuader, evangelist. At first it was tough trying to decide what it takes to make a state-of-the-art salesperson. Then it became clear that the best in the business of selling have the ability to fill all of those roles.

Out of all of the people interviewed, not one mentioned a closing technique! No one talked about keeping the upper hand or even much about overcoming objections. Instead, they talked about relationships, partnerships, discovering customer needs, listening, being sincere, providing service, asking the right questions and keeping promises. These skills make closing natural and almost automatic.

Sales success is based on common principles and values, and these are very simple. What isn't simple is finding the best ways to apply them. We hear companies across America talking about customer service, but finding it very difficult to develop the systems that ensure that good service is delivered day-in and day-out. There is a similar situation in sales. It is easy to talk about building relationships and listening to customer needs, but far more difficult to do it. How do you develop the complex set of skills it takes to be a sales master? You can start by listening to the best in the business as they tell you how they did it.

State of the Art Selling is divided into four sections to help you focus on the areas that are important to you. Here is a brief description of the sections:

Section I: Personal strategies

The sale starts with you, the salesperson. Your attitude, enthusiasm and ability to convey your vision to the customer are all critical parts of the sales cycle. In this section, you will hear how the sales masters maintain their motivation, how they deal with rejection and failure and how they organize themselves for success. You will learn how high-impact networking can propel you to new levels of success and how attention to detail can help you break through customer barriers.

Section II: The customer side and relationship strategies

It takes two to tango and at least two to make a sale. Focusing on customers and their needs and problems is the first step to developing good customer relationships. This section will give you fresh ideas on how to establish strong bonds by effective questioning and listening, by developing trust, and by walking in their shoes.

Section III: Product/company strategies

Customers expect expertise from salespeople. While product knowledge has long been emphasized in the sales world, the stars have found unique ways to develop their expertise above and beyond the norm. They provide service that is truly uncommon and associate themselves with companies that have a commitment to service and quality. State-of-the-art salespeople know that sales success is not a stationary target and, in order to keep succeeding, they need to keep improving. They have an overriding commitment to the sales training process.

Section IV: Solution strategies

Establishing good customer relationships and having outstanding product knowledge and service almost guarantees above-average success in sales. However, the very top level of success comes through creativity and innovation. It's only when the salesperson provides strategic solutions to customer problems that he or she is admitted to the level of partnership with the customer. The ability to think strategically and creatively for the customer differentiates the stars from merely good performers. Top performers find ways to leverage their efforts so that they achieve far more results. This section shows you how to put it all together to establish your own uncommon, extraordinary, outstanding level of success.

More thanks than can ever be expressed go to the many people who helped piece together a picture of the outstandingly successful salesperson. Each person interviewed for this book is extremely busy and has an acute awareness of the value of time. Yet each state-of-the-art salesperson generously volunteered time and insight in order to help others achieve success in a profession that can be very rewarding and extremely tough. Each person here has survived the rigors of the "early years"—the cold calling, the canvassing, the building of new relationships, the development of new territories and the rejection. Their interviews are a helping hand through the tough times—a small thing, perhaps, but sometimes all we need is a slight lift to help us over a major hurdle. The sales stars gave their time to help you succeed. They want you to find new strategies, new techniques, new tools and new motivation in these pages. They want you to become a state-of-the-art salesperson.

Artist Dean Peter has a unique way of describing his life. He states, "I ride the hurricane, I walk the tightrope of sanity. I live on the edge of the world." I live on the edge of the world—that also describes the life of a salesperson. Charting new territories, exploring new grounds, finding new ways to meet customers' needs and new ways to differentiate our products, our services and ourselves. Each of us is an artist—our life is our canvas. How well our life canvas develops depends to an enormous extent on how well we sell. This book is dedicated to not only helping you become a better, more successful salesperson, but also to helping you become a better artist, painting a life full of color and vibrancy.

So sit back and enjoy, but be prepared to ride the hurricane!

"Everyone lives by selling something."
—*Robert Louis Stevenson,*
  Scottish writer

Personal strategies

"Run through walls!"
—Jan Carlzon, CEO,
Scandinavian Airline Systems

Jan Carlzon took over a troubled airline, and within two years created a turnaround success that has become a legend. He says, "Your goal may seem impossible, but don't stop trying to accomplish it until someone really says no! The walls towering before you may not be as massive as they appear. Maybe they're not stone walls at all, but cardboard facades that you can run straight through."

In sales, perhaps more than in any other profession, we have to learn to run through walls. The rejection, disappointment, competitive pressures, fear and discouragement really are just cardboard barriers standing between us and our goals. Breaking through those barriers leads to incredible success.

The chapters in this section will introduce you to state-of-the-art salespeople who are at the top of their industries and will give you insight into the techniques they used to break through to new success levels. These stars discovered new methods for maintaining an enthusiastic attitude, for getting past personal fear and for developing a vision that motivates them to achieve their peak performance.

Richard Waller, vice president and director of manpower development for TeleRep, a marketer of television air time, believes that attitude is the most important trait of a sales star. He says, "The most important element of a successful salesperson is attitude. The attitude that stars need is different from what a lot of people come out of school with—that the world owes them a living. The attitude they need is that they are totally responsible for their level of success. They need to believe that the company is just a vehicle to enable them to achieve whatever they want in terms of income, upward mobility, industry recognition, security and so on. They have to take responsibility for making it happen. They need to have the feeling of 'Do it now...keep moving...be productive.' We want them to have an attitude of professionalism—they have to stay up with what's going on in their industry and to prepare and constantly improve themselves through reading, tapes and studying." Waller demands a lot of his new reps, but as a result of their rigorous selection process, their intense training and support program, more than 90 percent of them are successful.

It is impossible to become one of the best in the business without a success attitude like that described by Waller. Rich Luisi, regional vice president with Electrolux, vacuum cleaner manufacturer, is typical of the many state-of-the-art salespeople with that intense drive and "I-can-make-it-happen" attitude. Luisi's office is cluttered with the trophies, plaques and mementos of a successful career in sales. "Selling is fun," Luisi laughs. "When I do a demonstration, I get the kids involved or the husband involved. It's a fun thing. I keep it strictly business but I try to have a lot of fun with it. The kids love it and they try to get their parents to buy." Having fun selling and delivering the best service possible has helped Luisi break every record in Electrolux's history. When he sold 1,000 vacuums in one year, he was invited to appear on the David Letterman show.

I interviewed sales stars who sell computers, jet engines, insurance, training seminars, telephone systems, sunglasses and many other products and services. While the products differ and the daily activities vary, the basics from industry to industry, product to product, were incredibly similar. And, it all begins with the right attitude.

Selling vacuum cleaners is about as hard-core as selling gets—knocking on doors, cold calling and unlimited rejection. Most salespeople never get past the first few months. How did Luisi succeed under such formidable odds? "I quickly realized that not many people were selling door-to-door, but that the people who learned the art were making a fortune. I worked my hometown to the point that I knew exactly who lived in each house and what kind of vacuum they had. I kept records. If I knocked on a door, I made it worth my while—maybe not immediately, but over the course of the following years.

"I knew all the competitors' equipment and that it would break a lot faster than ours would. So I put my name and number on every vacuum—regardless of who made it—and asked the homemaker to call me anytime she needed something for her vacuum, even if it was only a $1.50 belt. There wasn't anyone else in the whole area who was working like I was. Vacuum cleaners eventually break, so I made service my business. I would personally deliver the $1.50 belts because it helped me build a relationship with the customer. I called every four months to see if she needed anything. Other people couldn't be bothered with that type of follow-up.

"Whenever I went up to a door," Luisi explains, "I would give the person my name and my company and tell her I was just stopping by to see how her cleaner was working. I would offer to test the machine for her and I would put my sticker on it. No one else is doing this—Avon doesn't knock on doors anymore, Tupperware doesn't, no one does. I figure I have the inside track because I'm doing something that most people don't like to do. Of course, a lot of people aren't home anymore so now we use a lot of telemarketing."

Salespeople aren't born, according to Luisi. There isn't some innate talent that makes a successful salesperson. When the need to succeed and the desire to be of service to people combine with a positive attitude, the result produces the potential for success in sales. Luisi states, "I noticed early in my career that the successful salespeople in the company had a good positive attitude. They enjoyed life. I started concentrating on that and reading all the positive thinking books...Napoleon Hill, Earl Nightingale and the others. I listened to tapes and now that I'm in management, I give tapes and books to all my sales staff. I surround myself with positive people and positive ideas. Negativity in my house is unheard of. You never say, 'I hate this.' That's the way I am."

Luisi believes in his product and has a great time sharing it with everyone he meets. During my interview with him, he received a wrong-number phone call. Before the end of the call, he was cold calling the caller! He asked the caller about his vacuum cleaner and then tried to recruit him.

He does it all in such a friendly, caring manner that you find yourself wondering if maybe you shouldn't replace your old clunker.

When Luisi moved into management and took over a branch that was making about 50 to 60 sales per month. He hired some new people and, in the first month, sales went to 300 units and by the third month, the branch had more than 900 sales! One of the things he works on most with his staff is attitude. They meet every morning and talk about goals and being positive. He says, "If a salesperson isn't positive and doesn't think that his product is the very best on the market, there is no way he is going to sell it."

Luisi has taught his salespeople that one of the ways to keep a positive attitude is by providing the best service possible. Helping people and giving them excellent service promotes a feeling that you are helping the customer rather than just making money from the sale. While the monetary rewards are a critical part of the salesperson's report card, the truly successful people do not tie their actions to the financial outcome. They offer service even when it isn't immediately clear that it makes financial sense. They go out of their way to be helpful, to solve problems, to help clients get what they want. The result is that they feel good about the service they are providing and they succeed financially. Luisi unquestionably has achieved enormous financial success—he has won more than 25 cars in sales contests and has traveled all over the world. The incentives have been fabulous because he has been able to give people a good product and excellent service.

"The criteria for a successful sales career," says Luisi, "is to have a burning desire to give the best service that no one else gives, treating everybody the way you would like your mother or your spouse to be treated, and to have a burning desire to be successful within your company."

Luisi achieved all the sales goals he set for himself. Now that he is in management, he has a new set of goals. One includes running the Electrolux company. "It's a goal that's in the future," he states, "but if I do the right things along the way, there is no reason why I can't do it." And, he just might.

Keeping a positive attitude does not mean being unrealistic or looking through the world with rose-colored glasses. It doesn't mean that nothing will ever go wrong. It means, rather, that you look for the information, the lessons, present in each failure or setback. It means viewing every day as a new opportunity to meet your goals. It means putting one foot in front of the other on the path you have chosen. It means having confidence that the path is taking you where you want to go. It means knowing where you want to go so that you can chart the path in the first place. It means knowing that you control your destiny. The stars you will meet in the following chapters are guides to help you chart your path.

"The longer I live, the more I realize the impact of attitude on life. Attitude, to me, is more important than facts. It is more important than the past, than education, than money, than circumstances, than failures, than successes, than what other people think or say or do. It is more important than appearances, giftedness or skill. It will make or break a company...a church...a home. The remarkable thing is, we have a choice every day regarding the attitude we will embrace for that day. We cannot change our past...we cannot change the inevitable. The only thing we can do is play on the one string we have, and that is our attitude...I am convinced that life is 10 percent what happens to me and 90 percent how I react to it. And so it is with you...we are in charge of our attitudes."
—*Charles Swindoll*

Chapter 1: I dare you!

Every sales book, every sales training course, every salesperson emphasizes the need for a positive attitude. The ability to take large doses of rejection and treat it as information rather than as a personal indictment, and the ability to know that the last "no" means you're that much closer to the next "yes" are central to sales success. Although everyone knows the importance of a positive attitude, staying positive in the face of rejection requires persistence and attitude strategies. This chapter gives you several different techniques for maintaining a positive attitude.

Included are tools for conquering your own fears and for making fear work for you. By understanding the fear we all experience, you can harness fear's energy and use it to drive you to better preparation and further honing of your skills.

Chapter 1's Action Plan will help you increase your income immediately through fearless cold calling.

Chapter 2: It's not who you know

It's really who knows *you* and what they know about you. Having a Rolodex full of names is not enough to build your success. You need to make an impression on people. They need to know who you are and what you stand for. Learn how to do high-impact networking.

Learn new techniques for breaking the ice with your customers and learn how the sales stars use profile sheets to build success.

Chapter 2's Action Plan will help you develop the information you need to develop a profile sheet for better networking and account management.

Chapter 3: The 5-percent difference

The difference between being good and being the best frequently means thousands and thousands of extra dollars for the best. But, often it doesn't mean that much more effort. The difference between the salespeople in the top 5 percent and the second 5 percent is generally a matter of organization and attention to detail. In this chapter, you will learn some of the small things that have enormous payoff. Learn a simple organization technique that will revolutionize how you look at your territory. Learn how to "sprint" to your goals and how to mentally rehearse your way to star status.

Chapter 3's Action Plan will help you develop a tool that has helped salespeople organize their accounts and dramatically improve their sales success.

Chapter 4: Managing for early success

This chapter is for managers who want to help salespeople develop early successes, as well as for new salespeople or those who are having problems breaking through to the level of success they want. Learn how to decide what mix you need of the four basic sales qualifications.

Chapter 4's Action Plan is a checklist to help you stay on track with your sales calls. Use this check list to evaluate each of your calls and improve your sales productivity quickly.

Chapter 1

I dare you!

"Do not let anyone else determine your success or failure."
—*Corporate Motto of Imagetec L.P., from Rich Cucco, General Partner*

Coming attractions:

Developing the success attitude

- ◆ Breaking through fear
- ◆ Fearless cold calling
- ◆ Mental rehearsal

At the Marriott Marquis Hotel in Atlanta there is a legend known as Smitty. His full name is Albert Smith and he is the concierge captain at the Marriott. Although Smitty has never held a sales position, he is responsible for a significant portion of the hotel's revenue and was recently recognized with the J. W. Marriott Award, Marriott's highest honor, reserved only for its very special heroes.

Twenty-one years ago, Smitty joined the Marriott selling hot dogs and hamburgers at poolside. Today he plays a key role in Marriott's sports marketing program. Dressed each day in his favorite attire—a tuxedo—he greets guests, remembering an incredible number of their names, and dedicates himself to providing service.

Roger Dow, vice president and general sales manager for Marriott, describes Smitty, 'He is completely customer-focused. Everyone loves Smitty. He is a sports nut and delights in taking care of the teams that stay at the Marriott. When teams arrive at the hotel, he sets up a greeting table of cold drinks and snacks. The welcome area is adorned with that team's pennants, bumper stickers, balls and memorabilia collected over his years working with the teams. Throughout their stay he caters to their needs— and anticipates them." Through the years Smitty made sure that Dr. J had Perrier water in his room after a game, Vida Blue had ice-cold watermelon waiting for him at the stadium, Pete Rose had strawberries, and Tim McCall had his English muffins just the way he wanted them—burned completely black! Players often call Smitty long distance to tell him what they would like to have waiting for them. The Cincinnati Reds appreciated his dedicated service so much that on Father's Day, 1985, they had a surprise presentation at the stadium and gave him a team ring.

"All the football teams used to stay with us when they were in Atlanta," Dow explains. "When a new hotel was built here, it offered the teams extremely low rates in order to get their business." The teams moved. But when the players weren't getting the service they wanted, they started calling Smitty. "With no authorization and using his own time," Dow explains, "Smitty would take hamburgers, fried chicken, anything they wanted (including hot pie a la mode to the 30th floor!) to the competing hotel. Single-handedly, through his efforts, every football team rebooked at the Marriott. The low rates of the competing hotel didn't offset what Smitty did by providing them service one-on-one. Smitty has become one of our heroes and inspirations."

Smitty's program is so unique that the players often complain that other hotels don't provide a similar service. He started his service on a hot day when a team was arriving—he thought they might enjoy a cold drink so he set up a table with a few sodas. "They liked it so much I just kept doing it," he explains. His table of cold drinks grew into the mainstay of the hotel's sports marketing program.

When Smitty was asked how he keeps motivated, he explained, "I look at my job as part of a game. I always ask the individuals around me to use positive words. When you think negative, send negative, you will perform negative. To beef yourself up, you think about winners, you think about champions. All of this runs in my mind all during the day. I just keep turning, like a generator in a car. When you turn me on, you are going to turn on positive energy.

"When I have nothing to do," Smitty continues, "I go around the hotel and take pictures or I go into a department and just listen because then I can learn something. If they're having a meeting, I just go in and sit down because maybe I can help them since I work all over the hotel. I want to know what is going on in my hotel."

In *my* hotel. Ownership, pride and commitment fill his voice as he talks about his hotel, his teams, his players. Smitty is a legend at the Marriott and he demonstrates the power of service, commitment and a positive attitude.

Even though Smitty has never held an official sales position, he exemplifies the personal qualities found in the best of the business of selling. He is a total professional, doing what he loves. He wants to know everything that is going on in his hotel and spends time outside his own area. He willingly goes out of his way to carry out his mission of taking care of the teams. He has positive persistence borne from his knowledge that he can give outstanding service to his customers. And, he constantly reinforces his positive attitude by studying champions and surrounding himself with positive energy.

Attitude. Throughout all the research and interviews conducted on what makes the top selling stars excel, attitude was mentioned more than any other attribute to success. One Harvard Business School study determined that there were four factors critical to success in sales: information, intelligence, skill and attitude. When these factors were ranked as to importance, this particular study found that information, intelligence and skill combined amounted to 7 percent of the sales effectiveness and attitude amounted to 93 percent! Could it be that 93 percent of our success in sales, at work and in life, results from our attitude?

What is this thing we call attitude? What makes it good or bad? Can we change our attitude? And how do we change it? William Danforth, founder of the Ralston Purina Company, considered this problem over 70 years ago. He described himself as a youth as "sallow-cheeked and hollow-chested." One of his teachers challenged him to change by saying, "I dare you to be the healthiest boy in the class."

Danforth wrote, "That brought me up with a jar. Around me were boys all stronger and more robust than I. To be the healthiest boy in the class when I was thin and sallow and imagined at least that I was full of swamp poisons!—the man was crazy. But I was brought up to take dares. As he talked something seemed to happen inside me. My blood was up. It answered the dare and surged all through my body into tingling finger tips as though itching for battle." Danforth took the dare and developed a healthy body and a new philosophy of life. Later in life he discovered that he could issue a dare—a challenge—to others and it would have the same galvanizing effect. He believed that each individual represented vast potential and it was their task in life to develop that potential. For 35 years, every Monday morning each of his employees received "Danforth's Monday Morning Message." These messages were full of inspiration and motivation. An example of one of his messages:

"Life is a glorious adventure. Face problems aggressively—opportunities do not come to those who wait. They are captured by those who attack. I am daring you to think bigger, to act bigger, and to be bigger. And I am promising you a richer life and more exciting life if you do. I am showing you a world teeming with opportunity."

In 1920 he put his philosophy in a small volume called *I Dare You!* He challenged all readers to develop to their fullest potential. On his statue at the National Headquarters of the 4-H

Club Foundation in Chevy Chase, Maryland, the inscription reads:

"I Dare You to be your own self at your very best all the time."

One of Danforth's dares was, "I Dare You, whoever you are, to share with others the fruits of your daring. Catch a passion for helping others and a richer life will come back to you!" Danforth lived this dare and was one of the founders of the American Youth Foundation (AYF). The mission of the AYF today remains the same as it was 65 years ago—"to motivate young people to achieve their best, to live a balanced life, and to serve others." The proceeds from *I Dare You!* provide scholarships for young people across the country to attend the AYF leadership conference, which has been attended by over 60,000 young people. Among the graduates of the leadership camp are Richard Gephardt, congressman from Missouri.

I Dare You! has been reprinted 32 times and has sold more than 1.75 million copies. As I interviewed top sales people, I found many who cherished this volume and its philosophy. The belief that we have enormous potential and that our task is to discover that potential and use it is the basis of a positive attitude. Sometimes we equate a positive attitude with optimism or a vague feeling that everything will turn out all right. But, it is more than just thinking positive. A positive attitude is the positive expectancy that if we do all that we can do, if we develop our potential to its fullest, that we will achieve the results we want. We expect positive results because we have done everything possible to achieve them.

In sales, a positive attitude, a positive expectation is critical. The prospect mirrors the salesperson's attitude and expectations. If the salesperson does not expect the prospect to buy, he creates doubt and negative expectations in the prospect.

So how do we develop this magical attitude of positive expectation? We could take a clue from Bob Shatney, number-one sales rep in his category for Minolta Copiers. In his rookie year, Shatney set records for the President's Club trip—qualifying in only nine months. Shatney was hired as a telemarketing rep but kept asking for outside sales. Once he reached that goal, he laid out a schedule of accomplishments that he wanted to reach and the exact time schedule for reaching them. His next goal is to be a branch manager and to help others learn to develop their sales skills and success levels. "I enjoy selling," Shatney states, "and I think it's important to do what you enjoy. I have fun. I have a good time even when I'm cold calling. If you don't enjoy it, you should get out of it."

Shatney maintains a positive, winning attitude in a tough selling field. That by itself is impressive, but

Shatney also faces the added difficulty of being handicapped. A motorcycle accident left him paralyzed from the waist down several years ago. Shatney was hired to do telemarketing, a safe although challenging position. But in spite of the physical difficulties involved, he wanted outside sales. Every day he told his sales manager he was ready.

Minolta had never had a sales rep in a wheelchair so Shatney had to convince them that he could drive to the appointment and demonstrate equipment as well as sell it. His manager finally agreed to let him demonstrate his abilities and he quickly convinced them that he could handle the job physically. Within a few months, he proved that he could become one of the best in the business.

Six keys to a positive attitude

By studying Smitty and Shatney and the many other sales stars who radiate a positive attitude, I found six keys to a positive attitude:

1. Professional pride

Sales is the highest-paying profession in the U.S. According to Dr. Thomas J. Stanley, professor of marketing at Georgia State University, there are more sales and marketing professionals than physicians in the six-figure income category. Sales is also a critical profession. It is the basis of our economy...nothing happens until something

gets sold. As we develop more and more complex products and services, it takes the assistance of highly trained, motivated salespeople to help customers determine which product or service meets their needs.

Although the financial rewards of sales can be great, they only come from whole-hearted efforts. Many jobs can be done on auto-pilot but a salesperson's efforts are only rewarded if he or she is fully engaged, totally immersed. To be successful, a salesperson has to define himself or herself as a critical link. The salesperson's self-image has to be that of a consultant, a partner, an assistant.

The top salespeople have risen above the sometimes shoddy image of the fast-talking, traveling sales hustler. However, rising above this image still takes effort. Recent polls of college graduates finds that less than 6 percent want to go into sales and yet by the age of 37, 76 percent of the U.S. business people find that sales is their primary responsibility. Because of the low public view of sales, many salespeople are never able to rise above that image and proudly announce themselves as a sales professional. However, Richard McGinn told me, "When I'm at a party and someone asks what my profession is, I tell them I sell computers, *not* that I am the president of AT&T Computer Systems."

Until you feel pride in your profession, you cannot develop the powerful, positive attitude that leads to sales stardom. Michael Finaldi, president of Tele-Solutions, a full-service telecommunications company, says you have to become identified with your profession, "If you plan on doing something, if you treat it as a life-long occupation, a life-long goal, it permeates your soul, then you become synonymous with it. Where I think people make a mistake is that they are not true to their heart. If people sat down and asked themselves what they really wanted to do and then went about the business of doing it, there would be a much greater success ratio today. You want to go into something because you are proud of it or because you might be able to add something to other businesses or people...and at the same time you want your little piece of the pie. The money is a come-along. The money comes because you are good at what you do. I have often gotten business because my name is so synonymous with telephones that they think of me as the 'telephone guy.' "

Being synonymous with their product or service is a trait of most sales stars. For example, Rich Luisi drives a van with Electrolux, his name and phone number printed on the side. Everyone he meets knows that he sells Electrolux. When his friends and acquaintances think of vacuum cleaners, they think of Rich Luisi. "I was one of the first guys in the company to put my name on my van," Luisi states, "but I learned that you have to keep your name out there. I always pass out fliers and magnets and anything else to keep my name and product in front of prospects."

2. Do what you love

Top salespeople love what they do. They believe in their product or service. They believe that it delivers an important value; they believe in its quality. They are proud to be associated with it. In order to reach the top levels of success in sales, you must be so interested and intrigued with your product or service that you want to know more about it. You must want to know how it can be used by your customers. There are thousands of products and services to be sold. The most successful salespeople stay with a product or industry for many years or for their entire career because it continues to challenge and fascinate them. The old saying, "Follow your heart and the money will follow," is especially true in sales. Love for what you do is that intangible something that picks you up when times are tough and keeps you going when you think you can't.

Love is contagious. If you love your product, you want to share it with others. You have enthusiasm for it. You are energized by being involved with it and by sharing it with others. This love and enthusiasm creates a positive attitude.

Jeff Weiss is a top technical analyst with Shearson Lehman Brothers. His love affair with the stock market started when he was in the sixth grade. His math teacher gave the class a project of investing $50,000. Jeff did very well on this pretend project and wanted to invest real money. When he received $400 for his birthday and Bar Mitzvah he bought five shares of Mattel Toy for about $80 a share. A year later and two splits, the stock sold for the equivalent of $160 a share and a career was born. "I got on my bicycle every day after school and zoomed to the closest brokerage office to see the close of the market," Weiss recalls. His fascination with the market gave him the energy and the motivation to learn all of its intricacies.

Weiss eagerly shares his love by frequently speaking to different groups. He explains the market as a metaphor for life. "I travel around the country," he explains, "speaking to brokers, clients, families, kids, college students or at community functions. I talk about a technical subject, technical analysis. But, if I talked about it in technical terms, they wouldn't understand it so I talk in non-technical terms. For instance, there is a technical tenet called the *50-percent retracement principle*, which states that over a period of time a stock or a market can retrace up to half of a prior intermediate gain without reversing its primary direction. Rather than saying that, I talk about trying to move forward two steps for every step backwards. That is the principle of the stock market." That is also a principle

for life. A positive attitude allows for the occasional backward step but tries to come back with two forward steps.

3. Invest yourself

Once you have found a product or service that you are genuinely interested in—one that commands your love and enthusiasm, then you have to commit yourself thoroughly. You have to invest your time, your energies, your enthusiasm to developing mastery of your skills. In order to stay 100-percent invested, you have to have something at stake—your self-esteem, money, reputation, the well-being of your family—something.

Once you are invested in the process of sales, you are rewarded for the accomplishment of your goals. Your rewards might be the sense of accomplishment that comes with a successful close, fat commission checks or the respect and admiration of your peers. Whatever the rewards are, you are aligned with the process. You believe that what you are doing is right for yourself and you believe that it is right for your customers. You also know that if you do not reach your goals, you are shortchanging yourself and your prospective clients.

Betsy Martin, advertising sales director of *Money* magazine, says, "The fire has to come from within. I love people, I love talking to people, I love accomplishing something. Selling advertising pages, you can see the product, you can feel the product, you get it every month. It gives me a sense of accomplishment on a month-to-month basis. I think salespeople measure themselves against others and against themselves."

Rich Cucco is the president of Image Tec, a large office equipment dealer. After spending several years as a successful sales rep, branch manager and chief operating officer for two other distributors, Cucco decided to pursue his lifelong dream of owning his own business. But, before he made that move he was earning a comfortable living, managing 300 people, and enjoying a solid position in the marketplace where he grew the company from $6 million a year in sales to over $23 million in less than seven years. Cucco states, "Many people talk about starting their own business, but never put a detailed plan in writing and then give it their all. I mean 110 percent and never looking back. I know I was leaving a successful operation and risking my life savings to start a business in an industry the experts say is matured and over 90 percent of new businesses fail. But there is never any reward without the risk. So I worked nights and weekends knowing what I had at stake."

That's being invested in the process! Sink or swim. Win or lose. When you are so heavily invested that you cannot afford to leave one stone unturned, one opportunity unexplored, then you will perform at your maximum level. After three years in business,

Cucco has 65 employees and a business level of approximately $8 million.

4. Invest in yourself

The most important asset a salesperson has is himself. He has to continually upgrade his product knowledge, understanding of the industry, understanding of his customers and his sales skills. The top sales stars take advantage of every training opportunity they have. They listen to tapes and read books on positive thinking, sales techniques and psychology. Rich Luisi states, "A salesperson has to read good positive-thinking books like the books *I Dare You!*, *Think and Grow Rich* and others." Several top sales stars have tape libraries valued at thousands of dollars.

5. Positive persistence

Before founding Electronic Data Systems (EDS), which eventually made him a billionaire, H. Ross Perot was a salesperson for IBM. His biography, *Perot*, written by Business Week correspondent Todd Mason, states that Perot was always in IBM's "Hundred Percent Club." Each year he met his quota earlier and earlier until one year he met his quota on January 19! But, when Perot launched EDS on his 32nd birthday with $1,000 of his own money, he did not meet immediate success. Perot made 78 sales calls before signing up his first client for EDS.

Top salespeople are extremely persistent but they find positive ways of being persistent. It's more than just showing up on someone's doorstep day after day and saying, "Are you ready?" The stars always have a reason for a call...whether it's a new piece of information about the product or service or just an article that they think the customer might be interested in.

However, the sales axiom of never taking "no" for an answer, also carries a hazard. Probably one of the toughest decisions for a salesperson to make is when to stop pursuing a customer. Eventually top salespeople develop an instinct for when a prospect truly isn't interested or qualified. Beginning salespeople tend to keep all prospects rather than working on the most promising ones. Knowing how to stay positively persistent is a skill learned over time.

Jim Euwer, winner of the 1989 President's Award for Armstrong World Industries, describes an instance where being persistent long after most people would have thrown in the towel paid off. Euwer was trying to land an account that had shown no interest in his product. He finally managed to get an appointment with a merchandise manager who showed some interest. When he called back, that manager had left the company. He obtained another appointment with the new manager who was interested enough to get him an appointment with a buyer. "I moved about halfway through the sales process (about seven months)," Euwer relates, "and the buyer quit. At that point I called the merchandise manager back to find out who to see and found out that he had been fired. So I started the process over with a new merchandise manager and buyer. The new people were not familiar with the product so I was starting over completely again. I went through two and a half years of buyers, merchandise managers and vp's."

Euwer's persistence and care impressed the customer. He explains, "Finally I worked with someone long enough to close the sale. I wound up talking to the president who made the final decision and I think he decided in our favor on the basis of my sticking with it for so long. He knew that anyone who had persisted that long would take care of the account. Anywhere along the way I could have decided that they weren't interested or that it wasn't worth my time."

6. Learning from failure

John Dryden wanted to be an insurance agent and for 10 years he struggled unsuccessfully to establish an agency. Despite his repeated failures, he learned a lot about the insurance industry and he thought he had a new idea for offering life insurance to the working class. In 1875, it was a new idea and Dryden developed his idea into The Prudential Insurance Company of America, now the largest insurance company in the nation.

An English proverb tells us: *"A smooth sea never made a skillful mariner."* We learn from life's ups and downs. Perhaps if John Dryden had been successful at his attempts to establish an insurance agency, he would not have learned enough to have founded "the Rock." Failure isn't failure if we discover its lessons.

Michael Finaldi, president of TeleSolutions, has probably sold as many telephone systems as anyone in the United States. The walls in his office and conference room are covered with letters from delighted customers, including one from James Florio, former governor of New Jersey and another from Senator Bill Bradley. One tip that he passes along to new salespeople is to learn from their failures.

He explains, "One of the ways I got better was when I lost an account. I would call the customer up and ask as nicely as possible why I didn't get the account. I told the customer that I felt bad about not getting the account but I would like to know as candidly as possible why the decision was made to go with another vendor. I told them that I really wanted to know even if they had to say something that would hurt my feelings. I got a lot of information from customers and if they told me that I needed to clean up my act, then I did. I was always looking for ways to get better. That gave me more confidence as I kept eliminating the old mistakes—perhaps making new ones but never making the same

ones. I became what I felt was a true professional salesperson who was not afraid to open doors or walk in on new accounts." Thomas Watson, founder of IBM, once said: *"The way to succeed is to double your failure rate."*

Challenge each day

One cold, wet blustery day as Rich Luisi looked out his window, thinking of catching up on paperwork and an extra cup of coffee, he decided to challenge the day. He went out in the pouring rain and headed for a neighborhood of high-priced homes. He knocked on one door and the maid answered. As it turned out, her vacuum was broken and she was interested in a new one but she couldn't make a decision until the owner returned, which was supposed to be shortly. Luisi recalls the day, "I demonstrated the vacuum to her and then showed her a rug shampooer—she loved that, too. We were looking at the product and waiting for the owner to come home when she went to the phone and called the maid next door. I went next door and gave her a demonstration— she liked it and called the maid across the street. In an hour and a half, I sold six machines for almost $4,000 in business, just getting out and working on a lousy, rainy day."

Luisi met the challenge of the day when an average performer would have stayed warm and snug inside. What if we challenged every day?

What if every single day got our very best performance? And, what keeps us from performing at our highest level every day? Most people recognize that their biggest personal barrier is fear— fear of failure, fear of being ridiculed or rejected, fear of testing our skills and talents against actual situations.

Breaking through the biggest barrier: fear

Marie Curie, the Nobel prize-winning physicist, once said: *"Nothing in life is to be feared. It is only to be understood."* But, John Dowling, executive vice president and top sales star of Cushman & Wakefield, a commercial real estate company, for almost 28 years says that he still feels fear. "Despite the bravado and the appearance of confidence, if I have to speak or do a client interview, I'm perspiring clear to my waist band. It's fear...fear of failure, fear of letting myself down, fear of letting my expectations down, fear of not being professional. No question that's my motivation. And it's a far stronger motivation than economics ever could be."

Fear is the biggest barrier to successful sales. Fear keeps us from making the cold calls, from meeting new clients and from closing sales. While fear is a formidable barrier, it can also be an enormous source of energy. As Dowling states, it's his major source of motivation. Fear of failing makes him constantly improve his skills and push himself toward success. Harnessing the energy from your fear gives you incredible power and drive.

Here are four primary tools that sales stars use to break through fear:

- ◆ Self-confidence
- ◆ Product knowledge
- ◆ Relationships
- ◆ Vision

Self-confidence

Goethe, the German philosopher, said, "Every individual is a marvel of unknown and unrealized possibilities." Too often, we aren't even aware of what we are capable of doing and becoming. Before Roger Bannister broke the four-minute mile, athletes, coaches and scientists said it was physically impossible for a human to run a mile in less than four minutes. In the months after Bannister broke through that barrier, more than 25 other athletes ran the mile in less than four minutes! Suddenly people realized that it could be done, so they did it.

Two beliefs are required for success in any field. We have to believe that it can be done and we have to believe that we can do it. When new salespeople are given achievable goals— goals that others have reached—they can easily see that the goals are achievable. The remaining critical belief, then, is whether they can reach those goals. Overcoming the lack of self-confidence is the first barrier to sales success.

Rich Luisi, one of the most successful salesmen in Electrolux's history, says, "Fear is what cripples most people...mostly fear that they can't get the job done." Developing confidence that we can do what is required comes from taking one step at a time. Setting achievable yet challenging goals for ourselves, meeting those goals and setting new, more advanced goals again and again.

Product knowledge

Jack Jackson, vice president of U.S. pharmaceutical sales for Upjohn, states that the $1.8 billion pharmaceutical company has chosen a scientific niche for the company's sales force. The majority of its people have science degrees and many are pharmacists. Training is geared toward giving salespeople the tools to talk with medical professionals about various forms of therapy and treatments. The salesperson develops a high level of understanding not only of the products but the methods of treating diseases with those products. Jackson states, "If you are going to have a 23-year-old sales rep walk in to talk to a neurosurgeon, that rep has to have confidence. We instill this confidence through our training program and this confidence changes the salesperson from someone pushing a product to someone helping a physician find a better method of treating a disease."

The successful salesperson understands his or her product and company thoroughly. He or she is committed to the product and believes that it offers customers valuable benefits. Product knowledge and understanding gives the salesperson confidence and provides the tools to solve customer problems.

Relationships

One of the first business people to recognize the importance of relationships in business was J. C. Penney, who said, *"All great business is built on friendship."* But, until the salesperson develops a friendship with his or her customers, there is fear. Fear or wariness of strangers is an inborn survival mechanism. The first cave salesperson was never sure whether he would be greeted with a club or a beaver skin. While we're seldom greeted with clubs today, every time we cold call or canvass, fear pumps a little adrenaline into our system just in case. Getting the first seeds of a relationship established with the prospective customer reduces our feelings of fear—and turns off the adrenaline that is pumping through the customer's veins, also.

Vision

Northwestern Mutual has one of the most impressive training programs in the insurance industry. Dennis Tamcsin, senior vice president with Northwestern, states that the company conducts over 100 different courses, schools and programs per year. However, Tamcsin states that a company must also offer a salesperson a vision. "The vision is really important," says Tamcsin. "The company sets a tone in an agent's mind about achievement, success, goals, setting standards, about the mission of life insurance, and what it can do for the people an agent comes into contact with." Many people at Northwestern consider theirs a true profession, a calling, because of the beneficial effect they can have on people's lives.

Truly successful salespeople almost always have a vision that their product or service actually improves lives. They know that their product or service can solve problems and offer benefits that will be greatly valued by their customers. The commitment to this vision provides the extra energy that drives salespeople to success. It makes them willing to provide extraordinary service, to search for solutions to problems, and to build lasting, important relationships with their customers.

Terry Crane, manager of Apple Computer's Market Center in Dallas, spent 13 years in education before catching her vision of the future of personal computers. During an experimental program with computers in a gifted and talented class, she caught a glimpse of how computers could have an impact on education. After becoming a self-taught personal computer expert, she decided to make a

career change and was one of the first people Apple hired who wasn't a computer science major.

Crane was one of 12 business development managers who rolled out the entirely new desktop publishing industry. She has won four Golden Apple Club awards, three Golden Odyssey trips and the business development manager of the year award, but her favorite award is the national sales impact award. "This award is given," she explains, "to the project that has had the most impact on the way we are going to do business." Only five were given last year. She won the award for the Market Center in Dallas that she championed and managed. "Our marketing center is now a model for a concept of developing more demonstration/briefing centers," she states proudly.

In the first year of operation of the Apple Market Center in Dallas's InfoMart, Crane's staff made presentations to more than 22,000 customers and their direct, trackable sales-to-expense ratio was over 18 to 1! InfoMart has more than 90 computer vendors on-site and Apple won the InfoMart award for the highest customer satisfaction rating on seminar events held there.

Crane describes the importance of vision. "I think you have to believe that the world needs the product you are selling. When I wanted to get into the computer world, I didn't consider going anywhere but Apple (although I didn't tell them that) because I believed in the product so much and believed in what they were trying to do in education and in business to empower people. The hardware is just the vehicle with which you get there.

"It is interesting to me," Crane relates, "that such a small percentage of the people have true vision. Many people go through the daily routine of things, but the people with vision are the ones who come up with the innovations and the ones who make things happen. The difference vision makes is between people who just accept their circumstances and people who change the way those circumstances affect them. One is the ordinary performer and one is the superperformer."

Charles Malone, vice president of international sales for Federal Express, caught his vision early. He was on R&R from his tour with the army in Vietnam when he ran into a friend who was working for American Express in Hong Kong. Malone recalls the meeting, "He started telling me about what he was doing and how much fun he was having and how on weekends he went to Katmandu and Jakarta and Bali. I said, 'That's for me.' I returned from Vietnam and used my GI Bill money to attend the American Graduate School of International Management. They were preaching globalization well before it was in vogue. I just happened to see something that looked exciting."

Malone credits the ability to develop a vision of what can be and not accepting the status quo for his success. "It's important to be open to new ideas," he says. "To always look for improvement rather than just managing for today. Never be satisfied with managing the present business. Always ask 'why not?' "

Conveying the vision to the sales force is the prime mission of leadership, according to Malone. In truly successful companies, leaders are able to take the vision, translate it and send it down through the middle management levels so all the employees understand where the company is going and why.

Malone also believes that consistency is a key for effective management. He states, "The companies that are successful rarely come off their main track. Every time a company changes course, employees become a little more cynical. They think that management doesn't mean what they say or that they don't know where they're going. When management is inconsistent, employees don't feel compelled to follow the leader. Maintaining a consistent course is difficult to do because there are a lot of events that require a certain degree of change. You must be flexible, but also consistent. So, it's not easy.

"You must have enough strength in your vision to weather the storm," continues Malone. "You can't be a victim of circumstances. Right now, Federal is confronting rising fuel costs—over 100 percent increase in the past six to seven months—plus competition that we have never faced before in the domestic market. We are also trying to gain market share internationally. There are a lot of reasons to look at the situation and say perhaps we should change directions. Maybe we shouldn't go international. Maybe we should stop investing in training and start furloughing people. Some people from the outside would say that's what we should be doing. But, as soon as you start reacting to those kinds of comments, you lose your credibility. The key is to remain committed to your company values and operating philosophy while exercising enough flexibility to take advantage of unforeseen opportunities."

Federal Express has an extremely consistent and ingrained philosophy of *people-service-profit* with heavy emphasis on people. The strength of this philosophy and vision has allowed the company to weather many setbacks that could have been fatal for other companies. When Zap Mail folded, Federal Express took a huge loss but it did not lay off people. Tough, seemingly inappropriate decisions such as these, keep the vision and the philosophy consistent and keep Federal people performing at the super-performer level.

Whose fear is bigger?

Many of us as children were told that snakes (or rats or mice or spiders or whatever) were more afraid of us than we were of them. Customers are like our childhood fears—our customers fear us as much or more than we fear them. They are afraid that we are somehow going to trick them into making a decision they will regret. Somehow by using a fancy closing technique or manipulation, they think we can force them to buy a product they don't want or need. Or, that we are going to make them pay too much for the product, or sell them something and then never deliver. Because the customer's fear is often greater than ours, our job is to reduce this fear. In working to help the customer overcome his or her fear, ours often disappears.

Fearless cold calling

Maybe cold calling will never be fun or even easy, but skillful cold calling can make the difference between success and failure. Sales is still partially a numbers game—you have to make so many calls, get so many "no's", before you get a "yes." Experienced salespeople know their closing ratios. They know they will get one appointment for every five (or two or 20) calls they make and close one sale for every 10 (or three or 30) appointments. They understand that every time they dial a number they are one step closer to a sale.

One salesperson who kept records for over 10 years was able to calculate that every call he made, every time he picked up the phone and dialed a number, was worth $22. Simply developing the discipline, the mental stamina to cold call or canvass is the first step that separates successful salespeople from those who will not be successful. Jack Kolker, vice president with Bear Stearns and one of its top bond salespeople says that at the beginning of his career he was glued to the phone. "I spent as much time as I could cold calling. After awhile it gets easier and you start getting accounts."

Of course it's not ever easy. If it was easy, salespeople wouldn't be paid so well for succeeding. If it was easy, minimum-wage order clerks would replace salespeople. Sales will always involve large doses of negative input, usually called rejection. Kolker talks about the rejection of the early years, "By the end of the day, if I didn't feel like I had been beat up in a boxing match, I figured I hadn't worked hard enough. But, eventually you just become calloused to it. Having a positive attitude helps and goals help."

Nine ways to say "no"

Bear Stearns is one of the most successful brokerage houses on Wall Street. In the recent turbulent times of the investment industry, Bear Stearns has been untouched by scandal and has prospered, remaining profitable in each of its 66 years of history. The company's mission is to make money for its clients and it has been extremely successful at fulfilling that mission. Bear Stearns has also built a system that allows its sales force to prosper—its average commission generated is three times the industry average. According to a Kidder, Peabody & Company study reported in *The New York Times*, the annual commission revenue generated per retail broker for Merrill Lynch (the second highest firm listed) was $133,000. For Bear Stearns, the average was $504,391. Since the salesperson's income is directly related to productivity (revenue generated), brokers at Bear Stearns are at the top of the income stack.

Obviously, the sales staff at Bear Stearns is doing something the others aren't. The difference is even more amazing when you learn that brokers at Bear Stearns are not given any accounts and are strongly discouraged from opening accounts with friends and relatives. Kolker explains, "We were encouraged not to contact our family and friends. Because that's the worst place to start. If you end up losing them as clients, you lose them as friends and then you have nothing left. So, you spend your first year cold calling."

Bear Stearns helps the sales staff learn how to perform at a level three times the industry norm on a regular basis. One manager for Bear Stearns states, "I take sales people doing $150 to $200,000 per year in commission revenue and if they do everything I tell them to do, they will do three times that by end of their second or third year."

The first skill they learn is cold calling. Opening accounts with people over the phone is a tedious business requiring consistent cold calling to find someone who is interested. Bear Stearns has an excellent reputation and is known in the industry as a good place for an individual investor. But, the people it deals with are successful business people who are being called daily by other brokers and investment representatives. To be successful in that fiercely competitive environment requires skill and a strategy.

Before anyone at Bear Stearns makes a call, they remind themselves of their goal for that call. It isn't to sell the latest stock recommended by research, it isn't even to open an account, it is to begin the client relationship. Everything that happens during that call should promote the relationship. "During the first call," states Kolker, "we introduce ourselves and Bear Stearns, and ask them if they would be interested in hearing about opportunities in the bond market." That approach gives the broker a nonthreatening way to find out more about the potential investor's interests and strategy. "Then when Bear Stearns gets involved with a bond issue that the investor might be interested in," Kolker continues, "I call him and ask him to buy. Most of the time his answer is 'no.' "

But what Kolker and other salespeople have discovered is that the prospect doesn't actually say "no." He generally says things like: "I need to talk to my spouse, a friend, my accountant, my lawyer or my brother-in-law." "I need some more information—send me a report, a brochure or research information." "I need more time—I can't do anything till spring, till after tax season, till the new budget cycle." These are all polite ways to say "no." But, they aren't the real objection and until the real objection is revealed, progress cannot be made. Most of the time, the real reason for saying "no" is because the client doesn't know you. You're a stranger and he or she is uncomfortable doing business with you over the phone. He or she doesn't trust you. The first job of a sales rep is overcoming that obstacle.

Kolker states that, regardless of what the client says, he tries to hear the client saying, "You're a stranger to me—I don't know you and I don't trust you." Constantly keeping this in mind helps Kolker stay focused on building a relationship of trust. Rather than being confrontational, Kolker works on building a relationship with clients. He provides extensive information and works with them to make sure they understand every aspect of the bond offering they are discussing. Kolker does what he calls "blue printing"—he gets as much information about their goals and objectives as possible. When he hears a "no," he knows that he either has not established the client's trust or he isn't meeting their needs or objectives.

Breaking through the brick wall

Once we know the real objection is that the client doesn't know us and doesn't feel comfortable with us, then we have one primary goal: to make the client feel more comfortable. There is a brick wall standing between us and the client—the client wants it there because it is protecting him or her. We want it down because it is blocking the client from receiving the benefits of our products or services. Being confrontational makes the client even more sure of the need for the brick wall—he or she may even add another row of bricks for further protection. How do we get around the wall?

A child's story tells about a challenge held between the Sun and the Wind. A man was walking down the street with a big overcoat on and to prove who was the stronger, the Sun and the Wind decided to see who could get the coat off the man. The Wind said, "I'm so strong, I'll blow his coat off." He blew and blew but the more he blew, the harder the man held onto his coat. Finally the Wind was blown out and he gave the Sun a turn. The Sun turned its warmest face to the man, radiating heat and light, and soon the man willingly took off his heavy coat.

We want clients to willingly come from behind the brick wall—we want them to feel comfortable with us. For them to feel that level of comfort, they must believe that we have their best interests in mind. Kolker states that it's all about trust and that trust has to be built; it can't just be asked for or demanded. The top salespeople, time after time, emphasize how important it is to always be completely honest with customers and to provide them with the service and support they need.

Just do it!

When Rich Luisi moved into management with Electrolux, he began to help others break through their barriers. One of the first salespersons he helped was Rich Kwaak. Kwaak had been with the company about a year and a half and was performing at an average level. He had experienced one outstanding month and Luisi thought he had the potential to be a star salesperson.

"He didn't have the confidence he should have," Luisi explains. "He had lots of ability and all the right tools. But, he didn't know how to get there. I got him working on tools and positive thinking and he wound up selling 40 machines the first month we worked together and 101 the second month! By then, he had so much confidence that he started working with the new reps."

Kwaak credits Luisi with helping him learn how to create a winning attitude and to look for ways to identify new business areas. "The main way to get past fear," Kwaak says, "is to just do it!" He believes action creates its own confidence. If you are doing the cold calling or canvassing, you are bound to have some success and that leads you on to more confidence and greater skill. "Now whenever I go out to service a machine, I automatically knock on all the doors in the neighborhood," Kwaak states. He is now the number-two salesperson in the entire Electrolux eastern region and has won trips to the Caribbean, Vancouver, Holland and San Francisco!

"Just Do It!" is more than a slogan from the Nike commercials—it is a philosophy of life. More than the planning, more than the positive thinking, more than the resolutions, we need to "Just Do It." Success comes to us because we are willing to do the things that others are not willing to do. In sales that means cold calling, canvassing, following up, keeping promises, listening to the customer's needs, and paying attention to details—it means "just doing it." On the next page is an Action Plan to help you get started.

"There is nothing in this world that's worth doing that isn't going to scare you. The moment you make the commitment to going for your dreams, you've begun to venture into the unknown."
—Barbara Sher, Wishcraft

```
┌─────────────────────────┐
╎      Two Ideas:         ╎
└─────────────────────────┘
```

What two ideas did you get from this chapter?

_____

_____

I dare you! to use these ideas to break through to a new level of success.

Action Plan

> Cold Calling/
> New Accounts

1. Additional income I would like to make this week (month, period)
2. Number of sales it takes to make this much income.
3. Number of product demonstrations/appointments necessary to close the number of sales in Step 2.
4. Number of calls it takes to schedule the number of demos/appointments in Step 3.
5. Am I willing to make that many additional calls this week (month, period)?
6. If yes, how many calls do I have to make each day (week, period)?

	Calls		Demos/Appts.
	Plan	Actual	Scheduled
Monday	_____	_____	_____
Tuesday	_____	_____	_____
Wednesday	_____	_____	_____
Thursday	_____	_____	_____
Friday	_____	_____	_____
Saturday	_____	_____	_____

1. Total new sales/accounts _____
2. Total new sales dollars _____
3. Total commission _____

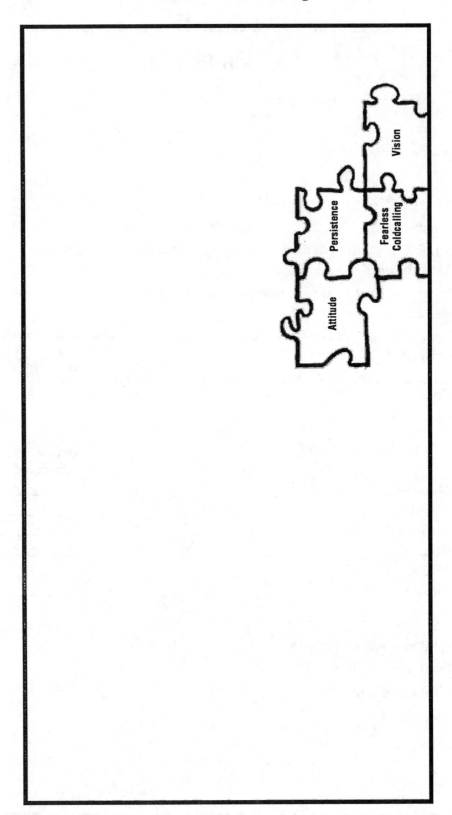

Chapter 2

It's not who you know

"The most important word in the English language, if you want to be a success, can't be found in the dictionary. It's Rolodex."
—Harvey Mackay, CEO, Mackay Envelope Corporation, author of *Swim With the Sharks Without Being Eaten Alive*, rated the top business book of 1988

Coming attractions:

♦ Star networking

♦ Ice breakers

♦ Gaining referrals

♦ Profile sheets

Mackay's Rolodex wisdom tells only half the story. A Rolodex filled with names is not enough. It is not enough for you to know lots of people. It isn't enough for you to collect and pass out a lot of business cards. It really isn't who you know that makes you successful—it's who knows you and what they know about you.

How do we let people know who we are and how do we make ourselves stand out from the crowd of competitors? Jeffrey Smith, national marketing manager in charge of training for Minolta Corporation, says the critical element is differentiation. He states, "I believe the key to sales is differentiation. At Minolta, we are trying to set ourselves apart with the training of our people. Products are reaching a parity level, so we believe that what will set us apart is the abilities of our people."

Top salespeople spend a great deal of time and effort exploring what makes their product or service different, what makes their company different and what their particular advantages as a salesperson are. They discover ways to differentiate themselves. Many of their methods are almost pathetically basic—things like returning phone calls, sending thank-you notes, calling back after a sale, providing information, keeping promises. Even with the abundance of information available about good sales techniques, too many salespeople neglect these basics.

Getting attention...the hard way

One of the most effective ways to let people know who you are is to define yourself sincerely—to be a real person. Sometimes just by being yourself, you can make more of a connection with people. Just as people want you to care who they are and be interested enough to find out their likes and dislikes, they also want to know who you are.

Tamara "TJ" Twitchell, vice president of sales and marketing for Arc Tangent, a developer of mailing-list management software, discovered this recently on a publicity trip. She was flying from Santa Barbara to New York to meet with the editor of a major publication about a potential review of the Arc Tangent software. She had been trying to meet this editor for several weeks and had finally talked him into spending 20 minutes looking at the software. During a layover in Dallas, while walking through the terminal, she dropped a bottle of champagne that had been given to her by a stewardess. Champagne bottles don't just break; they explode. Pieces of the bottle pierced into both her feet, instantly creating a bloody mess and pandemonium. She was whisked away to a hospital emergency room, complaining the whole way because she couldn't afford to miss her plane and the meeting she had scheduled in New York.

With the heroic efforts of the hospital and airport staffs, Twitchell was stitched, bandaged and back at the airport in time for a late plane. However, with both feet in bandages, she couldn't wear anything except boat shoes and, by the time the plane landed, she was already going to be late for the meeting and didn't have time to check into her hotel. She called the editor and explained her plight and he agreed to see her anyway. Twitchell laughs as she recalls the conversation, "I told him that not only was I going to be late but that I was coming in jeans and boat shoes...and was it okay if I brought my luggage? He asked if I was the cousin-from hell coming to stay forever. Anyway, it broke a lot of ice and turned out to be pretty funny walking through Manhattan looking like a bag lady. But the demonstration went really well and we spent an hour and a half together, and he was so impressed that he is doing a five-page solo review on the software.

"During the rest of the trip," Twitchell continues, "my feet and the story continued to break the ice and give me a real connection with people and built a lot of rapport. It was so comical that it got people's attention. I wouldn't recommend this as a way to break the ice for anyone else, but what I learned from it was to be myself as much as possible. Now I just try to be really friendly and have fun. Even though I stay professional, if I feel like doing or saying something stupid, I do. I let them know who I am in a human sort of way. I am very real with them."

Star networking

Products and services are purchased by people. Not purchasing agents, not computers, not corporations—people. They tell their friends and associates when they've gotten good service and they tell them when they've gotten bad service. It is impossible for a salesperson to sell without making contact with people. The more people you know who are potential customers for your product, the more you can build relationships which will eventually turn into sales.

Networking is a critical skill for all salespeople. Skillfully meeting new prospects can keep your sales pipeline filled and smooth the ups and downs of the sales cycle. Networking is not just a numbers game. For it to be effective, you have to have an impact on the people you meet. Walter Kaye, president of Kaye Insurance Associates, an insurance brokerage firm in New York City, states, "The whole basis of business is networking." When you talk to Kaye, he makes you feel like you're the only person in the world and definitely the most important person. He gets people to talk about themselves by asking questions. Kaye shakes his head and laughs, "Why people answer me I don't know. I guess everyone just wants to talk about themselves."

Networking takes connections

Kaye describes his methods and the impact it has in this example, "One experience happened when I was invited to a wedding in Las Vegas. I sat down at a table with a lot of people and a young lady sat down next to me—I didn't know her. It was time for me to leave and I mentioned that I needed to call a cab and she said she would drive me back to my hotel. On the ride back I told her how wonderful New York was and invited her to call me if she ever came to New York and I would show her around. A couple of years later she called and told me she was working at the Tropicana Hotel and asked if I was serious about my offer to show her New York. I was, so I had a chauffeur pick her up and my wife and I took her to the theater and to dinner. The next day we took her to breakfast.

"By the time the weekend was over she said, 'My boss and I are going down to Orlando. I know how crazy you are—would you come down and take us out to dinner?' I went down there and wound up getting their entire insurance account at the Tropicana Hotel and they just recommended Caesar's Palace to us. Next week I'm going out to have dinner with the risk manager there."

Obviously Kaye's meeting with this woman had a powerful impact. He could have ridden back to his hotel with her, handed her a card and said, "Call me if you ever get to New York," in such a way as to have no impact. Somehow Kaye gets past the fear of meeting new people, the fear of putting himself out there. He does this by concentrating so completely on the person he is with, that he forgets his personal insecurities. He not only makes you feel like you're the most important person in his world while he is talking to you, you feel like you are meeting a real person. This is the real Walter Kaye; good, bad or indifferent doesn't matter as much as the fact that he is a real person.

The purpose of networking is to start a friendship—not a friendship in the sense of a soulmate, but in the sense that J. C. Penney meant when he talked about all business being built on friendship. Business is built on trust, caring and a mutual understanding of what the other person is about. With friendship there is a natural desire to promote the interests of the other person. When Kaye made friends with the woman from Las Vegas, she naturally knew about his work as an insurance professional. During their time together she had a chance to understand his professional competence, his ethics, philosophy and his commitment. As their friendship grew, his interests also became her interests.

Too many networking functions and efforts are nothing more than business card exchanges. Rooms filled with eager people looking around for the hottest prospect to pitch gives networking a bad name. Good networking takes time, frequent contact, and a sincere interest in creating friendships. At the same time, for these efforts to have a positive impact on your career success, you have to be meeting people who have the potential to further your goals. You should identify groups of people who are the right type to have an impact on your business and spend your time and efforts with those groups. Once you have selected the groups you want to associate with, you put aside thoughts of immediate payoff and concentrate only on making friends.

One of the superstars of high impact networking is Marc Roberts. Barely into his 30s, Roberts is a streetsmart, boxing promoter whose career began and flourished, in large part, because of his ability to meet and build relationships with people.

Roberts had already established himself as a success in real estate and set records selling cellular phones (he sold 600 in 4 months) when he decided to establish himself as a major player in professional boxing. He is now into the boxing game with as much intensity as he brings to all of his other endeavors. He spent a small fortune building one of the best boxing gyms in the world. Perhaps sportswriter Carl Barbati with *The Plainfield Courier-News* best describes Roberts:

"The boxing business is loaded with crooks, thugs and ne'er-do-wells. The rankings are a joke. A slew of old-timers keep making comebacks, not for the championship belts but strictly and solely for the money.

"Sometimes it seems that every-body connected with boxing is there strictly and solely for the money. Then, along comes a guy like Roberts. Sure, he expects to make money on his boxers, but with him, that's not the point. He makes his millions with a string of businesses, from real estate to restaurants, from a modeling agency to a car telephone company. So far in his young life, everything this guy has touched has turned into gold.

"He got involved with boxing as a college kid because he loved it, and because he could see a few bucks in it. Several millions later, those are still his priorities, which makes him a distinct rarity. Roberts has single-handedly brought big-time boxing back to New Jersey. Not to Atlantic City, but New Jersey, which was once a hotbed of the sport throughout the 1940s and early 1950s."

While Barbati makes Roberts' entry into boxing sound like a corporate venture, it was hardly that when he took his first plunge at age 19. Roberts describes it thus: "I was a 19-year-old kid and didn't know anything. I called Bob Lee, who is now the head of the International Boxing Federation but who was then the state athletic commissioner, because you need a license to promote. I told him my name and he asked how old I was. I told him and he laughed. He asked if I had ever been involved with boxing and I said, 'No.' He asked if I had ever boxed and I said, 'No.' He asked if I knew anything about boxing and I said, 'No.' He said, 'Are you crazy? You'd better think about this and call me back.' We later became good friends and every once in a while he kids me about that first phone conversation."

But Roberts did get his license to promote even though everyone told him not to waste his time or his money. Roberts recalls that first fight, "I just decided to give it a shot. We were fighting in the fighter's home town so I thought a lot of people who knew him would come. And, I figured if the worst came to the worst, I had tried. At least I would learn a lot. You have to try.

"So when I decided to do it, then I went all the way. I was out till the wee hours of the morning putting up posters. The inspiration was all those people telling me I couldn't do it. I hit all the television stations and radio stations and did everything I could. We actually made a profit on that first fight and got written up in a lot of boxing publications."

Roberts invests himself completely in any project he tackles and believes that is a key ingredient in his success. He sometimes spends his Saturday mornings tacking up boxing posters and he promotes his fighters to Wall Street, television stations and anyone else who will listen. He states, "In boxing particularly, no one likes to spend money until the fighter has already made money. We realized that our three fighters have great potential. But boxing is a funny business. I'm really the first guy that has come along and put up big money to expose his fighters and get the word out. We spend money on sending out mailers all over the country—video cassettes and articles. It's all very costly and in boxing nobody wants to spend it until a fighter is already into the big money."

Investment means commitment. "You've got to stay focused," Roberts says. "You've got to understand what you're selling and you've got to live, breathe and sleep it. You can't get discouraged. You have to never give up and if someone says 'no,' you have to go right back to the book and figure out how to get the next person to say 'yes.' You're actually just paying your dues when you get 'no's.'

"You've got to know your priorities. If you want to be a supersalesperson, you've got to be relentless, aggressive and never get discouraged. If you want to be average, you can just work hard from 9 to 6."

Roberts has also been able to learn from his failures along the way. He lost a lot of money promoting a band but he states, "I've had my failures, but you learn from them. I wouldn't trade any of those experiences; they are all helping me now to move forward. Everybody has experiences of not going where they planned but the successful people take that and feed off of it positively. It helps them build a foundation for success."

Networking is an important part of Roberts' everyday business. He describes his style. "You have to do a little homework first to decide if it's someone you want to do business with. Once I determine that the person is ethical and is someone I want to do business with, then I invite him to lunch and get to know him. Then it's a matter of staying in touch and making the person feel like a king."

Make them feel like a king

Roberts explains how he makes people feel like a king, "You take them out to nice restaurants. You find out what people like and dislike. I study the person. You can look at the person's office, or dress or the way he moves. You find ways to give them compliments—sincere, honest compliments. I am always enthusiastic. I love going to a person's office and seeing that they are a little down but when I leave they are laughing. Eye contact and your tone of voice are extremely important. You also have to make sure that the person understands that you really appreciate their business. They could give their business to someone else. Being appreciative and loyal to people who buy from you or help you goes a long way."

Another super-networker is Bev Hyman. Today Hyman is the president of a powerful New York management consulting firm specializing in communication, training, and development. But, in 1978, she was a full-time professor with a wide range of skills making a minimal salary. She decided it was time for a change.

When she decided to go into business, she realized that she needed to have other people marketing for her. She focused on building such client loyalty that her clients would actually become her sales representatives. "I think that is critical for almost any business, particularly service businesses," Hyman states. She builds friendships with her clients and makes sure she connects with them frequently on a personal basis. She sends cards, flowers, balloons and other remembrances for different occasions. "Even if they're not a client," Hyman explains, "but maybe someone I'm trying to nurse along, trying to build a relationship with, I try to be a constant and generous presence and a humane and interested presence. What is helpful is that I like people and I feel genuine about it—it is not a ploy or a tactic."

Hyman talks about making contact with people, "I teach a seminar on networking with a marvelously successful chairman of the board of the largest privately held insurance brokerage firm in the country (Walter Kaye). He and I do a program on networking, which is a lot of fun. But we both agree. Networking means developing a supermarket of contacts. When we talk about making contact,

it means something different than what most people think it means. It means going outside of your circle of friends. You have to bust out of your circle. In recent years, I have broken out of my circle by becoming a community activist. I have joined the boards of several prestigious organizations like the New York Opera. While you don't go into these things primarily because you have a business point of view, you can't help but do business because it is in these places that you meet decision-makers and people who you can do business with."

In order for your efforts to have a high impact, people have to understand what makes you special, what differentiates you from your competitors. Hyman found two ways to differentiate herself. She explains, "The first way I differentiated myself was to find a niche within the market. I found my niche in training the trainer, and then differentiated myself through excellence. I mean 110 percent-every-day-and-never-a-failure kind of excellence. I think that the people who hold themselves to that kind of a standard, can begin to write more of their own tickets. It doesn't have so much to do with brains as it does with desire."

Get their "junk box"

Because Hyman has a burning desire to provide an uncommon level of service, she spends an extraordinary amount of time up front with her prospects. She goes through an extensive questioning process with them to determine exactly what their needs and objectives are. Then she asks them for a box of their "junk"—all of their brochures or annual reports, any training materials they have used, or anything that will give her a better understanding of who they are and what they are trying to do. The information she gathers through her questions and the "junk" box gives her a basis for designing a program that will exceed their expectations. Hyman makes a special effort to understand the career objectives of her clients. She wants her training programs to benefit her client's personal objectives as well as the company objectives.

Hyman believes that you should never apologize during a presentation because it sets a negative tone. She tells a story about how she always converts a possible negative into a positive. "I was going to do a two-day presentation skills program for a major client. It was a group of engineers—very high-level people. I left my house at 5 a.m. and usually that gets me to the client's at 7 a.m. in preparation for an 8:30 seminar. This morning, though, there was a fluke hurricane in Connecticut. There was nothing on the news about a hurricane but on the way, the hurricane hit and bridges were washed out, trucks were overturned—it was ghastly. I stopped at a roadside phone and told the client that I was going to be an hour late

and told them to have the people come at 9:30 a.m. rather than 8:30.

"All the way there I was thinking about how I always say never apologize because it is such a downer—forget all the excuses about flat tires, and so on. Go with the positive. So I was wondering what I would say to these people. Finally I got there and I walked in and said, 'Ladies and gentlemen, good morning. I came through a hurricane to be here with you!' And they applauded."

High impact networking ideas

All prospecting activities should have high impact. Star performers avoid low-impact, time-wasting activities. Attending meetings and handing out business cards is a low-impact activity—getting involved and elected to the board of directors of an organization is high-impact. Many of the top real estate agents have discontinued or limited their "farming" activities. Typically these activities involve the agent leaving calendars or notices at all residences within a predefined area. Most agents have found that these items have little impact and are often thrown away. They don't tell the prospect who the agent is; they don't begin a friendship.

Creativity can sometimes add impact to an otherwise unimpressive activity. Some salespeople print games, puzzles, quotes, mission statements or other catchy information on the back of their business cards. Delivering flowers or balloons along with a routine canvass call opens a lot of doors and creates an impact. In Southern California, Helice Bridges is known as the "the blue ribbon lady." She has developed a self-esteem program primarily for schools where students, parents and others are presented with a blue ribbon that states, "Who I am makes a difference." Some salespeople purchase those ribbons in quantity and present them to their clients, prospects and the people they meet at network functions. There are an infinite number of ways to differentiate yourself and add impact to your prospecting efforts. Here are some additional ideas from other sales stars:

Bill Stack, manager, Eastern Communications Region, GE Information Services, watches *The Wall Street Journal* in the "Who's News" section and sends the people mentioned a letter of congratulations and follows up later. One follow-up call with the vice chairman of the board of one company gave him seven leads. Stack has his own personal cards that he sends to his customers after a good meeting—he writes personalized, handwritten notes to these people.

Marc Rosenberg, vice president of Cushman & Wakefield, a large commercial real estate firm, uses his service orientation to bring him referrals. Rosenberg states, "About 50 percent of my business is from referrals or recommendations. The way I approach a client and provide service is to follow-up with them once a quarter. When they move into a new facility, I send them a small token gift such as a plant or a clock. I follow up with a card on their birthdays and on holidays. I try to be a friend to the people. One example is a deal I did a couple of years ago for a small computer company, leasing them about 1,000 square feet of space. Later they were merging with another company so the customer called and said, "Come over and speak to me." I did and he wound up taking 3,000 square feet. Later it was 9,000 and just recently they went into 30,000 square feet. That is a large deal—the average in this industry is about 5,000 square feet. He has recommended me to his wife's company; also to one of his clients, a large shipping company; and to his computer company. At this point I have probably done about 60,000 square feet worth of deals all coming from giving the best service possible to a small 1,000 square-feet client. In our business, the average person probably does between 50,000 to 100,000 square feet per year and I did that from one referral."

Buddy Olerio, an agent with Prudential Insurance, has won almost every award offered by Prudential, several times. Consistently in the top ranks of Prudential's sales force, Olerio maintains the same intense prospecting and networking schedule that he established for himself in his first year. He consistently prospects enough to set 20 appointments per week. Out of 20 appointments per week, he averages seven sales. Olerio builds relationships with the people he contacts. If he meets someone at a party he will get their card and a week later he will send them a letter commenting on the meeting and giving them an overview of his products and service. A week or so later he calls them and asks to set up an appointment. He takes the time to build a relationship rather than being seen as a hard-charging, fast-talking insurance salesperson.

Robert Montgomery, chairman of Montgomery, Zukerman, Davis, Inc., an advertising agency in Indianapolis, recommends finding four new people every month and getting to know them so well they'll tell you their problems. He says, "The salesperson who doesn't constantly make an effort to open new accounts will never be a true success. When you find out what people's problems are, you also find out what you can do to solve those problems. Often you'll gain a customer just by being attuned to his needs." Montgomery recalls how he got into one account. "I was trying to get into the account but the executive was refusing to see me. I found out that one of his pet projects was getting inner-city kids interested in the Boy Scouts. I joined the committee and we made progress in that direction." The strategy paid off—it became Montgomery's first million-dollar account.

Volunteer networking

If you want to expand your circle of acquaintances and contribute to a cause at the same time, you can volunteer your time and services to a nonprofit organization. It is important to pick a cause that interests you but also one that will attract the type of people who might become a valuable part of your network—typically people who are potential customers or people who could refer you to potential customers.

Ice breakers

Relationships cannot be maintained with tricks and gimmicks, but sometimes a bit of humor can be an excellent way to get past the awkwardness of the first meeting or first call. Here are several stories of ice breakers that worked.

Bob Benson, field sales manager for Sales & Marketing Management, tells of a salesperson who had been trying to reach a customer. He had a program worked out that he thought would be excellent for the customer, but he couldn't get through to him and all of his calls were unreturned. Finally the salesperson called the customer and left a message that the customer had won a red convertible. He got a call back in five minutes! In the meantime, he had a toy, red convertible hand-delivered to the customer and it arrived while they were on the phone. Since the customer was with an automotive company, there was a connection with the gimmick and the customer was intrigued enough with the ploy that he granted the salesperson an appointment, which resulted in a substantial sale.

Vince Espada, the number-one dealer support manager in the country with Konica Business Machines, was looking for a way to make himself different without being obnoxious when he cold-called clients. He knew that all of his competitors handed out business cards but that most of them were ignored and wound up in the trash. One day he was playing around with the copier and enlarged his business card. "I thought if I handed out an enlarged business card, maybe they would notice it and keep it. I enlarged it up to 11 x 17 and started handing it out. This was in Washington, D.C., and it's pretty stuffy—a lot of lawyers and trade associations. They weren't used to seeing something like this. It was before enlarging was a common feature so it was a tremendous ice breaker! The receptionist would look astounded and ask how I did it. Of course, that would lead me into explaining the enlargement feature. It got the interest going and soon I was known as the guy with the big business card. Often they put it on their bulletin boards."

James Euwer, II, star salesperson with Armstrong World Industries, a flooring and ceiling manufacturer, once ran an extremely successful new account campaign. A major part of the strategy was to send potential clients a letter of introduction followed by a Federal Express letter announcing that he would be calling the next day. The impression was that the call must be important if it was announced by a Federal Express package, and Armstrong wound up getting appointments with 90 percent of the people who received the mailing.

Kevin Patterson, national sales star with Marriott, wanted to talk to a meeting planner about the possibility of holding a meeting at a Marriott property. The customer was avoiding Patterson's efforts. He broke the ice by delivering a box of donuts to the client's office. That may not be all that original but taped to the top was a full-color, glossy picture of the property. Everyone who reached for a donut got a visual impact of the meeting site.

John Wimper, another creative Marriott marketer, was trying to convince Jack Sentell, senior director of the southeast region field operations for Chick-fil-A, to hold a meeting at Marco Island, Florida. Rather than just send information, Wimper bought a Chick-fil-A meal, ate it, and then filled up the empty box with Marco Island promotional items and sent it to Sentell. "I was impressed by his efforts to put

Marco Island together with Chick-fil-A and we wound up selecting them for our meeting," states Sentell.

Bill Czapar, CEO of Anaheim Custom Extruders, Inc., wanted to have an uninterrupted conversation with his client at lunch but was having difficulty getting him to break away. He came up with the idea of picking the client up in a chauffeured limo that would whisk him away to the restaurant. Now he invites his 20 top customers to lunch four times a year and seldom gets turned down.

Gimmicks and humor can be very effective, if they are related to the desired objective and are truly humorous and not intended to deceive. The toy convertible had to be delivered immediately to avoid having the potential customer think he had really won a car. Ice breakers of this sort also depend on the style of the salesperson. Some people can carry off this type of humor and some people can't. Not everyone could pull off some of these ice breakers. And they don't have to. Success in sales does not depend on gimmicks and ice breakers, but they can be effective at breaking down barriers. And, they can be a lot of fun!

Gaining referrals

One of the easiest methods to make cold calling easier is to turn them into warm calls. The more a customer knows about you and your company, the more comfortable he or she will be with you. When you send an introductory letter on your company's stationery, the prospect starts to form an opinion as to your legitimacy, your product and your ability to help him or her meet the company's needs. That letter should be a reassurance that you are trying to help—that you want a chance to see if there is any fit between his or her needs and your products or services.

Referrals are an excellent warm-up. The minute you can mention the name of someone the prospect knows, you have moved from the position of a possibly hostile stranger to a possible friend. When customers have received excellent service from a salesperson who has taken the time to build a strong relationship with them, they are almost always willing to provide referrals or references.

Art Mahony, regional sales manager with Ricoh Corporation, built his business by providing extraordinary service to his clients. When Xerox quit being the only game in town, the floodgates of copier salespeople were opened on businesses everywhere. Some small businesses felt that every other person who walked through their doors was selling copiers. In spite of that sales environment, Mahony sold over two years of quota in his first six months of selling copiers.

Because he does such an outstanding job of service and support, Mahony's clients are happy to provide him with references. Mahony tells about one instance when he had sold a machine to a real estate company. In the process of installing the machine and servicing it, he became friends with the husband and wife who owned the company and occasionally used them as a reference for other prospects. "Sometimes I took clients to that office to show them the machine," Mahony explains. "Once I took a nurse who was looking for a copier to this office and while we were talking, my customer walked in. I introduced her to the nurse and she said, 'Forget about the machine, the only thing it does is make copies—the best thing about this deal is that you get Art Mahony with it.' I was embarrassed and said 'Thank you very much,' put an original on the glass, and made one copy. The nurse looked at it and then at me and said, 'We'll buy it.' It really came down to one customer referencing another sincerely. The nurse got the sense that if she bought something through me and my organization, she would be taken care of. That's not a real fancy idea but that's it. When prospects get a reference like that, they really believe that I will be there to take care of them."

Emotional bank account

Kim Lundgreen, star salesperson with Franklin International Institute, does almost all of his sales through referrals. Franklin sells productivity improvement systems and seminars and Lundgreen builds what he calls positive emotional bank accounts with his clients so that they are happy to give him references. Lundgreen explains his 'bank account' theory. "Basically you either have a positive balance or you're in the red. If you have deposits on hand, you can take out withdrawals. If the client really likes me and I have spent a lot of extra time with him and I need him for a reference, he will want to do it because I have a positive emotional bank account with him.

"My big thing is reference selling— to get someone with whom I have a high bank account to call or write a letter to someone. I try to find someone who will be an in-house salesperson for me. I don't like to go in cold—I like to preheat the company. I'll research the company and find out whatever I can and then I'll go in with something I can talk to them about. Or I will try to get someone else to say 'Hey, you'd better look at Franklin.' I'll try to get them into a public seminar or a corporate seminar.

"Sometimes I find someone in the company who has been through the training and is excited about Franklin. I try to get that person to talk to the person I need to talk to. I qualify upfront in a hurry. I make sure that I'm talking to the right person. I introduce myself and let them know what I'm about and tell them about Franklin. I let them know that I am looking for the decision-maker who has access to spend money for our training. I ask them in different ways. From there, I'll use the reference or spend some time warming them up. I spend a lot of money—I'll send them a day planner kit and get them to try it. I want them to touch it and get used to it so they keep it. Our key is the training that goes with it—so I try to convince them to experience the training or have them send someone to the training. There is no magic. I try to practice smart selling. I will spend half an hour thinking about an account or prospect—doing research, finding out the divisions of the company. Most of the time I don't go through the training department. I go to the sales department because I can relate to them. Or through the vice president of production—someone who needs the benefit of productivity. I find someone who is excited.

"I always tell them that if they have any dissatisfaction at all, we won't bill them. I have such a positive attitude that this program will have a major impact and I try to let them know that. 'This will empower you and your people and it will make you a hero as the training director.' I let them know they can't go wrong in doing this. We start out with a pilot so they can see the program. If I can do one seminar in a company, then I'm there.

"I went through the old-style sales training with all the closing techniques. But, in the end if you are friendly, responsive and sensitive, it just happens automatically. I will use the techniques but that is just part of it. I think a key to my selling is just being friendly—maybe even overly friendly. If people are busy, I say, 'No problem, I'll call back. When's a good time?' I try to be real sensitive to their needs. Sometimes I call with no business reason at all just to say 'Hi, how's it working out?'

"Our mission statement is to help people gain control over their lives. It's fun to be in a business where you feel like you are making a difference. I show clients our governing values all the time. As part of a seminar I will custom-print the client's mission statement or governing values and make it part of the participant's book. That's the kind of stuff we do that makes a difference."

Profile sheets

The more you know about a prospective client, the easier it is for you to know how to approach the client, what to talk about and what his or her needs might be. Every successful salesperson has a system for collecting information about prospective customers. Perhaps the most thorough system around is Harvey Mackay's. He has a 66-question profile of every customer, which includes where the customer went to school (high school and college), the names and interests of all his or her children, previous employment, favorite places for lunch and even medical history! The process of collecting this information makes the salesperson extremely aware of every aspect of the customer's environment and would almost certainly provide a common point of reference. It is a lot easier to call on someone when you find out that both of your 6-year-olds are playing soccer in the same league. (For a complete sample of the "Mackay 66," see *Swim With the Sharks Without Being Eaten Alive*, pages 46-53.)

The "Mackay 66" is probably too lengthy and intense for most salespeople. The best form is one you design yourself and includes things like birth date, marital status and children, special interests (including favorite sports), product interests, goals and objectives and so on. If you are selling beauty products, your profile sheet will probably be very personal and have notes about colors and style preferences. If you are selling telecommunication systems, profile sheets will include the decision procedure, corporate strategy, notes on current equipment configurations and so on. For high-ticket, long sales-cycle items, you may even develop a book about the customer with information sheets on all the decision-makers, pictures of the facility, diagrams of equipment, product sheets, organization charts, important dates and deadlines and

anything else that helps you understand the company and its people.

The profile sheet at the end of the chapter comes from Kevin Patterson, national account executive with Marriott. Kevin tells the following story about one of his profile sheets. "I had one customer who happened to get a copy of his profile. The comments on the sheet said he was a native New Yorker who needed to be handled with kid gloves. It also said he was a screamer and had a strong ego. He called me one day and said he was faxing me something. It was a copy of his profile sheet. He said, 'You think I'm a screamer?' I said, 'Tom, you can be.' He said, 'You think I have a strong ego?' I answered, 'Yup.' He said, 'Well, I am a native New Yorker,' he paused and then continued, 'I think it's pretty neat that you take the time to analyze me. Just wanted to let you know that I know.' Of course, honesty was the key."

If you have your profile sheets printed on the same size paper as your day organizing system, the sheet can go right behind the date when you have a meeting or a scheduled phone call with the client. It then serves as a reminder and a quick review of the account status and what's important to that client.

The Action Plan at the end of the chapter will help you add impact to your networking.

Two Ideas:

What two ideas did you get from this chapter?

_____

_____

I dare you to use those ideas to broaden your network and increase your level of success.

Action Plan

```
Develop Your Own
Profile Sheet
```

Profile sheets need to be tailored to your specific situation and client base. If you have a lot of accounts, you can probably only keep a relatively small amount of information on each. It you only have five or six accounts, you will want to know almost everything about them and you will have profile sheets on several people within the accounts.

1. **What format do you need?** If you use a day planner, you may want the pages to fit the size of your planner. Will the data go into a computer? You may want the layout to match your computer database.

2. **What personal information do you need?** What information has been important to you on previous calls? Do you need to know a lot about your prospect's personal life? Do your prospects expect you to remember their birthdays? The names of their children? Their hobbies or favorite sports? Personal ambitions?

3. **What product/service information do you need?** What information will help you service this account better? Goals and objectives? Buying patterns and product preferences? Decision-making authority? Purchasing process?

4. **What miscellaneous information would help?** What general information would help you keep track of this client/prospect? Client hot buttons? Company structure? Personality quirks?

5. **Design a form that meets your needs and use it.**

Meeting Planner Profile

Company Name: _____

Name:_____ Birthday:_____

Title: _____Age:_____

Job description:_____

_____

Reports to: _____

Secretary's name: _____

Work phone:_____ FAX:_____

Home phone:_____

Home address:_____

_____

Spouse's name:_____

Children's names/ages:_____

_____

Hobbies:_____

_____

Favorite room amenity:_____

Dining preference:_____

_____

Hot buttons/comments:_____

_____

_____

_____

_____

_____

_____

_____

_____

_____

_____

Sample Profile Sheet from Marriott

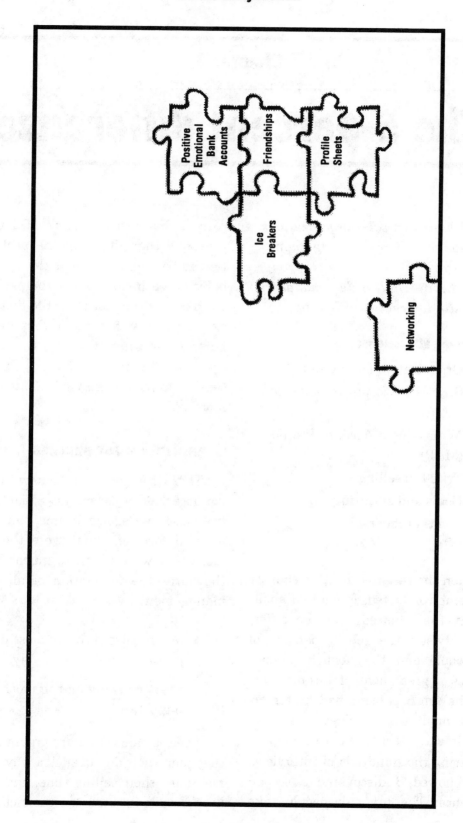

Chapter 3

The 5-percent difference

"I have seen sales organizations turned around by sending thank-you cards."

—Kevin Hall, sales manager, Franklin International Institute

Coming attractions:

♦ Organization for success

♦ Strategic Account Management (SAM)

♦ Management Account Profile (MAP)

♦ Trim tab selling

♦ Goals and sprinting

♦ Mental rehearsal

When the research for this chapter was being conducted, I was told about a study that showed that the difference between the top 5 percent of salespeople and the next 5 percent (besides a great deal of income) was that the top 5 percent had better organizational skills. They managed their time and territory better.

During the hundreds of interviews that followed, I discovered a second difference: The top salespeople take care of that last 5 percent of details; they buy the gift, wrap the package, tie the bow and then add the sprig of baby's breath that makes the package sparkle. It's the last step, the little bit extra, the last 5 percent that distinguishes the sales stars. Do these add up to a 10-percent difference in success? I think they may add up to even more.

Organization for success

There is a story that Andrew Carnegie once paid a consultant $25,000 for two ideas. In Carnegie's time, that was a small fortune. What were the two ideas that were worth so much? Here they are—the foundation of all time management:

♦ Make a list of the 10 most important things to do today.

♦ Start working on the most important.

The top sales stars are organized—they plan their day in such a way as to maximize their selling time, and they keep detailed records on their clients.

Most top salespeople have day organizers such as those produced by Franklin, DayRunner or DayTimer—and they use them. All the canvassing in the world, all the sales skills in the world can't produce a sale if you miss a meeting, a follow-up, a phone appointment or a planned event.

Kim Lundgreen with Franklin has three books on an otherwise clean desk—his day planner, a book of profile sheets on his corporate clients and a book of profile sheets on his government clients. Lundgreen explains his system, "On my day page, I write down the first name and company of everyone I want to call that day. I do most of this planning the night before but I prioritize my activities in the morning. Of course, I also write things down throughout the day. Then I get on the phone and start through it. I only spend 10 to 15 minutes doing the organization."

Lundgreen's organization also helps him make a statement to his prospects about how he follows through. "I'll make a future telephone appointment three weeks down the road at 9:20 a.m. By using my system, I'll be prompted to make that call and when I call, I'll say 'Hi, Sally, what time is it?' and we'll laugh." But, Sally understands that Lundgreen does what he says he will do—he calls when he said he will and follows up on all his promises.

One of the benefits that Lundgreen has identified about using his day planner is the motivation it gives him to actually do what he has planned to do. "The planner is a good tool because it just keeps staring at you. Sometimes when I come in, I'll just sit here and stare at the phone for a while. The planner tells me to call Don at the Coast Guard—and even though I don't feel like calling him, I do. I think about what I can accomplish if I just make that call and move on. I'm big on checking things off—when you check something off, you get a little endorphin. It's really fun. I want to get those items done."

The day planner also helps him deal with rejection. "When I have a good call," Lundgreen explains, "I'll get really excited and I'll do a victory salute. I'll be so high that I'll make three or four more calls right away. Then there are the downers—after one of them, I'll walk around and get a drink and regroup. It'll bother me for awhile. But, I get out of it by going back at it. Sometimes I'll call and be getting rejection and negative feedback and I'll get frustrated so I turn in my planner to my list of all the seminars I've ever done. The list shows me how many people came, what type of program it was and who taught it. I'll go back and look through this list again and try to see who might be ready to do another seminar. I'll focus on that and write up a short list of five companies that I should call again." By going back to his list of successes, Lundgreen is automatically dealing with people who know him and like him—people he has been successful with before. So he moves from failure and frustration back to success. That gets him pumped up again.

Marc Rosenberg with Cushman & Wakefield states, "I try to maximize my time—to touch every piece of paper only once—everything has a file. A key thing in sales is to be very orderly. All my deals are on the computer with a tickler file so when I arrive in the morning, I know exactly when something is coming up. People have to have an inner feeling about whether they want to be successful or not. I come to work every day and I want to leave feeling like I've done something constructive. I think you have to appreciate life and want to do the best you can. You have to go for the best you can be."

SAM: Strategic Account Management

Organization is extremely important for sales reps dealing with major accounts. Jeff Mandel is the director of sales support for Ascom Timeplex, a company that provides telecommunication and data networks worldwide. In his office is a poster with a picture of Yosemite Sam and the caption says, "Sam says plan or die!" Timeplex developed an account management model they call SAM—Strategic Account Management. Mandel says, "SAM is a planning function that looks at a salesperson's territory and customer base then builds an approach for managing it." SAM helps the salesperson understand the customer's needs and then plan the necessary activities and time frames around those needs. "This type of planning exercise is worthless unless salespeople understand its value," says Mandel. "SAM has become a proven and valuable sales tool for us." Using SAM, the sales staff and sales management review their current account/prospect list and group them into the following categories:

- Current clients
- Current clients with significant growth potential
- Current accounts that are vulnerable to competition
- Prospects with significant revenue opportunities

Accounts in each category are prioritized and plans are developed for targeted accounts. The account plan provides a current assessment of the customer's situation and outlines future activities and time frames for the salesperson. Questions that should be asked to develop the account plan include:

- What are the sales objectives for this account?
- What is the account's current situation?
- Where does the account want to be?

◆ What resources are at the client's disposal?

◆ What time considerations are there?

◆ Who are the key decision-makers?

◆ How will progress be monitored?

Timeplex has developed a four-page SAM form that leads the salesperson through a customer profile, a review of existing communication systems and networks, an analysis of who the competition is and what their strengths and weaknesses are, a forecast of the opportunity with the identification of appropriate tactics and the actual activities necessary to accomplish the objective.

SAM is designed for major accounts involving long lead-time products or services. It is especially good for focusing the efforts of sales teams and for keeping everyone concerned in tune with the sales efforts made for that account. Similar forms can be designed by individual salespeople to meet their own needs.

Management Account Profile

One of the most effective tools for organizing your territory and your efforts is the Management Account Profile—MAP. After years of selling, managing and observing sales professionals, I realized that 80 percent of the deficiencies in salespeople aren't in their sales skills or in their product knowledge. Most of the time it has to do with their activity level. They aren't doing enough canvassing, presentations, demonstrations, etc. The reasons for not doing the necessary activities could be lack of self-confidence or motivation, but more often, it's just a lack of organization and understanding.

Many sales managers use daily or weekly cold call or account report sheets in order to manage the activities of their sales staff. The salesperson spends a lot of time filling out these reports and usually thinks of them as more of a hassle than a help. Because of the cumbersome nature of these report sheets, managers often don't spend a lot of time with them and opportunities for coaching are lost. The old adage, "Don't expect what you don't inspect," comes into play and the whole exercise is viewed as merely paperwork.

The idea of MAP is to take all the information about the account status and throw it up in front of the salespeople and managers in a simplified way that actually affects activity levels. MAP becomes your territory-at-a-glance. MAP boards can be done on cork boards (most salespeople use 2' x 3' boards) with cards and push pins or on magnetic white boards with small, magnetic strips. You need to be able to move the information. The board is divided into columns to represent the various stages of the sale from first appointment to close. Typical columns are: First appointment, needs analysis, demo, presentation/proposal, close. Additional columns might be added for training and implementation or follow-up, or a separate board could be established for service and follow-up.

Manage people not paperwork

Cards are made up for each prospect showing the prospect's name, company, phone number and the date that the stage was completed. Prospect cards are moved to the next stage only after that stage is completed. Prospect cards are not even put on the board until after the first meeting. The card would not be moved to the needs analysis column until the salesperson had met with the client and had developed a clear understanding of his needs. By establishing the MAP board, you can instantly tell where you are. Do you need to do more prospecting? More demonstrations? More proposals? What actions do you need to take to move prospects into the next stage of the sale? Allen Nettleton, sales manager of Quality Office Products, says, "Implementation of MAP has cut the sales reps' paperwork in half and has increased their activity by over 10 percent." By decreasing paperwork, sales managers have more time for training, coaching and planning.

Charting your sales stages

The definition of a successful sales call is one that advances the sale or moves it forward. Unsuccessful sales calls are where the salesperson receives a "no" or a no-advance response. Successful salespeople identify the stages of their typical sale and the increments of progress that it takes to advance the sale to the next stage. Activities can then be planned to achieve those increments of progress. The MAP board helps the salesperson visually track progress through the stages.

Rick Dyer, director of sales operations with Apple Computer talks about the organization philosophy behind MAP. "I tend to use the funnel selling methodology. This means I've got prospects who are in the close phase, I've got prospects who are in the analysis phase, and I've got prospects who may be only suspects at this point. And what I try to do is maintain an organization that moves people from one step to the next. That keeps me on top of the business in terms of the status of those prospects. The idea is that a lot of the work that I'm doing today may not come to fruition for six months or more. What you want to do to keep up the flow of orders is to say, 'I need to be investing time at all levels of the selling cycle all the time, and if I'm only working on suspects, I'm not going to sell much this month.' The danger is that people will concentrate on just the closing. That's not sufficient—a lot of selling takes place in the initial contacts and what you've got to do is develop a stream of prospects that will in time convert into customers." In order to manage that stream, you need a tool such as MAP. Having a visual picture helps you focus on all of your accounts and organize your territory.

Sales managers also find the MAP boards extremely helpful since they can get a sense of where a salesperson is just by looking at their board. Michael Sapere, sales manager with A-Copy, states, "MAP has made a big difference for me because now I can walk around and see exactly where my reps are in each stage of the sale. The best part is that now that the boards are in full view, sales reps tell me the areas they need to work on instead of me having to tell them. No one likes to have a board with only three cards showing! My reps agreed to use MAP on their own because they saw the benefits of the system right away. Some of the reps even carry the board in the car with them for constant exposure to their account activity."

Phillip Harbour, sales manager with Modern Business Systems, states, "MAP has made a tremendous difference in my own productivity. Now I can view my sales reps' activity in a much clearer picture and plan strategy right away." Another difference the MAP system seems to make is in forecasting. One manager found that before using MAP, about 50 percent of the forecasted sales actually closed. After establishing the MAP system, about 80 to 90 percent of the sales closed. Putting the prospect on the board in full view seems to have a motivating effect on the salesperson. No one wants to pull a card off without a sale. Many managers require the card to come off if some activity hasn't happened within 60 days or whatever time frame is appropriate.

Eliminate marginal accounts

Reviewing and removing marginal accounts is one of the most difficult things that reps do. No one likes to let go of an account that you have spent time on. Louis Slawetsky, president of Industry Analysts, Inc., says, "Sales reps are afraid to qualify. The reason is that their manager told them that they should have 30 or 50 or 100 prospects in their prospect books and if the person they are talking to is not qualified, they would have to go get another one. It is easier for them mentally to carry someone in their list of prospects, even if they aren't qualified, than to find a new qualified person. This is probably one of the leading causes of failures of salespeople." Salespeople who reach the highest levels of success fervently weed out a lot of clients. They aren't afraid to let go of marginal prospects because they are time-wasters. It's tough to let go but it is a key difference between the sales aces and the average performers.

Rick Dyer states that analyzing his prospects and the stages of the sale helped him manage his territory and get rid of marginal accounts. "I found that it helped me prioritize my time and it also set off alarm bells real quickly if I found out that I was empty in a particular area. You have to develop your territory, you can't wait for it to appear.

"The other thing that is critical is that you've got to analyze your probability of success and invest your time, which is your primary resource, into those that have a high degree of probability. The failures that I have seen are people who look at a big deal and think, 'This is a big deal and if I can get this I'll be set.' The problem is that they have a 10-percent chance of getting it and in the meantime they are missing out on deals which might have a high probability. If they lose the big one they are in trouble."

MAP helps sales reps identify and eliminate marginal accounts. Prospects who haven't moved to the next step within so many days (or weeks, or months) can be moved to an inactive file. This file can be worked periodically to see if the prospect's status has changed.

The next page shows an example of what a MAP board might look like, and the Action Plan at the end of this chapter will help you develop your MAP board.

Trim tab selling

There is a small device on the elevator of an airplane known as a trim tab. The trim tab is critical to maintaining a straight and level attitude of the plane. But it takes only minor adjustments of the trim tab to have a major effect on the plane's attitude. In selling, details are the trim tab. Details like thank-you letters, follow-up phone calls, punctuality, small gifts or cards are all examples of details, little things that have a major effect on our sales success. Most of the details involved with trim tab selling are very basic. They aren't sophisticated techniques or complicated maneuvering, they are just basic things that, too often, we forget.

Kevin Hall with Franklin International Institute runs a different sales campaign every two months. A recent campaign was called FOCUS: Furnishing Our Customers Unmatched Service. Hall states, "We asked the sales reps to send out five thank-you cards a day. If every salesperson would send out at least one thank-you card per day, whether it's to a prospect or an internal customer, it would change an organization. I've seen this one action turn around an entire organization in 90 days." Mike Lupfer, director of national accounts for Marriott, gives a different twist to saying thanks. When his region won Marriott's top region award, they sent all of their accounts a gift of Missouri Ozarks smoked bacon with a note that said, "Thanks for helping us bring home the bacon."

Management Account Profile

First Call		2nd Stage Presentation	3rd Stage Demo	4th Stage Proposal	5th Stage Close
A	R	C	H	J	B
E	S	I	F		
K	T	D			
L	U	V			
M					
N					
O					
P					
Q					

Sample Management Account Profile Board

ACCOUNT NAME *ABC Company*

Stage Completed   **Date**   **Product**

✓ **Stage 1**   5/2/91

___ **Stage 2**   ___   xxx

___ **Stage 3**   ___   **$ Potential**

___ **Stage 4**   ___   #15 K

___ **Stage 5**   ___

Reprinted with permission from *Reseller Management*

Throughout the interviews with the top sales stars, I found a commitment to the basics, to the details. Top salespeople seem to find the time to do the thank-you notes, to provide the extra little bit of information, to do the after-the-sale call to make sure the customer is happy, to find ways to add value to the sales process.

Arthur Bragg, former senior editor of *Sales and Marketing Management*, says that what differentiates the very top level of salesperson from the average performer is concern for the client's business and the willingness to take care of the details. He says, "Today's top salespeople all consider themselves business managers, concerned as much about their client's businesses as their own. Also, they're there for the client even after the sale has been made. They're at the installation of the product or checking on the billing...whatever. They take the extra step."

Chocolate lobsters

An example of trim tab selling comes from Gail Wargo, national account executive with Marriott. Wargo works out of Washington, D.C., primarily with trade associations. Because there are a lot of decision-makers involved with trade associations, a major focus for Wargo has been helping meeting planners make sales presentations to their association boards. Often this means providing them with audio-visual materials or coaching them on benefits or presentation skills or anything else they need to make a good presentation. Wargo explains how this worked at one presentation, "We had one group that was trying to decide between Boston and Toronto and we wanted them to choose Boston. We scheduled the meeting for a Marriott facility in Boston and when the board arrived, at each place was a little wire lobster cage with a chocolate lobster inside of it and a watercolor card of Boston inside with a poem about the meeting. It made a tremendous impact on them."

David Poznak, president of Vision Products also believes that it is the little things that make the difference in sales success. "I always do the little extras," Poznak explains. "With most salespeople, after you get the confirmed purchase order, you don't hear from them until next year or until time for the next order. I always make sure I call them about a week after the delivery to make sure everything was okay. Was the packaging okay? Was everything received? I put it on my calendar book to call them once every three to four weeks, just to see how things are going and to see how the line is selling. Sometimes if a line is going slow, I will offer them a small extra discount to help get sales going.

"Sales to me is secondary," Poznak explains, "and the relationship is first. It is more important to have an honest relationship. I want everything nice and open and if I can't fit their needs, I come right out and tell them." Poznak once turned down a $200,000 order because he didn't believe he could deliver the quality the customer wanted. In the short-run it was a painful decision, but it built trust with his customer and developed into a strong relationship. The customer was Kids 'R Us and because of his honesty he got their business. At the time they had about 30 stores. Poznak smiles as he recalls that incident, "Who knew then that they were going to be the power they are with 160 stores?" Poznak was awarded the Kids 'R Us "Vendor of the Year" award for his outstanding service and quality.

Steve Albano, president of Offtech, a large office products company echoes these comments. "Success doesn't come from one big thing, it comes from a lot of little things. Each day, it requires consistency and follow-up with the customer to make sure they are receiving the kind of service that we are committed to. It requires constant follow-up with our service organization—which applies to the people in billing, collections, the people who answer the phones, everyone. It is a constant, daily kind of reinforcement." Albano's commitment to the highest level of service is somewhat unique in the office equipment industry and earned him a write-up in the August, 1987, *Inc.* magazine, which stated, "To most manufacturers and distributors, the service department is a necessary

evil. To Offtech, Inc., it's the source of half the profits." By developing a high-level, professional service department, Offtech can provide fast, reliable service to customers and make it a source of profit.

Set goals

John Stuart Mill, the English philosopher and economist, once wrote: "One person with a belief is equal to a force of 99 who have only interest." One of the differences between people with interests and people with beliefs is that the people with deep-seated beliefs set goals and act on them. Anthony Robbins in his book *Unlimited Power* reports a study conducted by Yale University. Graduates of the class of 1953 were asked if they had a clear, specific set of goals written down with a plan for achieving these goals. Only 3 percent had written such goals. Twenty years later the researchers went back and interviewed the surviving members of that class. They found that the 3 percent with written specific goals were worth more in financial terms than the entire rest of the class put together. Researchers also found a higher level of happiness and satisfaction with the 3 percent group.

Salespeople thrive on feedback. They constantly want to know how they are doing. They need to be able to measure their performance against other salespeople, national averages or their own standards. They do this not only because of their desire for financial rewards, but also because they like the feeling of winning, of accomplishment. In order to have a standard to perform against, salespeople need goals and objectives. A useful model for goals and objectives is that they should be SMART—Specific, Measurable, Achievable, Realistic and Trackable.

Having goals allows us to make life an enjoyable game and helps us focus on the specific direction that we want to take. Goals are subjective and negotiable. We create them; we can change them. While they shouldn't be treated so lightly that they don't affect our actions, they also shouldn't become a burden. Goals are like a roadmap for personal and professional growth. As our lives evolve and change, our goals will be adjusted. We will always be in a position of *arriving* rather than *having arrived*.

Harvey Cook is an insurance salesperson. However, he only sells two days a week for seven months out of the year—that's all the time it takes him to meet the incredible goals he sets for himself. He once sold $4 million of insurance in eight days! Cook recommends, "Don't just set goals or write to-do lists. Improve your effectiveness every day. Don't compete for number one! Compete with yourself. I owe everything I achieved to the fact that I've never tried to beat anyone else. I've only tried to beat Harvey

Cook's previous record. And I have beat that every day for 18 years." Cook sets a goal for every 15 minutes. He paces himself the way a runner runs laps. He sets small goals—appointments booked, calls made and so on.

Lynea Corson, a psychologist who works with sales teams to help them achieve their sales targets, takes a "whole brain" approach to setting goals. Working with one Farmers Insurance office on its life insurance sales, she helped the agency progress from selling 17 policies in nine months to selling 60 policies in three months. Corson teaches salespeople how to set goals that engage both sides of the brain. The logical left brain likes concrete task—goals that can be checked off. These goals are the ones that have a logical sequence, such as making 10 cold calls today, making three presentations this week, achieving a certain level of sales for the year, and so on. The right brain responds to more abstract visual goals such as being the number-one salesperson in the region or winning the trip to Tahiti.

Corson has her salespeople make a visual representation of their objective. They cut out pictures that represent the goal and place a picture of themselves in the goal picture. She recommends that this objective be just far enough out of reach that it challenges the right brain to create opportunities to reach it. Corson states that by getting the right brain working on these objectives, somehow opportunities are created. What you see is what you get. Goal pictures that have been effective for salespeople have been pictures of the type of clients they would like to attract, pictures of awards they would like to win, pictures of special recognition printed on their business cards or pictures of what they could buy when they achieved a certain level of success (houses, cars and so on). The goal picture needs to be one that builds enthusiasm and motivation.

Sprinting

In Rich Luisi's Electrolux office, the salespeople sprint, but not on a track. "We work six days a week," Luisi explains. "What I do is have my salespeople think that Monday, Tuesday and Wednesday make up the week. We sprint those three days and try to accomplish our week's goals by the end of Wednesday. Then we all get together Thursday morning and compare notes—what we did right, what we did wrong and why we did or didn't meet our goals. If we have met our goals, we double them. But even if you don't hit the sprint goal, at least you know on Wednesday that you are not on track. You don't find out Saturday night that you're not on track. We try to save the week. We have a monthly goal, a weekly goal, a sprint goal and a daily goal."

Goals have to belong to the salesperson. They can be negotiated within the framework of the company's needs but if a salesperson feels that a goal cannot be met, that goal becomes a demotivator. Goals need to be measurable and realistically attainable. The salesperson should be able to develop a plan that assures that the goals will be met.

Kim Lundgreen states, "When I first came to Franklin, I sat down with my manager and set goals. I set an income goal and then I did the 'pencil sell.' If I've got to do this many seminars per week, what's my closing rate? How many phone calls do I need to make? I would log every phone call. I thought it all out logically then I got obsessed with following that plan. Now when I want to, I can take off and go golfing."

When a salesperson is completely invested in the process of selling, the goals become a certainty. They aren't something that a salesperson tries to do; they are what the salesperson does. Yoda, the Jedi Warrior, says there is no such thing as trying—there is only doing or not doing. Goals become the steps of the plan that the salesperson will do. If you aren't going to do the steps, then they shouldn't be on the plan.

Goals can be divided into A Goals and B Goals. A Goals are the things you are going to do in the specified time period *regardless* of what occurs. The B Goals are the things you intend to do, but there is some flexibility in time. It is very important that once something is designated an A Goal that you honor it. Part of building a good attitude is trusting yourself to do the things you want to do. It is a matter of staying in integrity with yourself. It is more than self-discipline; it is being the person you want to be.

For instance, if you sit down on Sunday evening and plan your week and decide that you are going to do 25 cold calls per day as an A item, then you must do those cold calls. If there is any doubt that you will do them, then put down that you will do 25 cold calls on three days this week. Put the other two days on your B list.

Building up your goal muscle can take time, but eventually if you say you are going to do something, you do it. You 'understand how much you can get done during a week and you start to know where your priorities are. In the beginning, as you list all the things that you would like to get done, you will probably overwhelm yourself to the point that you either don't get them done or you find yourself at 11:30 p.m. Sunday evening trying to get the last tasks done. But when you establish your list for the coming week, you'll be more realistic. You'll start to find ways to use your time more effectively. Each of us has the same 10,080 minutes to spend each week. How many can we afford to waste?

Mental rehearsal

Athletes discovered long ago the magic of rehearsal. Studies show that the process of mentally rehearsing an activity has as much impact on improving the performance as actually doing the activity. Mental rehearsal can help sales performance in the same way it helps to improve skill at basketball, tennis, skiing or any other sport.

Charles Garfield, in his book *Peak Performers*, states, "Peak performers, particularly in business, sports and the arts, report a highly developed ability to imprint images of successful actions in the mind. They practice, mentally, specific skills and behaviors leading to those outcomes and achievements which they ultimately attain."

Garfield describes how Brandon Hall with Wilson Learning used mental rehearsal to break through to the level of success he wanted. "Brandon Hall told me about a graph he kept on his office wall, depicting his sales goal. Its ascending line conveyed the direction he wanted to go in selling corporate training programs. His production in 1982 had been $175,000. Even in the recession of that early part of the decade, he decided to set his goal for 1984 at $1 million—a peak that was talked about but never scaled at Wilson Learning Corporation. Hall would envision himself topping it. He envisioned himself trouble-shooting each customer's training needs. He envisioned himself deciding which Wilson products were right for each situation. This was not mere wishful thinking. As he learned the ropes in his early, less lucrative days, and as he used the dual process of mental rehearsal and effective follow-through, he acquired expertise and confidence. The result? He was the first Wilson Learning account executive to pass the $1 million mark."

Mentally rehearsing a sales call through to a successful conclusion builds self-confidence and versatility as you mentally decide how to handle different situations and objections. Perhaps you can't logistically make 20 successful sales calls per day. But, in your mind, you can be successful 20 times or 50 times every day. Each mental success builds your skills and confidence level.

Mentally rehearsing is more than just positive fantasizing however. In order for mental rehearsal to be effective, you need to rehearse the call from beginning to end, seeing each move you make and hearing each comment you say and the customer's comments and responses. When you rehearse your sales call, you should see yourself in your car driving to your appointment, feeling confident and knowledgeable. See yourself reviewing your objectives for the call and all the information you have about the client. Make mental notes of points you want to cover.

See yourself parking your car, entering the client's building and office. Mentally greet the receptionist and confidently announce your scheduled meeting with your client. See yourself being escorted to your client's office. Smile and extend a warm handshake and greeting. Mentally examine the client's office and appearance for connection points. Feel yourself making contact with your customer; feel the beginnings of a strong working relationship.

Mentally rehearse the questions you would like to ask the client and hear how he responds and the problems he identifies. See yourself responding to his questions and needs—skillfully leading the conversation toward your objectives for the meeting.

See the client thanking you for bringing him the information or ideas you have brought. See him happily agree to your next meeting or demonstration. Or see him give you the information you need to present a winning proposal. Visualize yourself closing the meeting on a warm, positive note, agreeing on your next step of action.

You can also rehearse pieces of sales calls. If you want to improve your opening statement, see yourself walking into a variety of situations and making an opening statement. Have your customers respond and watch to see what statements are the most effective. Rehearse cold calls until they feel completely natural. If asking for business is difficult for you, visualize your customer benefiting from your product or service, getting so much value from it that it would be a shame not to allow him to buy. Visualize that until it feels automatic to ask for the business in order to allow him to have those benefits.

"You cannot climb uphill by thinking downhill thoughts."
—*Wilfred A. Peterson*

71

```
┌ ─ ─ ─ ─ ─ ─ ─ ─ ─ ─ ─ ─ ─ ─ ┐
│        Two Ideas:            │
└ ─ ─ ─ ─ ─ ─ ─ ─ ─ ─ ─ ─ ─ ─ ┘
```

What two ideas did you get from this chapter?

_____

_____

I dare you to find a way to use one of these ideas to become more organized or to add that extra step that makes the difference between star success and average performance.

Action Plan

```
┌─────────────────────────────────┐
│                                 │
│         Develop Your            │
│            MAP                  │
│                                 │
└─────────────────────────────────┘
```

Developing your **Management Account Profile** will help you develop an action plan for success. Start today.

1. **Get a board.** This can be a white board with magnetic strips or a cork board, cards and push pins. Some salespeople use 2' x 3' cork boards so that they can carry them with them in their cars.

2. **Analyze your prospect base** and make a card for every active prospect. List their name, company, and telephone number. Date the card in the upper left corner—this is the beginning date for this prospect. After each stage is completed, you will indicate the date that the stage is completed.

3. **Analyze your sales cycle** and determine what steps are necessary in your normal sales cycle. Typical steps are:
   - First meeting
   - Needs assessment
   - Demonstration
   - Presentation/proposal
   - Close

   Each sales cycle will be different and it's important that you identify the critical steps in your cycle. Maybe instead of doing a demonstration, a critical step in your process is to get a prospect to attend a free seminar, or to give you specific pieces of information. Whatever those critical steps are, they form the basis of your sales stages.

4. **Analyze each of your prospect cards** to determine what stage the prospect has completed. Prospects aren't moved to the next stage until the action is completed. If a prospect has had a demonstration, the card is in the demonstration column. Put the stage on the card plus the date the prospect finished that stage.

5. **Establish a marginal account cut-off date.** Decide how much time you will work an account before it goes into the inactive stage. This could be 60 days, six months, or six years, depending on the nature of your sales cycle. But once you have established that cut-off, it means that you will pull the card. You may develop a schedule for recontacting inactive accounts, but that will be an activity that's outside of your mainline MAP activities.

6. **Eliminate marginal accounts.** If you have any prospects cards that have dates greater than your cut-off, immediately put them into your inactive file.

7. **Review your board** and determine what activities will move each of your prospects to the next cycle.

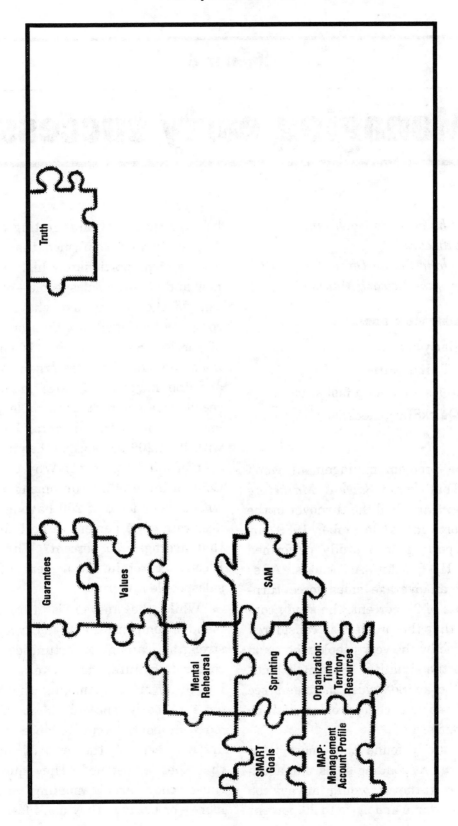

Chapter 4

Managing early success

"Who dares to teach must never cease to learn."

—*John Cotton Dana, former director of the Newark Museum*

Coming attractions:

♦ Early success

♦ STAR qualities

♦ Teleselling for a fast start

♦ QuickStart checklist

"The problem management won't face." That's what *Sales & Marketing Management* called the turnover of the sales force in its November 1989, article reporting on a study performed by R. H. Bruskin Associates. After finding an average sales force turnover rate of 27 percent, the study concluded that the problem is considered insolvable by the very people who could address the situation. "Succinctly put," states the article, "sales managers see turnover as an ongoing problem with no solution in sight."

The study found that more than half of the responding sales managers felt that turnover would always be about the same and close to 20 percent

believed the situation is getting worse. The study also confirmed that turnover is disproportionately high among new and younger salespeople—60 percent of the salespeople who leave a company have had less than one year of service. So, if turnover is such a major problem for sales organizations and the majority of sales managers see it as an almost unsolvable problem, why is it that Federal Express with its 1,200 salespeople has a turnover of only 2 percent? Why does A-Copy, a large office equipment dealer with a sales force of 200 have a turnover rate of 35 percent in an industry that averages 70 percent? Why does Electrolux retain 85 percent of the salespeople it recruits?

While the answer is a complex blend of compensation plans, company strength, career opportunities and corporate culture, the key to minimizing turnover is managing the sales force to early success. Most of the early dropouts occur because people are not reaching the level of success that they envisioned. They quit because they aren't making enough money or because they don't feel good about what they are doing. Consistent failure makes people feel bad so they leave. Companies with low turnover rates find ways to ensure the success of their beginning sales force. They design rigorous selection processes to help pick the people who best fit their sales positions and they commit to an intense, ongoing sales training process.

Early success

A study of the backgrounds of Olympic champions showed a common experience of early success. Regardless of the sporting event, most Olympic champions won some type of recognition or praise for their early performances. Whether it was winning a track meet or receiving praise and notice for their ice-skating, because they received positive strokes for these activities, they were motivated to work even harder to improve their skills. A similar thing happens in sales.

The rookie salesperson who succeeds enough to win positive strokes (contests, praise, recognition, bonuses) will be motivated to strive for even more success. *Success is the most powerful motivator.* Federal Express builds early success into its sales training program. During the three-week sales basics program, the new sales representative has a chance to work on actual accounts in his or her own territory. Almella Starks, manager of basic/intermediate sales training explains, "There is a business writing

section of the basic sales training. During the class event, the trainees write letters to assure that they will have appointments set up when they leave the class. There is also a telephone sales module where they actually make calls to their clients."

When the new Federal Express sales reps return to their territories, they have an exact plan of what they will do—appointments are set up, and they know where to start and how to handle their territory. Everything is designed to guarantee success.

Debra Palmer, sales training manager for Comdoc Office Systems, focuses on individual development rather than specific turnover numbers. She explains, "We try to maximize the success of our people through proper recruiting, orientation, training, and support. One of the most important things is that candidates understand what is required in their position. They can't come in thinking that they are going to make a lot of money quickly or without a lot of effort. Thoughts determine what you want but actions determine what you get. So we have a rigorous selection process and then we concentrate on making our salespeople successful."

Managers of small sales staffs and new salespeople who aren't lucky enough to participate in a comprehensive sales training program, have to develop their own early success program. They should design a self-training program that gives them time to learn the products and the company, their territory and the customers (including the benefits customers receive from the product) and sales skills. Then they are ready to develop a sales plan with the help of their sales manager or other experienced sales reps. Whether this learning and planning time is three days or three weeks, it is important that the new sales rep be ready for the challenge ahead. This preparation time is the foundation for success in any sales position.

Early success often comes from focusing on the right targets. Most managers recommend that the new person approach easy, nonthreatening prospects first. They should start with people who are most likely to say "yes," gradually building their skills until they are ready to tackle the toughest prospects. Once a prospect has said "no," it's doubly hard to convince them to say "yes."

The talent/position fit

Sales is a unique profession—it is very intolerant of misfits. Few other professions offer such constant and relentless feedback. Sales are either made or they're not; credit is not given for close or almost. Performance is subject to public scrutiny and salespeople can never rest on past successes.

In order to be successful in sales, a person needs to be able to accurately assess the needs of the sales position

being considered. If an honest evaluation of the needs of the position and the talents of the sales candidate does not result in a match, the candidate would be much better off choosing a different sales position or profession other than sales.

Countless studies have demonstrated that there are several common traits that are necessary for success in sales. We call these talents STAR qualities.

STAR qualities

There is a Chinese proverb that states,"One beam alone, no matter how stout, cannot support a house." Success in sales is like that house. Just as it takes many beams to support the house, it takes many talents to support sales success. Many of these talents or qualities will be discussed in the following chapters but the basic four are:

Service motivation
Tuned-in; empathetic
Action bias
Rejection tolerance

Service motivation: In today's economy when many products will solve the same problems and fill the same needs, customers are increasingly turning to service as the determining factor in a purchase. The salesperson who adds a service motivation to empathy and an action bias quickly pulls away from the pack. In all of the interviews, I found the motivation to provide unequaled service to be a common factor.

Tuned-in; empathetic: When a salesperson is tuned-in to a prospect or customer, he or she understands what the customer is trying to say, what the customer really means. The salesperson is operating on the same channel as the prospect and therefore has little interference in understanding the message. The tuned-in salesperson is even able to understand needs that the client might not fully recognize. Without empathy—the ability to tune in to a prospect—the salesperson will be severely limited in his or her attempt to be successful.

Action bias: The successful salesperson combines empathy for the customer with a bias for action. She knows where she wants to go and she acts to get there. When a person has an action bias, she needs frequent "successes." These could be sales closings or they could be predefined intermediate steps. For a salesperson selling major computer systems the success steps might be: 1) making contact with all the decision-makers; 2) doing needs assessment; 3) gaining agreement on system needs; 4) making a formal presentation; 5) negotiating price

and service agreements; 6) closing the sale. The salesperson has to have well-defined, achievable steps in order to satisfy the action bias. The process of achieving each step creates so much satisfaction that the salesperson is motivated to take the next step. There is a hunger for the satisfaction that comes from achieving goals.

Rejection tolerance: The sales process is often likened to a funnel. A whole bunch of prospects go in the top but only a trickle of customers comes out the bottom. Prospects drop out because they can't afford it, because they just bought it from their brother Harry, because they tried it and didn't like it or because it's Wednesday. There are a zillion reasons why someone won't buy your product or service. And, the difference between the nice wide prospect-top of the funnel and the narrow customer-bottom is...REJECTION.

Many potential top salespeople have been stopped by the rejection barrier. The ability to accept the "no's" as part of the process, while still focusing on success, is the critical factor that allows the salesperson to stay in the game long enough to succeed. Salespeople with rejection tolerance understand that the rejection is not about them personally—it doesn't make them a bad person. Rejection is data. As much as possible, each rejection is analyzed to see why. Was it a poor match of product and customer needs? Was the timing off? Is there a possibility of a future match?

Human beings have a strong tendency to do what makes them feel good. If being of service to someone makes us feel good, we will find ways to provide service. If being extremely persuasive and accomplishing our objectives makes us feel good, we will find a way to do that. So part of the process of matching the right sales position with the right salesperson is understanding the abilities and talents of the person and the requirements of the sales position.

Sales position types

There are many different types of sales jobs, each requiring a different mix of skills to excel. Here are three basic types of sales positions:

1. Action emphasis/quick close. These positions require someone who can do a lot of cold calling and who thrives on action and being persuasive. Sales of insurance, vacuum cleaners and securities broadly fall into this category. The salesperson who thrives here will have a high rejection tolerance and an overriding bias for action. He or she is persuasive, empathetic and goal oriented.

Prime "high" comes in closing. Combining these traits with a service motivation often creates spectacular incomes in this type of sales position.

Jack Kolker with Bear Stearns was so successful when he started that many of his friends followed him into the business. But it wasn't easy for him in the beginning. Kolker describes his early days, "In sales and brokerage there is a high rejection rate. To be able to handle that emotionally, you have to have the right attitude. You have to believe in what you are doing and stick with it. The first thing is to set a goal and focus on the objectives and not worry about the stuff in between. Anybody who is a rookie in the brokerage business has to realize that they are not going to make it in one day and they have to stick with it. I think in our business, the number one thing for success is persistence.

"The next thing," Kolker says, "is that you have to treat everyone—from the receptionist to the traders, the people who are making markets for you—you treat them all well and give them all the respect you can. You have to focus your attention on your business, reading, keeping abreast of your industry. You have to keep abreast of this business moment by moment. Everybody else has the same products and the same ability. To make a difference, you have to service your accounts, keep on the phone with them and be patient with them. Some of your clients aren't whizzes at this business and you have to realize that.

"You have to develop trust. I do 95 percent or more of my business over the phone. I've probably only seen 30 percent of my accounts. You have to be able to get on the phone and tell someone to send you $100,000 or $200,000. The way you do that is to gain their trust. You have to be honest all the time. You have to believe in yourself. If you think you're a million dollar producer, you are; if you think you're a failure, you are."

2. Service emphasis/moderate cycle. The successful salesperson in this category loves to provide service, and the longer sales cycle offers him or her an opportunity to build a warm and friendly relationship. The longer cycle generally means there are fewer initial prospects and, thus, fewer rejections, so rejection tolerance does not have to be quite so high as with the shorter cycle. A high level of service motivation is necessary plus enough bias for action to keep it a sales process rather than just a friendship. Some of the products in this category are: most office equipment, pharmaceuticals, computer software products,

advertising, standard industrial products and commercial real estate.

Charlie Payseur was bored with his job in corporate finance when he decided to try sales. He tackled one of the most challenging sales areas—commercial real estate—and became Coldwell Banker's rookie of the year in his region. In an industry where legends of the "big deals" abound, Payseur focused on consistency and service, targeting one geographic area and specializing in small apartment complexes. "I'm not a deal chaser," he explains, "I don't try to find the monster deal. If you get one, it's great, but if you don't prospect for your small to average-sized customers, you don't eat. I try to be consistent and that helps my peace of mind. If I didn't have a steady base of cases from my farming of the territory, I'd be a mess. It's a matter of knowing the owners, doing more for them than anyone else has ever done for them. I provide them with a lot of information and I'm not always hitting them up for a listing. I just provide steady information and after a while they get to know me and when it's time, they call me."

Payseur provides an unusual level of information and service to his property owners. He starts by taking a picture of the property he is interested in, framing it with a special frame and giving it to the owner. He also provides them with a three-ring binder of information about their property, which shows pictures of the property and provides a history of rents and comparisons with the apartment market around them. It also contains blank sections, which allows Payseur to follow-up with more information at later dates. "They get this book and picture before I've actually met them," Payseur states. "Then I send them more information about every month and call them every two to three months to see what is going on."

Payseur has a typical service approach providing his prospects tender, loving care and an endless supply of information. Another high-service provider is Cheryl Ricketts Basinger, star salesperson with Franklin. Basinger established her success by making everything easy for her clients. Basinger tells her clients, "I like to describe it like this. If you get a headache, you take a Tylenol or an aspirin. I want you to think about me as your aspirin or Tylenol. If you have a problem with anything that has to do with Franklin or our seminars, even though it isn't something I'm directly involved with, I want you to call me and give me a chance to make the headache go away. I want you to think about me as a partner in making this happen and I want any program you might do with Franklin to be absolutely

the easiest seminar you ever do. My role is to make that happen."

Basinger states that this approach has been the basis of her success. "The thing I have found is that most people aren't used to this approach so it's a breakthrough. Of course, I have to make sure that I fulfill their expectations."

3. Solution emphasis/long cycle. In this category, the salesperson needs the ability to take the long overview not only of the sales process but also of the needs of the customer and capabilities of the product or service. The successful salesperson in this type of position possesses an extraordinary amount of empathy in order to fully understand the needs of the customer. Part of the bias for action is channeled into knowledge of the product, the industry and the customer's needs. Top salespeople generally are, or become, industry experts. This sales category is a joint search for solutions, more of a partnership arrangement, so rejection is more infrequent than the other categories. Closing normally happens at each step of the process and empathy guides the salesperson along the right track. Typical products include: computer systems, large telephone systems, and high-tech medical equipment.

Frank Byrd, general manager for GE Aircraft Engines, understands solution selling and long cycles. There may be five to 10 years between the purchase of jet engines by an airline and there are only a small number of airlines in the world. Byrd manages the sales cycle by maintaining a strong relationship throughout the long cycle. "We have a very long cycle," explains Byrd, "and a very small total number of customers. One of the things we do to differentiate ourselves is to own our customers all the way through this very long cycle. There may be 10 years between purchases but the salesperson continues to stay in touch with the customer, answering questions and resolving problems. We have to have a long-term relationship with our customers." Successful sales reps with GE have to develop criteria to judge their personal success other than just closing a deal. They have to be able to concentrate on gathering information, anticipating directions and problems and maintaining strong relationships in order to handle the extremely long sales cycle.

Trying to squeeze a salesperson into a slot that doesn't fit his or her skills and talents is an exercise in frustration and failure. Many of the companies with low turnover rates have hired outside consulting firms to help them evaluate candidates prior to selection. These firms develop a profile of the successful salesperson within that firm and then interview candidates against that profile.

"Fun" isn't at the top of a sales manager's criteria for hiring a salesperson, but maybe it should be. Most of the top salespeople I interviewed talked about how much fun they have with their job. They like what they do...they like the challenge...they like working with people...they like the sense of accomplishment they get from closing a sale.

Mihaly Csikszentmihalyi in his book, *Flow, The Psychology of Optimal Experience*, states, "Paradoxically, it is when we act freely, for the sake of action itself rather than for ulterior motives, that we learn to become more than what we were. When we choose a goal and invest ourselves in it to the limits of our concentration, whatever we do will be enjoyable. And once we have tasted this joy, we will redouble our efforts to taste it again."

Define your company success factors

Each company has its own criteria for success. Salespeople who learn what the rules are have a better chance of succeeding. They can begin to get a sense of what those success guidelines are by talking with the sales manager and top salespeople in the company. In the December 1990 issue of *Think and Grow Rich Newsletter*, Hideo Yoshida, chairman of Dentsu (the largest advertising agency in the world) offers some success guidelines:

1. Initiate projects on your own, instead of waiting for work to be assigned.
2. Take an active role in all your endeavors, not a passive one.
3. Search for large and complex challenges.
4. Welcome difficult assignments. Progress lies in accomplishing difficult work.
5. Once you begin a task, complete it. Never give up.
6. Lead and set an example for your fellow workers.
7. Set goals for yourself to ensure a constant sense of purpose. This will give you perseverance, resourcefulness and hope.
8. Move with confidence. It gives your work focus and substance.
9. At all times, challenge yourself to think creatively and find new solutions.
10. When confrontation is necessary, don't shy away from it. Confrontation is the mother of progress and the fertilizer of an aggressive enterprise. If you fear conflict it will make you timid.

Problems equal success

Many star salespeople got their careers off to a fast start by going for the problems. Jerry MacLean is one of the top insurance agents with Prudential, ranking in the top 20 out of more than 17,000 agents. He once left a successful territory to open a new territory in Vermont, leaving his entire client base behind. He explains how he used problems to build his new territory, "I always started off with the idea of looking for problems. When I went to Vermont, I asked everyone to give me all of their problem cases. If you want to be successful, all you have to do is take everybody's problems. That's the kind of direction I took. For example, I took people who had claims that they couldn't resolve, clients who were difficult to deal with, and people who didn't pay their premiums on time."

MacLean focused on solving the problems and providing outstanding service to these customers. "I visited with them," he explains. "I kept focused on the fact that the customer is always right. You don't go in to win the battle and lose the war—you go in to win the war even if you have to lose the battle. I went in and said 'I'm sorry for what has happened in the past and I will correct the problem.' When I talk to people, I consciously sit back in my chair and listen. I don't care whether they buy something or not—I just want to take care of the problem. Eventually that focus will become very successful. That type of thinking gives you unlimited people to see—I am currently backed up about six months with people who want me to review their insurance situation and make recommendations."

MacLean has developed excellent listening skills and it helps him know how to help his clients. He derives great satisfaction from knowing how much he has helped people. "Most of my clients have become friends," he says. "I sold my insurance to one couple who listened to my advice from the very beginning and agreed to all of my recommendations. Six months after we wrote the policy, the husband was killed in a plane crash. When I delivered the check to the wife, she refused to take it. She said, 'You told me that if something ever happened, you would take care of everything. You do something with this money. I'm not capable.' Over the past several years, we invested it through Prudential and it has grown and maintained the family's lifestyle. We have become friends and I have sold many policies over the years to her family and friends. That makes me feel good."

Randy Gotthilf, vice president of Garden State Business Machines, also built his success on problems. He explains, "The first company I went to work for told me I had 30 days to work out and if I didn't, I would be out of a job." In the early days of the office products industry, there was very little training available and Xerox had about 85 percent of the market. In order to avoid losing his job, he took on all the company problems. He explains how this got him started, "I took all

the company's inactive accounts. I made hundreds of phone calls—all to companies that had dropped us because of dissatisfaction with some aspect of the company—and scheduled 12 demonstrations. Out of those 12 demonstrations, I closed 11 sales. That taught me that the best opportunity you have to sell your product is to someone you've had problems with in the past. If you can solve the problem and prove to them that you have corrected whatever caused the problem, you have an excellent chance to get their business."

Teleselling for a fast start

The challenge for all new salespeople is to become productive quickly. This involves gathering together an incredible amount of information about the product and services offered, the territory and customers and sales skills. It generally takes years before a salesperson has all of this information firmly in place and can handle everything the customer throws out.

Bob Thornton, division marketing manager with ITT Commercial Finance, was struggling with how to help his sales staff be more productive and how to get new people off to a faster start. Statistics showed him that his division was doing more than 84,000 face-to-face calls nationally and it was taking an average of five calls to close a client. He decided that if even 25 percent of those calls could be handled by phone, it would give the sales reps more time to make face-to-face calls and could drastically increase sales with the same level of staff.

Thornton initiated a teleselling pilot program against heavy opposition. He explains the early opposition, "One reason for the delay in going to telemarketing is that it doesn't fit with previous experience. Experienced sales reps have always done sales face-to-face and a lot of the sales slogans revolve around getting in front of the customer. We sell an ongoing service of financing support to dealers and it requires a consultative type of sale. It is a large sale based on a relationship of trust and understanding the client's needs. The salespeople did not believe that this could be done over the phone. Also, most people have a negative view of telemarketing because they think of it as being dinnertime calls to your home from fast-talking, boiler-rooms sharps."

In spite of the skepticism, Thornton felt that teleselling was a way to add the advantages of technology to the sales process. He even calls it tech-selling. Tech-selling means sales through technology—using the telephone, video conferencing, video training and all the other new technologies available. "Tech-selling," Thornton explains, "allows resources to be applied in the most efficient way. It also forces you to do more pre-planning. That's probably another reason why some salespeople don't like it. But, that's also why it's good for new people."

10 steps to implementing teleselling

Planning is the key to teleselling. All the information needed for the sales process is laid out in front of the salesperson. In Thornton's pilot, he prepared a set of visuals to be hung on the walls around the person doing the teleselling. The salesperson wears a phone headset and can actually walk through a sales cycle, reading through features and benefits and being able to walk to the sheet on objections when one is raised by the customer. Actual scripts are available on wall sheets or on index cards that can be quickly accessed by the salesperson.

The process of building a teleselling "success zone" can be invaluable for both new and experienced salespeople. Here is an outline of steps:

1. **Product sheets.** For each product, prepare a sheet listing the features, benefits and proofs.

2. **Reasons-for-buying   sheet.** Prepare a sheet showing why customers would buy your product or service. Talk to as many customers as possible to determine what is important to them and what problems are solved by the product or service.

3. **Objection sheet.** Prepare a sheet listing all the objections you've encountered with this product. Talk to experienced salespeople to identify as many objections as possible. For each objection, have a complete strategy for handling it.

4. **Competition sheet.** Prepare a sheet showing the comparison between the competitors' products and services and yours. Develop a way to show your product or service in a favorable light so that you do not have to bad-mouth the competition.

5. **Stages sheet.** Prepare a sheet that shows you the normal stages of a sale and what you are trying to accomplish at that stage. If it is an initial contact and you are trying to explore the customer's needs, you may have several typical questions listed on the sheet. You should also have a visual reminder not to leap to a close.

6. **Results sheet.** Prepare a sheet that shows customers who can act as references. Show their name, address and phone number and the results achieved for each customer. Have a mix of types of businesses and needs satisfied.

7. **Pre-call planning and strategy.** Develop a strategy for each call. Who are you calling? Why?

Do the necessary background research to obtain information necessary to connect with your client and to show understanding of the client's business or needs. Is a third party reference appropriate or available? What potential problems might the customer have? What is the objective of the call? What action do you want the customer to take at the end of this call? Possible actions are to schedule an appointment, provide information, commit to buy, suggest other people to talk to, and so on.

8. **Scripts.** Develop scripts for opening the conversation. The opening script is critical. It should identify you, your company, your product and your competitive difference in about 30 seconds.

9. **Reminders.** Put reminders on your walls that are important to you. Examples are: Get down to business quickly. Don't talk about solutions too soon. Concentrate on questions. Investigate! Find out what they need.

10. **Assemble your success zone.** The equipment you will need includes a phone headset, a recording system plus a telephone listener. You will need poster sheets with information placed strategically around you so that

you can access the information quickly and smoothly. Make this space *your* space by adding any personal quotes or motivating pictures.

Recording calls

One of the advantages of teleselling is the ability to immediately review a call. While taping is illegal in some states, several legal counselors have advised that as long as the tapes are used only for review or training and are immediately erased, they can be used.

The tapes give the salesperson a chance to make sure he or she understands what the customer was saying and a chance to review sales techniques. Were enough questions asked? Was the objective of the call met? In Thornton's pilot, they found that salespeople were asking for commitments or the business before establishing value. By reviewing the tapes, this was obvious. The powerful part of the process was that, by reviewing the tapes, the salespeople recognized this weakness themselves and were able to adjust their approach.

Many salespeople who have implemented this system immediately review their taped calls and make notes on their client contact sheets. Tapes can also be reviewed during commute time to listen for ways to improve the sales process.

Another potential benefit of the teleselling process is in training and coaching. By using a telephone listener, a device that allows a third party to listen to a conversation without the effect of a speaker phone, a manager or coach can listen to the conversation and point out possible strategies or approaches. The manager can also provide immediate feedback after the call and play back the tape to demonstrate weak areas and suggest methods of improvement.

"The bottomline," Thornton says, "is that if you could go on a sales call with all this information laid out in front of you, you would have a major advantage. But, in a face-to-face situation, you can't rely on scripts and prompts." Thornton's pilot convinced others within ITT Commercial Finance, and the program is now being rolled out to the rest of the organization. Even some of the most skeptical experienced salespeople in the organization were so impressed by the results of the pilot that they are incorporating teleselling into their own activities.

Of course there are also disadvantages to using the telephone—it's difficult to connect with people when you can't see them and their surroundings and it's sometimes easier for the prospect to terminate the call. You have to review your own sales situation to determine whether, and how, teleselling might help you break through to new levels of success. Some salespeople use the teleselling methods to establish an appointment while others are able to sell their product using this technique. Each sales situation is unique and each salesperson must determine how this technique works best in his particular situation. Here is a review of the advantages that teleselling can bring you:

- Canvass more prospects in a shorter amount of time

- Less costly than face-to-face visits

- Allows earlier qualifying of the prospects

- Allows the salesperson to use scripts and prompts

- Prospect may give more frank answers than in an early face-to-face meeting

- More likely to reach the decision-maker

- Can be taped and reviewed

- Allows the salesperson to recognize weaknesses and take action

Star advisers

A consistent response of the sales superstars interviewed was their eagerness to help new salespeople. They generously shared their time, their knowledge and their wisdom to be passed along to the next generation of superstars. Here are some of their insights:

Betsy Martin, advertising sales director for *Money* magazine:

"Probably the most important thing to do when you're junior and new is to do a lot. Your calls will not be as honed as a senior salesperson who knows how to go in and say the right things at the right moment. So obviously quantity helps. We encourage our new salespeople to share information with their customers and prospects—whether it's a circulation increase, new editorial section or whatever. Each call should have a purpose, otherwise you'll be known as someone who never has anything to say.

"Build relationships and don't make them phony. Relationships should last for a long time. Follow up. Respond to people. If a client asks you for something in the morning and by the end of the day you don't have it, call back and tell them what's happening. Don't leave people hanging. Never lie—that is an absolutely major mistake. Trust is very important. Don't run away from a problem. Seek answers. Don't carry a problem by yourself. Get help."

Charlie Garrison, number-three sales agent for Farmers Insurance:

"If there was one thing that helped me most, it was taking a sales course when I first began. We learned about the sales cycle and about the personality of the buyers. Parts of the course were videotaped and it was an agonizing experience but I chose to do it because my objective was to be in sales and ultimately in sales management. It made me aware of a lot of sales techniques and concepts—such as finding a viable customer, getting before them, being able to communicate a need that the person has for your product, asking for the sale and asking again.

"I learned to find out why someone says 'no.' If he needs it and can afford it, but says 'no,' there must be something that you don't know so you have to find out what it is. Either they don't like you or they think your company is bad or they didn't understand something. You get that clarified so you can go on."

Mike Rakosnik, national program marketing manager, Minolta Corporation:

"There are many skills and factors that must be mastered in order to achieve a high level of personal and business success. Here are the cornerstones I have identified for reps to start out on the right track.

"Attitude: More than the normal interpretation, it is the smile on your face, the spring in your step, the willingness in your voice, the commitment in your soul. Customers will see it, and respond.

"Homework: Commit to the time needed to find out about your prospect and their needs. One size does not fit all and it is your opportunity to demonstrate why.

"Knowledge: Become a student of your industry. Read all the information that is available concerning it and how it effects your customers. Learn your products, and those of your competitors, better than anyone else.

"Resilience: Realize that, even with the best of efforts, you will never be consistently 100 percent effective. So, accept that each customer encounter is a learning experience. Some of them will pay better than others, but, you will gain value from each."

Jerry MacLean, top sales representative with the Prudential Insurance Company of America:

"When my oldest daughter went to work for the Prudential a few years back, I told her that making money was immaterial in the beginning. Go in there and soak up as much knowledge as possible. Go to work for a company with the idea that it's forever and learn all you can. The money will come. You have to be honest and do a thorough job. Be nice and smile. Make it easy for the customer to buy insurance. I keep it as simple as possible. I tell people what their options are and where they are protected and where there may be holes in their programs."

Steve Rauschkolb, director of sales and medical education, Schering Plough Corporation:

"Selling skills are primarily good people skills. People have to trust you, they have to be able to understand you. A good place to start is to join Toastmasters and learn to speak in public. Another way is to volunteer to get into a community or charitable group. This will give you a chance to work with people on committees and learn how to sell your ideas and move into a leadership role."

Randy Gotthilf, with Garden State Business Machines:

"New salespeople tend to get intimidated in front of customers and they start talking too much. If you let the customer do at least 50 percent of the talking, you will sell your product. You have to use open-ended questions; you have to find their needs. I always stress that you should never promise something you can't deliver. (Harvey Mackay states: 'Always deliver more than you promise.')"

Travis Young, Jr., recently retired as one of Prudential Insurance Company's top reps for over 29 years and winner of almost every award offered by Prudential and the insurance industry:

"If I were a new agent, the question I would ask every person I talked to would be, 'If you went into the insurance business today, who would be the first three people you would call?' I could make a living with just that one question. I would ask them if they would mind if I showed my information to those three people. I would tell people that I was going to provide them with the best service they ever had and ask them to give me a call if they ever hear of someone who needs insurance. That approach will bring you as many referrals as you can handle."

Young has a unique approach to servicing his clients. He tells them he will do anything for them as long as it isn't physically impossible or illegal. He wants them to call him about anything, even if it isn't related to insurance. When one woman called him to ask for his recommendation on binoculars that she wanted to buy as a gift for her husband, Young insisted on sending her an extra pair that he had. "Problems create sales," Young states. When people call him with a problem, he has an opportunity to solve it and build their confidence, loyalty and friendship.

Young passes along two sayings for success in sales: the three STPs—*see the people, sell the people and service the people*. And, *ability plus attitude plus activity minus excuses equals success*. Simple formulas that contain a lot of power and wisdom.

If you always do...

There is a popular saying that states: *"If you always do what you've always done, you'll always be what you've always been."* Sales is not a profession that allows you to coast. You have to keep finding new and better techniques, novel ways to tell your story, more effective ways to prospect and more efficient ways to manage your time and efforts. This section has focused on the personal qualities needed for a successful career in sales. Section II will show you the other side of sales—the customer side—and how to build powerful customer relationships.

"It is our duty as men and women to proceed as though limits to our abilities do not exist."
—*Pierre Teithard de Chardin, Jesuit Father, author, paleontologist*

> Two Ideas:

What two ideas did you get from this chapter?

_____

_____

I dare you to find a way to use one of these ideas to build your success.

Action Plan

```
Quick Start
Checklist
```

The checklist on the next three pages will help you stay focused. You may need to tailor it to your specific product and sales cycle. Every time you make a sales call, run through this check list to see what you could have done better.

Introduction: Did I...

- Learn something about the person, company or industry before the meeting?
- Observe prospect's office decor (i.e., trophies, awards, pictures and so on)?
- Find out prospect's personal interests, hobbies, family and so on (something unique)?
- Bridge to the business topic smoothly?
- Start building a relationship throughout the entire sales call?
- Listen a lot (80 percent listening; 20 percent talking)?
- Ask customer about the philosophies of the company?
- Ask the customer what challenges the company is facing?

Qualifying: Did I

- Find out who the decision-maker is by asking: 'Who besides yourself might be involved in the decision making process?'
- Ask what it would take for a vendor to get the business?
- Find out what the purchasing procedures are?
- Find out how and why they made their decision for their present product or service (assuming they are replacing a product or service)?
- Find out what their time frame is?
- Find out if funds have been allocated (and how much)?
- Find out their specific needs?
- Ask if they could change something about their present product or service, what would it be?

Surveying: Did I...

- Ask open-ended questions? (WWWWWH$—Who, What, Where, Why, When, How, How much; Tell me about; Describe.)
- Follow the funnel question method (described in Chapter 6) going from broad questions to more specific questions?
- Ask about the corporate structure?
- Ask about the prospect's role?
- Ask what's important to them?
- Ask what's interesting to them and focus on that?
- Ask what risks they perceive?
- Ask how we can help solve their problems?
- Ask what their feelings are toward vendors in the industry?
- Ask what they think about our company?
- Ask what they like and dislike about their current vendor?
- Ask how the prospect feels about his or her situation?
- Ask how industry trends or situations are affecting them?
- Ask "What if?" questions?

Handling objections: Did I...

- Listen to the entire objection?
- Pause three seconds before responding?
- Remain calm and not defensive?
- Answer the objection with a question in order to find out more specifically what the objection was?
- Restate the objection to make sure we both agreed exactly?
- Answer the objection?

Presentation: Did I...

- Prioritize the prospect's needs?
- Talk about benefits to the customer?
- Use layman's terms?
- Link the benefit to the prospect's needs?
- Verify each need before moving on?
- Present myself, company and product in a positive light?

Demonstration: Did I...

♦ Reestablish rapport?

♦ Give the prospect a tour of the company and make appropriate introductions?

♦ Review the prospect's needs?

♦ Ask if anything changed since our last meeting?

♦ Pre-commit the prospect?

♦ Give a general overview of the product/service?

♦ Convey the reason and purpose on the flipchart?

♦ Keep the demo focused on customer needs?

♦ Involve the customer in the demo?

♦ Summarize the prospect's needs and how the product/service meets those needs?

Closing: Did I...

♦ Ask for the order? ("Why don't we go ahead with this?")

♦ Get the customer to identify all possible problems that might be solved by my product/service?

♦ Get the customer to identify the value of solving the identified problems?

♦ Get agreement that the proposed solution provided the values identified?

Customer maintenance: Did I...

♦ Write thank-you letters for appointments, demonstrations, orders, and so on?

♦ Earn the right to ask for reference letters and referrals?

♦ Maintain communications for future considerations?

♦ Establish a schedule for follow-up calls and customer visits?

♦ Get a taped reference? (See Chapter 5.)

♦ Take a picture? (See Chapter 5.)

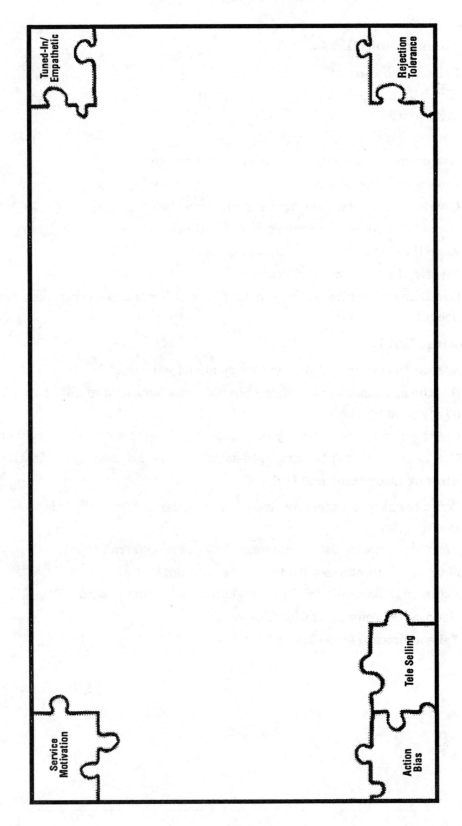

Section II

The customer side of sales: relationship strategies

"Selling is about the building of long-term relationships."
—*Bev Hyman, president, Bev Hyman & Associates*

There is a rumor floating around that people dislike change, that they are afraid of change and that change creates stress. Actually we love change. It is exciting, refreshing and stimulating. Entire industries are built on our love of change—the travel industry thrives on people who want to see something new, theme parks are built on the knowledge that people will pay dearly to have a dramatic change even if it's only for two minutes, the automotive industry depends on people getting tired of driving the same car after three years, the clothing industry knows that most clothes aren't bought because we need them but because we need something new to pick us up. We love to find a new computer that performs a microsecond faster or a pair of the latest running shoes with new technology built into the sole. We love the promise and excitement of new products and services.

So, if we all love new gadgets, toys, tools and services, why is it so hard to be a super sales star? Why doesn't every rookie easily double or triple his or her quota? There are two reasons—limited resources and fear. Each of us—individuals, corporations and organizations—have just so many resources that can be used to purchase goods and services. For all but the wealthiest of us, we buy one car at a time. So, if we buy a Ford station wagon, we can't buy that little Miata sports car. If we decide to take our annual vacation in Hawaii, we can't go to Aspen. If we buy a Minolta copier for the office, we can't buy a Xerox copier. Because of our limited resources, we have to make choices. And there's the rub.

Every time we make a choice, we have the possibility of making the wrong choice. There's always the possibility that we will go to Hawaii during the rainy season and wish we were in Aspen, or that whatever car we buy will turn out to be a lemon or that the office copier will break down all the time and everyone will blame us.

Increasing technology and change have made most of us technologically illiterate. We are surrounded by boxes that make our life easier but we have little understanding of how they work or what to do if they don't work. We are completely dependent on others to explain to us which box we need and what to do when it doesn't do what it should.

Not only is the technology and the vast array of products confusing, but the price possibilities are overwhelming. How do I best allocate my limited resources? If I buy a television for $500, will my neighbor tell me I could have gotten it down the street for $400 or that I could have gotten a bigger, better model for only $450? How long will it work? Can I get it fixed if it breaks?

Studies show that a problem occurs with almost 25 percent of all sales even if the problem is never reported. Almost every buyer has been burned with a purchase that didn't work out—the product didn't do what the salesperson said it would, it broke before it should have, a neighbor told them they should have bought a different model, or a friend told them they could have gotten it cheaper. Each of these experiences creates fear and insecurity.

We want new products—a car, a dream vacation, a new computer, a better copier for the office, but we are afraid to buy because we might make the wrong decision. The easiest way

we have of protecting ourselves from making that wrong decision is to avoid salespeople. We have this image of a con artist who tries to trick us into making a wrong decision. To ward off this evil, we set up our barriers and tell the receptionist that we don't want to see any salespeople. We throw away our "junk mail." We set up purchasing departments and pay people to make the decision for us. We say, "I'm not interested." "I'm just looking." "I have all I need." "I'm happy with my present car (computer, copier, stockbroker and so on)." What we are really saying is "I'm afraid to make a decision. I'm not sure you (salesperson) are telling me the truth. I don't think you care about anything except making money for yourself. I'm afraid to listen to you because I might make a bad decision."

For a salesperson to succeed, he or she has to get past this barrier of fear and allow the prospective customer to glimpse the excitement and promise of the new product or service. The customer has to view the salesperson as a valued adviser, someone who has the customer's best interests at heart. The only way to have the customer's interests at heart is to be close enough to the customer to know what those interests are. The very best companies and salespeople have developed elaborate listening strategies to find out what customers want and need. Once they know what the customer wants, they can design the necessary delivery systems.

One example of a listening strategy is Marriott's Customer Advisory Forums. At a recent Forum, a group of senior meeting planners told Marriott that they wanted sales reps who were more responsive to all of their needs—the little meetings as well as the major conferences. This led to a revamping of Marriott's national sales program. Jim Schultenover, vice president of group development, describes the transformation of the national sales group. "Before 1985, we were the typical example of the other way of selling. Reps had high account loads, often as many as 350 accounts. Now they average 35 to 40 accounts. We had a tendency to park new college graduates in national sales and now we have extremely seasoned people. The reorganization allowed the salespeople to focus on accounts rather than just individual events."

David Townshend, director of national sales for Marriott, states, "In national sales we know that service is the basis of sales. I want my customer to know that I am always available regardless of how small the need. Sometimes our competitors start to take business for granted. If you show desire and persistence, you are at least going to get people to listen, and that's the first barrier to be broken down. I travel to customer programs held at competitor hotels to get a better idea of what the customer is looking for—what's working and what isn't. To give customer service, you have to understand the needs and expectations of the customer. Sometimes it's a little easier to do that when people are away at meetings. It's a little more relaxed environment."

Kevin Patterson is Marriott's national account executive for the IBM account. He states, "The restructuring of our national sales program gave us the time to build relationships with the customer. The first thing is to develop a level of comfort and discover the customers' expectations. You really get a return when you can actually anticipate their needs."

Through his ability to build relationships, Patterson increased the number of room nights booked by IBM dramatically. "We worked hard to become kind of a friend of the family, a consultant. The customers start to look at you as a confidante, someone they can bounce ideas off of. But it takes time. Familiarity breeds business. I think for measurable wins, it takes at least 24 months for the customer to start looking at you as an ally, as someone who is in it for the long haul. IBM's own studies show that it often takes account reps three years before the customer starts to feel comfortable with them."

Schultenover says, "Because we now have seasoned account directors, we expect them to spend their resources in a way that will have the biggest payoff. If that means flying with customers to the Bahamas to do a site inspection, then that's what they do.

One of our reps actually had a job exchange with one of his clients. He worked a registration booth at a convention for a week and his client came in and worked sales leads for Marriott for a week. Activities like these continue to break down barriers. It's all about relationships. Kevin Patterson probably knows more senior managers at IBM than he does at Marriott."

When people at Marriott talk about building relationships, they start to talk about Rich Green, national sales director. Green is something of a legend at Marriott. He is "Mr. Relationship." His customers throw parties for him. Green has some interesting points about building relationships. "I genuinely care for my customers. Customers have to be treated like you want to be treated. We have all these distinctions between buyers, sellers, customers...there really isn't a difference. We're all just people. People really do buy from friends and if you can make a client into a friend, you have a much better chance of getting the business. I like to entertain so I take people to my home and cook dinner for them. Entertaining at home brings things to a totally different level. Clients love knowing how you live away from the office. They love getting to know the essence of a person, and what better way than seeing a person's home?

"I think it's important to create an experience that's fun. You have to find out what makes a person tick. I was working with a meeting planner who mentioned that she liked convertibles and that she had never been to the wine country. I rented a LeBaron convertible and we drove up to the wine country and went to a couple of wineries and had a picnic lunch. That was four or five years ago and she is still an account, but she is also one of my good friends.

"You can't be manipulative," says Green. "If you try to be a salesperson, you'll fail. The first thing you have to do is be true to yourself. You know that you have started to really build rapport when your client starts talking about personal experiences. Maybe it's just mentioning how his kid did in a school play or how he and his wife met. I know when that happens, that I have achieved something...a level of trust. In order to get to this point, I have to share a little of myself with them. They know who Richard Green is. I am easy to talk to and have a warm aura about me. But everyone has to find their own way to do it. It has to be true to their own nature."

The phrase "high tech/high touch" comes to mind. As our society becomes more and more technologically sophisticated, we seem to need even more personal contact to balance the equation. We not only need guides to lead us through the maze of bells and whistles, we need reassurance that someone who cares about our needs is there to help us. This process, above all, depends on trust and the development of truly professional salespeople.

The truly professional salespeople—the top sales stars—provide the trust and the comfort level necessary for a buyer to take the risk and drop the protective barriers. The following chapters will give you strategies for developing uncommon customer relationships.

"No man is wise enough by himself."
—*Plautus, early Roman philosopher*

Chapter 5: Three keys: like-trust-respect

To succeed in sales, the customer has to like you, trust you and respect you. He has to have a relationship with you and this relationship is built on a foundation of friendship and trust. Relationships require open, honest communication, service and honoring all commitments. Learn how to remove customer fear, what it takes to establish a firm foundation of trust with customers. Learn how to develop powerful customer references, the perils of iceberg selling and how to prove your commitment to service with customer surveys.

The Action Plan will lead you through the development of a customer portfolio to help you break through customer fear and resistance and help you get much closer to your customers.

Chapter 6: What's the question?

Selling is about asking questions. The top sales stars have learned that knowing how to ask questions and what questions to ask is more important than knowing the answers. Find out how to use the funnel of questions to build your sales success. Learn how to build a powerful listening strategy and how to find information that will help you understand your customers.

Asking the right questions depends on your understanding of the customer's situation and needs. Preliminary research can uncover a wealth of information that will help you prepare for your first customer meeting.

The Action Plan gives you a brief listing of research sources that have been used by sales stars to build the foundation of a customer relationship.

Chapter 7: Walk on the other side

Until you can walk in the customer's shoes and understand his or her needs and problems, you will not be able to establish the kind of powerful relationships that will rocket you to the top of sales success. In this chapter, you learn more about what customers look for and you will learn a dynamic technique for finding out more about what your specific customers want.

The Action Plan will guide you through the development of your own listening strategies.

Chapter 5

Three keys: like-trust-respect

"If you can call your client on a Saturday night and ask him for a favor then you have a relationship. If you can't, you're not doing your job."

—*Bill Stack, Manager, Eastern Communications Region, GE Information Services*

Coming attractions:

♦ Establishing TRUST

♦ Powerful customer references

♦ Iceberg selling

♦ Customer surveys

♦ Be the expert

In the fourth century B.C.E., an eccentric philosopher named Diogenes walked through the streets of Athens carrying a lamp in broad daylight looking for a good and honorable man, an honest man. Legend has it that he never found one.

Talking with buyers, purchasing agents and the typical consumer would make us think that it's as hard to find an honest, honorable salesperson as it was for Diogenes to find his honest man. But not until you talk to the top salespeople...the stars. There you find an incredible commitment to truth and honesty. Edward R. Murrow once said, "To be persuasive we must be believable; to be believable we must be credible; to be credible we must be truthful." The sales stars who have been extraordinarily successful over long periods of time discovered the power of being open and honest. They discovered that there are four requirements to developing powerful sales relationships: the customer has to know you (discussed in Chapter 3), like you, trust you and respect you.

Connecting

The first barrier standing between you and the customer is fear—fear based on the fact that the customer doesn't know you, doesn't like you, doesn't trust you...yet. The customer has to get a sense of who you are and what you stand for. He or she has to connect with you. Just as a cocklebur cannot catch onto a smooth surface, people cannot connect with you if you don't give them something to grab hold of. You need to connect as people before the sales process can begin. When you comment on a picture, book or award in someone's office, you are searching for a personal hook to the customer. When you mention your family, hobby or interest in prehistoric mollusks, you are providing a hook for the customer to connect with you as a person. Star salespeople have developed their skills in connecting quickly and sincerely. They don't spend a lot of time telling jokes or chewing the fat but they do connect powerfully on a personal level.

Establish TRUST

Sales are made on the basis of relationships and are an important part of all selling. However, the more risky the purchase decision is, the more critical the relationship. Cheap, throw-away products require only the basics of a relationship, while expensive, critical products require a strong, long-term relationship. While we have little hesitation about buying a hamburger from a new fast-food place, we consider long and hard before signing a long-term lease for a new office. We might pop in to an unknown office supply store and buy paper, but we

want to know who is selling us a mutual fund.

The difference in these buying situations is the amount of trust the customer demands before making a decision. Trust is the foundation for the sale and the sales relationship; therefore, I will use it as the acronym for the critical elements of a strong relationship:

Truth: To be totally honest.
Reliability: Never promise something you can't deliver.
Uncommon Effort: Go the extra step to earn the business.
Service: Superb service builds trust.
Truth: Openness and honesty, start to finish.

Truth

Susie Cox started her career with World Book, selling encyclopedias on the run. The day she got her kit, even before being trained, she sold a set of encyclopedias to her neighbor. Since then she has won many sales awards including the top district manager award. She often sells 10 sets a week—a very high level for a product that is sold primarily on a cold call, person-to-person basis where the basic product costs almost $600. Cox maintains this high level of performance by being able to quickly put her customers at ease.

She starts by being completely honest. "When I use the phone," Cox explains, "it's normally from a referral or a lead and I introduce myself and tell them what I'm selling. I am very straightforward. I am brief and to the point. I've always believed in disclosure—letting them know up front what I have and what I do. I will even give them prices over the phone. I don't believe in high pressure and I think people buy when they are ready."

Cox treats her prospective customer with respect and honesty. Most of us know that if a stranger calls us at home, it isn't to do a marketing survey or to ask about our well-being. We know they are trying to sell us something, so the top salesperson is honest with us, treats us like adults, tells us what he or she is selling and lets us decide whether we have any interest.

A frequent form of marketing and sales is the "giveaway." Someone calls you on the phone and tells you that you have won a fabulous trip to Hawaii and spends several minutes describing the wonders of the trip and how lucky you are. At the end of the conversation you are asked to spend 90 minutes seeing a demonstration of product X before you receive your free ticket (which actually only covers one airfare). This is a dishonest approach, a one-shot hit. The salesperson who uses this approach is saying, "I want to get your money and get out." It is obviously successful or so many people wouldn't be using it. But, not one of

the top salespeople interviewed across the country—people who have been at the top of their profession, making extremely high incomes for years—not one of them used short-term gimmicks or dishonesty to reach their level of success.

Be there when there is a problem

It is especially important to be honest with customers when things go wrong. Customer service studies have shown that if a customer problem is resolved quickly and effectively, the customer actually develops stronger loyalty than if the problem had never occurred. Top sales stars know how important it is to do whatever it takes to solve the customer problem and to be there working with the customer to resolve the situation.

Reliability

Time and again the top sales stars emphasized the importance of always keeping promises and commitments. This includes returning phone calls, making sure shipments are delivered, checking to make sure that everything promised was delivered, especially when someone else is involved in the delivery process. The salesperson who makes a sale and turns it over to "the system" and never checks to make sure the system worked is risking his or her entire relationship with the customer.

Uncommon effort

Customers want to know that you want their business and that you will go out of your way to get it. They want their business to be important to you. Little things can have enormous pay-off here. The special trip to deliver a piece of information, the personalized binding on a proposal, the invitation to lunch just because you want to see how things are going—these small efforts demonstrate your willingness to do whatever your customer needs. When the customer perceives you doing something you didn't have to do, that is when they really start to feel that you are on their side.

Bob Benson, field sales manager with *Sales & Marketing Management*, has consistently been one of its top salespeople and has set records with his performance. He tells about one of his early sales trips, "When I first started my career, I went on a sales trip to call on a small furniture manufacturer in Spring City, Tennessee, which is not even a dot on the map, wedged between Knoxville and Nashville. I had flown into Chattanooga and spent a day calling on customers and was planning to shoot over to Spring City when I missed my turnoff on the highway. The next turnoff was about 12 miles down and I'm running late. When I got to one of those u-turn intersections, there were some construction workers who told me that I could take this country dirt road and save some time getting to Spring City. So I'm hurrying down this winding, farm road in my Hertz car and I plowed right into a cow. I killed the cow...and the rental car.

"Shortly afterward, a farmer came down the road and offered me a ride into town (in back of the truck because his dog rode up front). So I'm in the back of this pickup with my suit and tie on when I saw my client's building where I was supposed to be. I banged on the back window of the pickup and the farmer stopped and let me out." Benson's client watched him climb down from the back of the pickup and listened with amusement as he described his ordeal with the cow, the rental car and the pickup truck.

"This manufacturer had never bought an advertising program in his life," states Benson, "but he was so impressed that I had taken the time to find Spring City, and with what I had gone through with the cow and the rental car, that he signed up for an exclusive advertising program. He is probably still laughing about the salesman who killed a cow and a rental car to get his business." Woody Allen says that 80 percent of success is showing up. It worked for Benson.

When a customer perceives a salesperson doing something he doesn't have to do, it creates an incredible level of trust. John Dowling whose extraordinary sales success in commercial real estate advanced him to Cushman & Wakefield's board of directors, treats his clients' business as his own. An example of the care he gives them occurred with a prestigious law firm in New Orleans. Dowling had negotiated a generous electricity allowance with the overage to be credited to overtime air-conditioning charges. But, the credit didn't show up because the electricity usage was much higher than estimated. Dowling went to New Orleans to find out why the usage was so high. The meters showed that the company was using more electricity at night than during the day. "My hotel room faced their office building," Dowling states, "so I sat in my room and photographed their offices during different hours of the night. We found out that they had five full floors of lights on so we got them to turn off the lights at night." When that still didn't achieve the results Dowling wanted, he had them install motion detectors to control the utility usage. His commitment to his clients makes him part of their operation and his job is to help them meet their objectives.

Service: the breakthrough tool

The service John Dowling provides is not ordinary. According to some people, it's almost unheard of. Because it is so rare, that commitment to extraordinary service is a tool for breaking through to new success levels. Rick Nixon, the vice president of sales for North America with Federal Express, started as a courier and came up through the ranks. Nixon says, "As we have seen, sales is becoming increasingly more personal. A recent study shows that 75 to 77 percent of the decisions that are made today are based on who the salesperson is, not the company or product they represent. More specifically, they are judged on how they represent themselves—their knowledge of the industry that they are in and their knowledge of the customer's industry. Knowing how your customer's industry works gives you the basis for knowing what questions to ask."

Nixon emphasizes the importance of service. "Service is what we sell," he states. "The salesperson can be the most intelligent person around; he can have a lot of experience in selling; and he can represent the best products on the market; but he still has to walk into a customer's office and do a needs assessment. He still has to determine what the customer wants to accomplish with the product and how it fits into the competitive market. Additionally, unless we have the folks to back up the sales effort with the service, it means nothing. It takes the efforts of everybody—from the time it's picked up by the courier and moves through the system till it is delivered at the other end. The biggest thing we have to sell is our reputation, our standing in the industry. I feel like my reputation as a person is on the line everytime we sell something."

Bob Benson maintains a service attitude that typifies the top salespeople. He does everything for his clients down to analyzing the copy in their ads. "I know our audience so well," he states, "that I know what will work with them. It's important to take an interest and learn your customer's business. You've got to always be thinking and giving him ideas about how he can develop more business. We try to turn problems into successful solutions. *Sales and Marketing Management* is set apart by our commitment to being cost-effective. We reach a corporate audience at about 25 percent of the cost of the bigger business magazines. We are always trying to fine-tune and improve results for our clients."

Although service is a surefire way to develop a successful sales career, it isn't particularly easy. "In an average year," Benson states, "I have about 125 advertising clients and that's a lot to keep in touch with. I maintain a strong contact relationship with them, spending a lot of time on the phone. I also do a tremendous amount of field work and make sure I follow up when I commit to something." A lot of effort and hard work, but the effort always pays off.

Reduce risk

The sales process progresses when enough trust is established to balance the perceived risk of the decision.

Therefore, to get the sales process moving, you can either build more trust or reduce the risk involved. Companies have developed many ways to reduce risk including money-back guarantees, free trials, samples and warranties. Saturn Corporation shocked the auto industry with its 30-day free trial. Drive a new car for 30 days and if you aren't happy with it, you take it back, no questions asked.

A risk reduction method that has worked well for many salespeople is to start small. Bill Baril, major account representative with Offtech, Inc., gives us an example. Some of his accounts have several hundred copiers, but when he establishes a relationship with a new account, he often starts small. He makes it easy for them to get involved with him, his equipment and his company.

When Offtech was first getting started, Baril called on Tufts New England Medical Center, which had more than 300 machines installed—and a contract with another vendor. During the process of getting to know them, he discovered that many of their machines were experiencing severe jamming problems. It was a nightmare for Tufts and for the person who was responsible for the equipment. Baril knew that his equipment had solved the jamming problem and could eliminate the problem for Tufts. The question was how to get around the contract that was already in place. So Baril and the fledgling Offtech offered to put their equipment into the areas where Tufts was having the worst problems at no cost to Tufts.

The equipment was installed and the jamming problems were eliminated. "The customer was elated," recalls Baril, "and he was able, on his own, to work out a way to end the contract. So we got an order for several machines—it was our first multi-machine order for more than 25 units. We still have Tufts. We started out with 50 machines and we now have about 350 machines installed there. In the beginning we were in there on a daily basis making sure that the machines were maintained and working properly. I am still in there on a weekly basis."

Baril reduced the risk and took the fear out of the decision. Even if there hadn't been a contract with another vendor, the chances are that Tufts would not have decided to go with a new dealer, and a manufacturer who was new to the United States. They would more than likely have gone with a "safe" decision—with a major manufacturer. By giving them no-risk option-free equipment and service— and solving some of their worst copy problems—Baril found a way to establish a relationship that has flourished for almost 10 years.

Trust begins and ends with truth. "Never lie to a customer," was probably one of the statements heard most frequently during interviews with the sales stars. Without complete honesty, there can be no relationship. Although it's possible to make a sale based on a lie, it's like winning the battle and losing the war. Eventually the customer will know that you did not have his or her interests in mind.

Customer references

Probably the most common method of making prospective clients feel comfortable about our products and services is to let them hear from other satisfied customers. References are used by every sales star, but there are a wide variety of styles.

John Dowling is called "Mr. Commercial Real Estate" and is widely known as one of the best in the business. Commercial real estate is tough—it is relatively easy to get into, the payoff for the winners is large and the competition is cut-throat. These traits lead to a huge turnover in salespeople and a short-term mentality among the sales force. By contrast, Dowling has been with Cushman & Wakefield almost 30 years. From the time he finished college, he knew he wanted to be in the real estate industry because, as Dowling explains, "In real estate you could leave something tangible behind. You could do a better development, you could change the way people experience their lives and cities."

The transitory nature of the majority of the industry's sales force has driven Dowling to prove himself different. "What has driven me all through my career," he explains, "and what may have contributed to the success I have achieved is the sense that I am going to prove to each client that I am substantially different from the other practitioners in the field." Dowling practically insists that potential clients contact references. He says that the normal process of interviewing a broker is just a beauty contest—it only reveals superficial characteristics and appearances.

"I tell my clients," explains Dowling, "that these interviews only demonstrate my salesmanship—they tell you absolutely nothing about my knowledge, my work ethic, my negotiating skills and my basic ethics." He gives his prospects a list of his current clients and insists that they call. "What you've got to ask them," he instructs the prospective client, "is how was it at the end of the project. Did I go the extra mile in every single case? And did I frankly exceed their expectations?" Dowling tells them who to call and what questions to ask. "I tell them," he explains, "to call IBM or GE, call the heads of real estate and ask them who the best guy in the United States is to help them solve their problems. Ask them who will really care, who is it who will allow you to sleep at night because they really care about your business? Real estate is often the biggest single commitment a business makes and it's more than just rent. Is the building clean, cool or hot? Does it have the

right image for prospective clients or for employees? Do you have an option to expand? Someone might find you cheap rent but if the building stinks, it'll wind up costing you a lot of money."

Dowling recommends that young salespeople who haven't built up a client base should avoid the first person singular pronoun. They should speak about their firm and build a real knowledge of the firm and what the firm's successes and strengths have been. The salesperson can then build on that reputation. "No matter what you're selling," Dowling emphasizes, "it's your personal services that are as important or perhaps more important than your product."

Story references

The industry standard for reference lists is a typed list of names, addresses and telephone numbers. The salesperson hands this list to a prospect and hopes the prospect gets a glowing recommendation. There is a better way.

For a reference to be truly effective, it should present a situation similar to the prospect's and it should be extremely positive. I'm assuming that you will be providing such outstanding service and support that all the references will be glowing, so let's address the first requirements situation similar to the prospect's.

When a prospective client gets the standard reference sheet, he or she knows nothing about how the product or service is being used and what the specific situation is for that person on the reference list. The prospective client probably gets a similar sheet from every vendor he or she talks with. Most clients won't call everyone on your list; so they may not hear the powerful stories of how well your product is working and what outstanding service you're providing. One way to differentiate your reference list and give the prospective client a much easier way of determining which references to check is to do a story reference. This simply tells the story behind the reference. Here is a reference comparison:

Old-style Reference:
Mary Smith
Westside Medical
Plainsview, DE
211-233-3334

Reference:

Mary Smith	Equipment: 742 with	Key Applications:
Westside Medical	10 bin sorter\auto feed	Book copying
Plainsview, DE	Monthly Volume: 10,000+	Duplexing
211-233-3334		Editing

Operations manager for a six-physician clinic. Old equipment was jamming frequently and office staff often could not provide important copies to patients. Three model 742's were installed in 1992. Since then, there have only been two repair calls with less than two hours of down time on each. Client just ordered two machines for a new office in Jonesburg.

When your prospects read about your customers' applications, they may come across one describing a situation similar to theirs. Any similarities increase the likelihood that the prospect will call that customer and ask why they decided to do business with you. Describing the situation makes the reference appear more real and gives the prospective client a basis for asking questions.

Different salespeople have added new twists to the story references. Steve Gold, one of Comdoc Office Equipment's top salespeople (and now a new sales manager), started taking pictures of his customers. He explains how he got started, "I found that selling office equipment was tough and it was hard to differentiate myself because copiers do two things—they make copies and they break. That was consistent throughout the industry. Almost everyone seems to kick their machines at some point in time. I wanted to find a way to prove to people very quickly that they would be happy with my copiers. I knew that if I could do that, I would be able to sell more and realize greater profit potential on my sales. So I started taking pictures of all my customers with their equipment. I would have them put their hands on the copier and smile. I did that with every copier I sold. I found that using those pictures was a great way to make a presentation. It seemed more realistic and backed up everything I had stated about the copier. At first people laughed but one customer said, 'You know the real reason why I want to buy your equipment, Steve?' I said, 'Why?' and he said, 'Because I want to be in your book.'

"It brought the process down to earth and made it something fun—something people could relate to. My sales and profit margins went up. People liked to see me and I started developing personal relationships with my accounts. It made it a lot more enjoyable. It was a real breakthrough for me." Pictures and stories make the references seem real, more believable.

Tape-recorded references

Some salespeople take their references the next step by recording them. Tape-recorded references have several advantages—they require little effort on the part of the prospect and hearing the customer's voice makes the reference seem even more real. Taped references should be used in connection with story references so the prospective customer always has the option of calling and asking questions on a confidential basis.

To develop your reference tape, take three or four accounts that have been using your product or service for six months or longer. These accounts should be ones you're in contact with frequently and you know are happy with your products and services. Contact the person who was involved with the initial purchase decision and ask if you can stop by to tape an interview about his or her positive experiences with your product and your company. If you've done your job by staying in touch with these customers and making sure they were satisfied, they should be more than happy to accommodate you. You should choose clients who represent a broad range of situations and who are using a variety of products or services.

After explaining the process to your customer, begin the taped interview by saying a few words that position the product and its benefits. The taped reference should include the following:

♦ An introduction of yourself and the person you are interviewing (name of the individual, title, name of the company).

♦ Mention of the type or types of products or services the customer is presently using.

♦ The customer then tells some of the reasons why he or she chose to do business with your company and how your products or services have successfully fulfilled his or her needs.

Generally, the customer will start talking about service, benefits received from your product, reliability and so on. You'll be surprised how much the customer will volunteer. However, if he or she fails to mention any important aspect, offer a reminder. After the interview ask for a reference letter on the company letterhead reiterating the points in the interview. The letter verifies the validity of the taped reference in case you run into a skeptical prospect.

Immediately following the taped interview send a short thank-you note and a small gift to the customer. It leaves a lasting, positive impression that can make a favorable difference the next time you call for additional business.

When a prospect asks about your ability to provide service, you can say, "I'm glad you asked. Here's a comment from a customer who had the same hesitation as you two years ago." You then play that reference and your prospect hears from a satisfied customer. Regardless of what your prospect's objection is, you can play a tape

that reassures him or her that your products and services have pleased and satisfied other customers. The tapes provide a high level of proof that objections will be handled to the customer's satisfaction. Reference tapes should never be more than five to six minutes and each customer should talk for only one or two minutes. You should play only the reference that is closest to your prospective client's situation. You may want to have separate tapes so you can easily access the specific references you want to use.

Video references

Bill Stack is the manager of the Eastern Communications Region for GE Information Services. Its product is a complex, high-level custom application of a worldwide data network. "We usually have a reference-type sale," explains Stack. "If I have a client in the particular application area of interest to a prospect, then we use that client for a reference. Since the items we sell are generally million-dollar ticket items, we often take the potential client in to see the application in use." Stack also uses video-tapes of client applications. "We try to get permission from all of our clients to use them as references. We have clients worldwide who have allowed us to videotape them. We have them talk about the application and we put three to four clients on a tape, each with different applications. We have them talk about how GE has come in and helped them solve their problem and helped them be competitive on a worldwide basis."

How well have video-taped interviews worked for GE? Stack states, "It makes it easier to close a deal and increases my percentage of closings by a minimum of 25 percent."

Everything you do with references should be designed to let the prospective customer see your level of service and concern for their needs. References should help the customer feel confident that if he chooses your product or service, it will be a safe decision. References should be part of the security blanket you provide your customers. The warm fuzzy feeling that says you are on their side, you have their interests at heart, you are the expert who is there to help them.

Story references, pictures, taped and video-references all help you build trust with your prospects. Mike Fields, president of Oracle USA tells a story that demonstrates how deep fear and mistrust can go in customers. "I was still at Burroughs," he explains. "There was a customer on Long Island in the fuel oil business. My salesperson came to me and said the customer wanted to buy our hardware, but the president of the company wanted to meet me to negotiate the contract. So I put on my best suit and went down to meet the customer. He was a big guy and I sat down across the desk from him with the contract in front of me.

He said, 'You want me to sign this?' I said, 'Yes, but if you have any questions, I'd be happy to go over them. I understand your technical people have evaluated the product and feel that it's the best solution for your company.' I was giving him the normal pitch. He said, 'Yea, yea, I understand that. But, what you want me to do is sign this contract?' Again I said, 'Yes, do you have any questions?' He said, 'No.' Then he pulls out a gun...a big gun...puts it on the table, takes his pen in hand, signs the contract and says, 'Don't ever screw me.' " What would you do differently if your clients had guns? In effect they do, only it's a pen. If they do not get the service they want, they point their pen in a different direction and your competitor gets their business.

Iceberg selling

The last piece of the formula for building relationships is that the customer has to respect you—he or she has to respect your product knowledge and your understanding of his or her business, needs and problems. The customer wants to think of you as the expert, someone who has information that will help the business. Gaining the information it takes to make customers respect you takes a lot of hard work and preparation. Many people, and unfortunately even a lot of salespeople, think of selling as the activity that takes place in front of a customer.

That's like thinking an iceberg is what sticks out of the water. The salesperson who depends on his or her presentation skills or persuasiveness without doing the necessary background preparation, is like an iceberg without a bottom...it sinks and so does the salesperson.

Michael Vandiver, national sales manager with Gillette Corp's Paper-Mate division, says, "My boss gave me this old saying, 'Selling is 90 percent preparation and 10 percent presentation.' It's really true. It's the work you do before you go in to make the call—knowing the customer and putting together a program—that makes the difference. Too many people in selling want to spend all their time in front of the customer. We want our people in front of the customers, but you've got to be sure that you're armed 100 percent. Too often, people go in and shoot from the hip. It just isn't as successful as when you go in with a good concept and a good idea as to what possible objections the buyer might have. Being prepared includes practicing mentally and physically."

John Dowling, one of the nation's top commercial real estate sales stars, says, "Everything in business is like trying a lawsuit—it's all in preparation. Most salespeople I know never read *The New York Times* or *The Wall Street Journal*, they never read general business publications. I don't know how much I read per week but it's a lot. You cannot relate to a man in business without understanding his business. A man in the oil business wants you to understand the oil business and what a drilling rig is and what upstream and downstream means and what crude and refined is and what's OPEC and domestic and who his competitors are and his recent history—has it been good or bad and why. Too many salespeople don't know anything about business let alone the client's business. It is a compliment to the client for you to know his business and the history of his company. It's preparation. A successful salesperson cannot be lazy. Too many people believe that the successful salesperson has secrets or that people are feeding him deals. It's absolutely nuts. The first thing you do is your homework."

Dowling has a special peeve with salespeople who don't understand the importance of appearance. "You have to empathize with your clients. I see people who call on a law firm and they have hair halfway down their backs and so much jewelry on their arm that they would sink if they fell into the Hudson River. One client from GE told me about a property manager with the company who lives on a plane and doesn't make an awful lot of money. If this guy has to go to Albuquerque to see some warehouses, he gets met by a real estate person in a Mercedes with a Rolex on his arm and a trunk full of golf clubs, tennis rackets and so on. He asked me, 'Why don't the people in your industry show some empathy for the guy who is working his ass off for an industrial company?' I've given that advice to a lot of people, but it doesn't seem to get through."

Customer surveys

One way to make sure you understand what your customers are thinking is to do frequent customer surveys. Some salespeople in high service businesses survey their customers as frequently as every month. Every month the customer receives a questionnaire asking about the level of service of the salesperson, the product and the company. The response goes back to the president of the company, or the salesperson's manager. This continuing feedback identifies problems early and gives the company and the salesperson a better understanding of what's important to the customer.

Salespeople who have implemented the customer survey program have also found that it is a dynamic sales tool. When a customer asks for proof that the level of service being promised will be delivered, the salesperson can explain the customer survey program. He explains that if the prospect becomes a customer, he will immediately be part of the program and will be asked to rate his service every month. The salesperson can pull out customer surveys from other clients that document superior service. They can also show responses that might indicate a problem and then discuss how that problem was resolved.

Many salespeople add the surveys to their story references and pictures to develop a comprehensive customer portfolio. Even the most skeptical prospects can be convinced when they are presented with story portfolios, pictures, reference letters, taped references and actual customer surveys testifying to excellent service. See Chapter 8 for details on implementing customer surveys.

Frequent contact

Relationships require frequent contact. You should have a schedule of contacts, a plan for keeping in touch and up-to-date with each customer. Real estate agents often maintain an appraisal file on properties so that every three or four months they can call the client and discuss recent sales that compare to the clients and see if the client is considering a move. Car salesmen keep in touch through the service cycle and by monitoring the life of the current car and car loan. Very few products are "one-shot" sales—almost everything is eventually replaced or upgraded.

Bill Stack of GE Information Services is quoted at the beginning of this chapter as saying if you couldn't call your customer on a Saturday night and ask for a favor, you didn't have a relationship. Stack also believes in doing favors and special services for his clients. "We had a client," he explains, "who was a vice president and his company got involved with a leveraged buyout that forced him out of his job. The sales rep actually carried the guy's resume around with him for months trying to help him connect with another job. The client wound up with a small pharmaceutical company that was about to place an order with another vendor. Our client flew to the home office in London, stopped the order and gave the order to our sales rep strictly on the basis of their relationship and our past successful implementations. That sale wound up being worth close to half a million dollars."

Customers have to like you, trust you and respect you before they will make a decision to buy from you. Developing that trust takes constant honesty, reliably keeping all promises, uncommon effort and extraordinary service. The next chapter will tell you more about how sales stars base their success on an exceptional level of service.

"Goodwill is the only asset that competition cannot undersell nor destroy."
—*Marshall Field, department store legend*

> Two Ideas:

What two ideas did you get from this chapter?

_____

_____

I dare you to find a way to use one of these ideas to improve your relationship building skills.

Action Plan

```
Developing Your
Customer Portfolio
```

Building the customer's confidence in your products and services is a critical step in the sales process. The customer portfolio is an excellent tool for establishing confidence. Here is a step-by-step process for developing your portfolio:

1. **Story references.** Develop a broad range of story references. Give the background of the account, what their concerns and objectives were, and how the product or service has met those needs.

2. **Pictures.** Take pictures of your customers—with your product or in the process of using your service. You might want to have one large picture or a collage of pictures showing different aspects of your product or service.

3. **Reference letters.** Get reference letters from each client who will be referenced in your portfolio.

4. **Taped references.** Make a tape of customers talking about different aspects of your product. Each reference should be no more than two minutes and you will only play one or two references. You might want to have five or six on the tape. You can space the references and mark them with a strip of tape so you can fast forward to the right spots—or you can use different tapes to emphasize different product benefits or uses.

5. **Videotape references.** If you have highly complex installations and products, ask permission to videotape the installation in the client facility. This should be professionally done but not too slick. Get customers to talk about the benefits of your product and the actual results that have been accomplished by using the product.

6. **Customer surveys.** Use the surveys as proof of your high level of service and as an example of your listening strategies.

7. **Customer portfolio.** Put all the materials into an attractive presentation book that can be shown to your prospects.

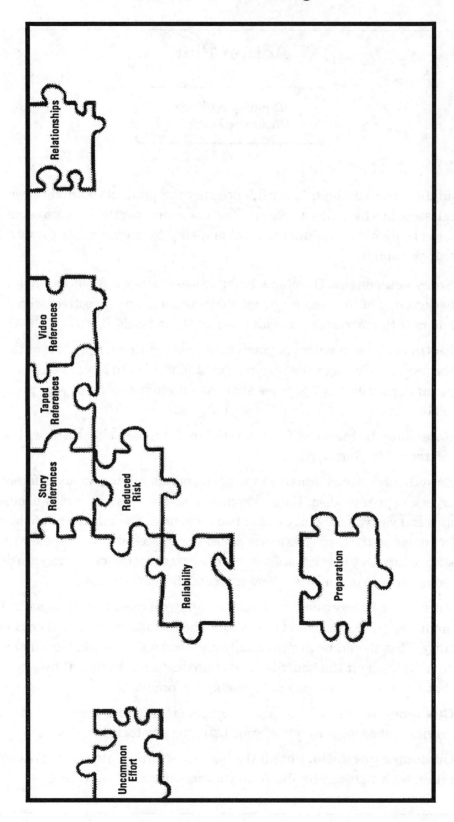

Chapter 6

What's the question?

"Every single word the customer says has value."
—*Richard McGinn, president, AT&T Computer Systems*

Coming attractions:

♦ The listening salesperson
♦ Listening keys
♦ Success through research
♦ Funnel questions
♦ The one best question

In real estate it is often said that there are three main principles: location, location, location. In sales the three critical skills are: listen, listen, listen. If you analyzed all of the interviews with all the sales superstars, by far the most frequently mentioned critical sales skill would be listening. New salespeople often feel like they have to keep control of a sales situation and they try to do that by talking, by making their pitch. They go through their canned presentation and flip charts or presentation book and hope they hit all the points of interest to the customer. Oddly enough, the way to keep control of the sales situation is actually by not talking. The listening salesperson hears information and clues, which leads to the next step of the sales process. By letting go, he or she keeps control.

The listening salesperson

Just as you cannot pour coffee into a full cup, a customer cannot give information to a talking salesperson. When the salesperson listens, he or she creates an empty space that the customer fills with information about needs and problems. This information leads to sales. No salesperson ever listened themselves out of a sale.

Studies show that we spend almost half of our time listening—far more time than we spend talking, reading or writing. Yet schools, including business schools, train people to read, write and speak, but not listen. Research shows that most Americans talk at about 135 words per minute but listen at between 400 and 800 words per minute. The difference in the rate of speaking and listening allows time for our minds to wander.

But, this "spare" time can be used to improve our listening skills by paraphrasing, organizing and questioning the material we are receiving.

Larry Frank, chief operating officer with Comdoc Office Systems, states that listening is the tool that leads to customer partnerships. "I see partnership as the theme almost everywhere I go. The reps who develop partnerships with their customers are the ones who are the most successful. The way they do that is by listening—asking a lot of questions and only talking when they have something to say. People who do primarily a sales presentation approach are about as effective as sending a brochure and a price list in the mail."

Over and over again, the top sales reps emphasized the importance of listening. But listening is one of those skills that is easy to talk about doing but hard to actually know when you're doing it. The following comments give you a better idea of what the top salespeople are actually doing when they are listening:

Mark Ochoa, top national account executive with Federal Express: "You have to discipline yourself to listen. I utilize a handy cue card in my notebook that states: 'L-I-S-T-E-N.' Listening is a key asset of successful sales professionals. It is through aggressive listening that you can detect or uncover customer dissatisfaction. After I have done my preliminary research on a client (prior to meeting them), I dedicate time to preparing specific questions regarding the client's requirements. By design, this process allows the customer to do most of the talking. By listening I avoid unnecessary time spent 'selling' the customer and I am actually focusing on the areas that are important to him."

Jeffrey Smith, Minolta Copiers: We don't believe in the 27 magic closing tricks and tools. The approach we take is that if the customer says something then it's true, and if we say it then it may not be true. We try to get our salespeople to involve the customer as much as possible and let the customer do 75 percent or 80 percent of the talking. If the customers can verbalize it and state it, they are also much more likely to believe that the solution is one that they need and can live with. They are also much more likely to feel comfortable with the salesperson. They don't feel like they're being "sold" something."

Bill Stack, GE Information Services: "We try to find out the strategic plans for a company we're dealing with—where they want to go in the next five years. We try to develop a trust that we are there and maybe we have a program that's appropriate for them. We are going to try to help them meet their goals. We ask them how they want to increase the productivity of their sales force. How do they want to improve client services? How do they want to be competitive in a worldwide market place? We try to get our sales-people to think about those types of things, to think strategically so we can develop our technology into a product that will solve a business problem."

Rick Dyer, Apple Computer: "For me, the key to listening was to be able to go back and re-explain what the customer told me. Did I understand it well enough to restate it in different words—either back to the customer or to my boss? If I didn't feel like I could completely explain his business and his needs, then I had to go back and talk to him some more. It is important to learn to recognize when you know what you need to know. And, by the way, you never know everything. You never reach the point when you un-derstand the customer's needs suffi-ciently. There is always more to be gained by more questioning, by more time spent with the customer."

Dyer has a "sales by walking around" philosophy: "I believe in going out and looking at their business. I found that talking about it was nice but I really wanted to look at the situation. I wanted to walk the floor, stand over someone's shoulder to see how they do their job. Because what you'll find is that you've probably got some informa-tion that the customer doesn't know about. And the customer can only de-scribe what they know. Hopefully you bring some additional expertise and can

come up with an idea that the customer hasn't thought of. The way to find that out is to go out and look at the situation firsthand."

Bev Hyman, Bev Hyman & As-soc.: "I listen to the clients, I listen to their objections, I really hear what they are saying. I listen to their body language. I'm not satisfied unless I can listen to what my clients want and repeat it to them in terms that make sense to them. Maybe its partly be-cause I'm in the communication busi-ness that I know how fraught with difficulties communication is. Probably one of the reasons for not making a sale or for the sale falling apart when you think you've closed it, is the basic lack of communication. I don't think salespeople listen enough, they don't force themselves to restate in the lan-guage of the person that they are selling. Because salespeople want to shorten the selling cycle, they push for the close too soon. You have to have patience to sell—at least to sell a big-ticket item. You have to be willing to go around on more than one occasion, to be willing to not take a 'no' per-sonally. You have to know what your objective is. You have to have a fall-back objective when you can't get the whole objective accomplished."

Sy Gardner, president of Gardner Carpets: "The most important thing is knowing and understanding the custom-ers...reading the customer...watching for facial reactions, body reactions, listening to them. Listening is probably more important than selling. When you're selling, you're not hearing what the customer's needs are. You are only telling the customer about your product and why he should buy it. It's like trying to sell a Mercedes to a guy who needs a dump truck. If you let the buyer tell you what his needs are, then you can tailor your offerings to his needs.

The top salespeople seem to be particularly adept at selective listening—hearing the main items of interest to the customer and hearing the problems of primary concern. They are able to pick up key phrases that can be used to advance the sales process. They listen for, and hear, links between the customer's needs and the benefits offered by the product or service. Top salespeople are detectives, finding information that will turn the product or service into a solution for the customer. Listening is the top tool in their tool box.

Listening keys

Listen for information. Information is the key to sales success. Too often, salespeople use this time when a customer is talking to get ready to launch their presentation. Learn to distinguish emotional messages from information. Here are some listening basics to help you develop this critical skill:

Watch body language. The customer's body often tells you more than his words. Is he bored, impatient, tired, excited, interested? Top salespeople can translate body language and they respond to it just as they respond to the customer's words.

Show interest and alertness. Your body language tells the customer whether you are really interested in him and his problems. Eye contact, leaning forward in your chair to hear what he says and note-taking tell him you are there to listen.

Eliminate distractions. You may not be able to control the distractions in your customer's environment, but you can eliminate your own distractions. Clear your mind of everything except the customer's situation. All distractions of the office and home should be put aside— they'll still be waiting for you when you are through with the customer.

Delay interpretation. Put yourself in the speaker's shoes and wait for the entire message. Too often, salespeople hear a key phrase and they jump to a conclusion and try to close the sale. Compensation isn't paid for the speed of the close, just for the close.

Put aside personal opinions. This isn't the time to work out political or religious differences. It doesn't matter if your customer has a different organizational philosophy. What matters is whether your product or service offers the customer an honest solution to his needs or problems.

Avoid expectations. Trying to force-fit what the customer is saying into some preconceived product or service solution doesn't work. It may be that your product or service doesn't meet the customer's needs at all. Trying to force him into a mold will just alienate him and shut off the information that might trigger a solution that would work for both of you.

Check your understanding. Even if you listen perfectly, the customer may not communicate perfectly. Unless you check what you heard, you will not know if it is what he said.

Boost your memory. Confucius once said, "Short pencil better than long memory." Take notes and use those notes to check your understanding of what was said. These notes will also help when you call back. You can start a conversation with, "When we were last together, you said..." and make an impression on the customer that you were really listening.

What's the question?

The *Little Brown Book of Anecdotes* tells us that when Gertrude Stein was dying of cancer, she turned to Alice B. Toklas and murmured, "What is the answer?" Miss Toklas made no reply. Miss Stein nodded and went on, "In that case, what is the question?"

Before a customer's problem can be solved, the salesperson has to understand the customer's business or needs. To get the information necessary to understand those needs, the salesperson has to ask the right questions and listen for answers and clues. First come the questions.

But there are good questions and not-so-good questions. Boring, simplistic questions can do as much damage as good. One buyer who gets hundreds of calls from prospective vendors said, "Vendors call me with the same stupid set of questions. They must copy them and send them around the country—it's very irritating."

Neil Rackham investigated sales for 12 years and analyzed more than 35,000 sales calls to determine the difference between successful calls and unsuccessful calls. In *SPIN Selling*, he says, "Selling is about the asking of questions." He discusses his conclusion that much of the difference depends on the type of questions asked. The success of the call did not depend on the number of questions asked, it depended on the type of questions. Here are the types of questions identified by Rackham:

Situation questions. At the start of the call, successful people tend to ask data-gathering questions about facts and background.

Typical situation questions would be "How long have you had your present equipment?" or "Could you tell me about your company's growth plans?" Although situation questions have an important fact-finding role, successful people don't overuse them because too many can bore or irritate the buyer.

Problem questions. Once sufficient information has been established about the buyer's situation, successful people tend to move to a second type of question. They ask, for example, "Is this operation difficult to perform?" or "Are you worried about the quality you get from your old machine?" Questions like these, which we call problem questions, explore problems, difficulties and dissatisfactions in areas where the seller's product can help. Inexperienced people generally don't ask enough problem questions.

Implication questions. In smaller sales, sellers can be very successful if they just know how to ask good situation and problem questions. In larger sales, this is not enough; successful people need to ask a third type of question. This third type is more complex and sophisticated. It's called an implication question, and typical examples would be "How will this problem affect your future profitability?" or "What effect does this reject rate have on customer satisfaction?" Implication questions take

a customer problem and explore its effects or consequences. As we'll see by asking implication questions, successful people help the customer understand a problem's seriousness or urgency. Implication questions are particularly important in large sales, and even very experienced salespeople rarely ask them well.

Need-payoff questions. Finally, we found that very successful salespeople ask a fourth type of question during the investigating stage. It's called a need-payoff question, and typical examples would be "Would it be useful to speed this operation by 10 percent?" or "If we could improve the quality of this operation, how would that help you?" Need-payoff questions have several uses, perhaps the most important one is that they get the customer to tell you the benefits that your solution could offer. Need-payoff questions have a very strong relationship to sales success. It's been common, in our studies, to find that top performers ask more than 10 times as many need-payoff questions per call as do average performers.

Rackham states that one of the worst selling diseases happens once a customer identifies a problem or a need. The inexperienced salesperson gets so excited that he leaps across the desk and starts to beat the customer with features and benefits, trying to close immediately. This salesperson never gets to the implication or need-payoff questions. While asking good questions is a basic key to success in sales, we found many sales trainers having difficulty with questioning "models." Too often, salespeople get so wrapped up with the questions they are supposed to ask, that they don't listen to the answers.

Bill Wilkes, a Federal Express Hall of Fame account executive, emphasizes the importance of listening as part of the questioning process. His soft-spoken, southern manner belies an intensity that has kept him consistently at the top at Federal Express and previously at Xerox. He was the Account Executive of the Year twice while Zap Mail was in operation. When Zap Mail was scuttled, Wilkes left the company. "I was one of the few people who was ever 'dumb' enough to leave Federal," he states. "I was fortunate enough to come back into worldwide sales a year and a half later.

"One of the most important things I learned early on," Wilkes says, "was to ask a lot of questions, appropriate questions about a customer's business, listen very carefully and then come back and make positive recommendations. I think that it is very important because salespeople too often do a lot of talking and not enough questioning. The right kinds of questions are important—not only what's important to

the individual personally and professionally but what's important to their company.

"Before you would ever go on a sales call, you would want to do the research to learn some obvious things about what their revenue is, what their earnings are, what kind of products they make and what services they offer. We do a lot of research first and that points us toward the right questions."

Wilkes offers this advice to new salespeople, "If I were starting out, I would want to know who my clients' biggest competitors were. Where are they positioned in their market? Which divisions are doing real well—which ones are the 'darlings'? Which divisions are starting to do not-so-well? I would want to know what kind of warranties they have—guarantees that distinguish them from their competitors. Basic things but things that a lot of salespeople don't ask."

The top sales stars know that developing a good set of questions is the basis of doing a good needs analysis. But they have to listen carefully, be able to change directions, and use other questions and probing techniques according to the reactions and responses of their customers.

Dan Gibbs, another top account executive with Federal Express, states, "You really have to take the time on the front end to get to know your customer's business. Most people do not want their time wasted answering obvious or poorly thought-out questions—especially if you are trying to talk at the highest levels. They have a short time span and expect you to do the basic research necessary to answer preliminary questions. If you can go in and let them know that you have something that might be valuable for them to hear, then they will spend time with you."

Wilkes spent a year working on a Kodak account. He identified a division that was growing rapidly and started meeting with them to find ways of solving their business problems. "I was just building layer upon layer of trust and confidence," he explains. "I brought in all the resources we have and matched them up to their business objectives. Nothing revolutionary but things that can't be short-circuited." Wilkes' work parlayed a few meetings into over $1 million worth of business by customizing Kodak's critical shipments to Europe.

Wilkes' philosophy of selling is demonstrated in his aversion to the term negotiate. "I don't like the word 'negotiate' because it has a feeling of win-lose about it. I like to use the word 'create.' Let's look at how we can do things. Let's get the adversarial stuff out of the way. You come over and sit in my chair and I'll sit in yours. Let's approach it with how we can come out of this with a win-win scenario and be strategic partners for the long-haul.

"It's like closing," Wilkes continues. "Closing should be natural. It

should not be manipulative. You're always asking questions like 'Are we on track?' 'Is there anything we need to do?' 'Are we in agreement?' 'Are there any obstacles to this?' You shouldn't have to get your way by manipulation, because it will always come back to you."

Captioning

One of the interesting sidebars of this book occurred when I interviewed Barry M. Farber, radio personality who is the founder and vice president of Talk Net. Farber, the radio personality, is noted for his interviewing skills and has interviewed hundreds of people from movie great Ingrid Bergman, to former chancellor of Germany Willy Brandt. Farber convinced some of the world's most powerful people to appear as guests on his talk show. I interviewed him because his book, *Making People Talk*, contained an excellent chapter on listening.

He told me how he developed intense listening skills including a particularly powerful technique he calls captioning. Farber states, "Listening is one of the most devilishly effective techniques of all. I do not listen because I am particularly interested; I listen very opportunistically. I believe in captioning. Captioning is when you pick up a spark from the conversation and later in the conversation, you play it back to them with the comment, '...as you said a while ago....' When they hear themselves quoted accurately, it proves you were listening and you prove you find them worth quoting. Then you have a blue ribbon around your cracker jacks.

"I have forced myself to learn to listen," Farber continues. "I have played games, pretending that the president called and told me it was a matter of national security that I remember everything the person said. A little listening goes a long way because people are not used to being listened to. I used to think that if the client caught me captioning or attending to him, it would sour him on me. But that is wrong. If he catches you, he just knows that you are a good player. Even if he sees through your act completely, he will appreciate the act."

Research first

Ellen Manzo is an area manager with AT&T Computer Systems and has been a consistent award winner, including receiving the Council Leaders award (for the top 2 percent of all salespeople), top national account team and top management award in the Eastern Region. Manzo states, "It is critical to do a lot of account research—especially if you are servicing a small number of accounts. There is a ton of information available. I go to the library, I go through Dun & Bradstreet and news clipping services and get the last 18 months of articles on the company. I buy a share of stock in the company so that I receive all of the proxy statements and quarterly information. Then I ask to see the customer's library and any information it might have on file. I try to get on the customer's mailing list. Another excellent source of information we've found is noncompetitive salespeople. Also, AT&T sells into almost every company in the country so we have a lot of internal resources. I require my salespeople to do all of this background research before they ever ask for an interview. They should know what the industry is doing as well as what the company is doing.

"We are the new kid on the block in the computer industry and by having all of the information about the customer's business, we are able to establish our credibility. We become a very quick study on the customer's industry. For instance, until I researched them, I never thought about UPS as one of the top 10 airlines in the country—they not only have all the problems of running a package delivery service, but they have all the problems of running an airline."

Manzo gives an example of how doing preliminary research pays off. "We were recently involved with a data network system for one of the now big-six accounting firms. We found out through all of our information gathering that one of our decision-makers on the West Coast had tight ties with another computer company and actually developed software in conjunction with that company. Since our system interfaced with the other computer company's systems, we realized we could use that interface ability as a benefit point for our system.

"Through our investigation and understanding of this connection, we not only sold the prospect, but we also actually wound up installing our data network system in the other computer company. By having that background information, we were able to accurately position our product and identify needs and sensitivities that would affect our position."

Manzo especially emphasizes the need to understand how the key decision-maker's compensation plan works. She explains, "Most key executives of large companies have bonus packages that range from $100,000 to well over $1 million. It's critical to understand what their key compensation points are. What do they have to do to make their bonuses and how can your product or service affect those points?

"An example of how critical it is," Manzo explains, "happened just after I came to AT&T. We had one account where we were cutting-over one PBX system per week. These were good-sized systems ranging from $150,000 to multi-million dollars. The manager of the project had 10 points he was measured on and one of the items was that if he missed his schedule on one cut-over, he could lose 10 percent of his bonus. This was a bank and they only had certain hours when the cut-over could

happen and if it didn't happen on time, the whole bank system would go down. Knowing about his compensation points was very, very important to selling to that client. We could design a plan to show him that we would make sure we met his due dates. We helped him succeed."

Manzo requires her new salespeople to be very research-oriented. She explains, "As a kickoff exercise with new people (all recent college graduates), we give them a list of questions and tell them to go find the answers. The questions include questions about AT&T such as: What is the current stock price? Who is the CEO? How many business units are there? They then go on a hunting exercise—they can use any resource they can find, whether it's calling a stockbroker, going to the library or talking to a manager."

Background research is critical for the salesperson who wants to walk into a major account and make an impression. They can leave a lasting impression with their client through their understanding of his or her business and needs. Manzo requires her new salespeople to do as much research as possible on an account and then to meet with her to strategize before making that first, critical call. She says, "After they have done the background research, I ask them to sit down with me and think through that first sales call since it is the critical one. If they are meeting the key executive for the first time, I want them to get an understanding of what that key executive's compensation plan is. Understanding what motivates that executive is critical. Understanding how we can affect that plan is critical."

One of the tools Manzo gives her salespeople for getting information from the executives on their compensation plan is to set up an "if-scenario." She explains, "If I were talking to a CEO, I would ask 'If I were the CEO of this company, how would you measure me? What would be the key criteria, the key performance items that you would measure?' If they mentioned executive bonus, I would ask them, 'Is that a big number or a little number compared to my salary?' "

This gives the executive some room to discuss compensation points without actually revealing the actual compensation plan. The client and the salesperson can discuss performance requirements in a way that is not threatening to the client. The client also understands that the salesperson is on his or her side.

At the end of this chapter is a summary of the research sources used by Manzo and other sales stars. Manzo laughs, "I'm not sure I want IBM to have all of my sources. I have found that a surprising number of salespeople, even ones who have been in the business for a long time, have not found out about these resources. They may have bought the one share of stock and discovered the trade periodicals and checked out the Dow Jones

News service, but they usually don't understand the extensiveness of *Standard & Poors* and what *U.S. Industrial Outlook* and *Value Line* can do for them. I think they underestimate the importance of the executive compensation plan."

Cheryl Ricketts Basinger, star account executive with Franklin International Institute, also believes in doing a great deal of research before she ever walks through the customer's door. Basinger explains her background research, "I use the library a lot...*the Harris Service & Manufacturing Journals, Moody's, Standard & Poors*, lists of top companies. I will go through back issues of magazines and try to find information on specific companies—where their locations are, their numbers, what kind of employees they have. If it's a subsidiary of a company, I try to find out about the parent company. I research what's happening in the industry as well as the company. I have targeted my top 50 prospects and so I look for articles and things about that company or industry—things about the people in the company.

"Another key for me is the company philosophy. Does it want to be number-one? Is it quality driven? What kinds of challenges does it face? Is going into a global market an issue? Is its growth rapid or stagnant? Is it relocating operations? My approach is different depending on what I learn. Our core product is a corporate and personal productivity program and it can be positioned differently depending upon the client's needs. All the information I can find out before meeting with the client helps me develop the right questions and positions me as a knowledgeable potential partner. If I'm setting myself up to be a partner, it's pretty tough to go in and be absolutely ignorant about the industry or the company. The approach of 'I'm sure I can help you no matter what you need,' is awfully arrogant and, quite frankly, ineffective."

Basinger explains how she approaches the investigation part of the sales process, "Typically, I say to prospects that I want to answer any questions they might have about Franklin or our productivity concepts or whatever else it is that I am there to talk about. However, for me to be most effective, it would be helpful for me if I could ask a few questions about their company. I ask if it would be all right for me to do that. You usually see a look of surprise go across their face because people expect you to pitch the product right away."

Funnel questions

"I use a funnel-type approach to questions," Basinger explains. "I start with very, very broad questions and then go into the specific. I usually start out with an opening statement that starts out something like, 'Franklin is really committed to making a positive difference in our client companies. In order for me to evaluate whether our program is a fit for your situation, I would like to ask you a few questions. Would you give me an overview of your company?'

Funnel questions

1. **Overview.** Philosophy, trends, mission statement, goals of industry and company.

   - Tell me about your company.
   - What is your company philosophy?
   - Does your company have a published mission statement?
   - What are your strategic goals?
   - Where do you want to be in five years?

2. **Problem identification.** Specific needs, problems and challenges.

   - How is X trend affecting you?
   - What is going well for your firm?
   - What's not going so well?
   - What challenges are you facing?
   - Is your growth rate causing any problems?
   - Is X causing you any problems?

3. **Problem effect.** How important are the problems identified in Step 2?

   - What effect does X problem have?

- Does X problem cause problems for your customers?

- Does X problem cause problems for your employees?

- Is your productivity affected by X problem?

- Could X lead to increased costs?

4. **Value of possible solutions.** Which problems have the highest payoff if they are solved?

   - Would it be useful if we could improve X?

   - How would it help you if we could change X?

   - What's the effect of having X problem?

   - What benefits would you see if X could be fixed?

   - Why is it important to solve X?

"They usually tell me about their product, their structure, whether they are centralized, decentralized, their philosophy, their sales volume, whatever," continues Basinger. If they don't give me all of that, then I will specifically ask them. I might also say, 'Tell me a little bit more about your company philosophy. Is there a published strategic direction, mission or values? Tell me more about those.' That gets me into their philosophy. If I want to know more about a specific area, I will just ask them to share more about it. I will ask about their goals. I will say, 'What do you think is going well for your firm? How is (blank) trend affecting you?' (I try to pick out a relevant trend). Here I am beginning to try to assess needs and identify problems. Other questions might be 'What challenges are you facing?' 'What's the work environment like?' 'How are people doing at completing projects on time and within budget?' 'If I asked an employee what makes accomplishing their job most challenging, what would they say?' 'Does top management expect to see return on investment from training?' 'What kind of return on investment do they expect to see?' "

Basinger continues to explain her funnel theory, "Next I start to funnel down to specifics of how many employees they have, what kinds of employees they are responsible for the development of, and what types of training they do. I might ask them, 'If we decided that there was a mesh between us, how might it work for you to implement this program in the company? What other kinds of training programs are being offered? Do you have a quality improvement program?'

"I have found," Basinger says, "that first you break down some barriers. If you want to build a partnership, you begin by finding out about the company. I once spent three hours with a sales training manager and almost two hours of that was the questioning process. Once I get important information, I tie it back into my presentation.

"Of course using the more specific questions is easier and quicker. One thing that is different about me is the amount of time I expect to spend in the initial sales call. I always expect it to be an hour to an hour and a half. Many salespeople assume that if they can get 15 to 20 minutes, they will be lucky. If you begin with that assumption, then you tend to start with very narrow questions. If you expect to have more time, then it is comfortable to explore the broader questions. If we run out of time, I schedule a time when I can come back and complete my understanding of their situation and their needs.

"Sometimes when I ask for the time to understand their needs better, they will ask what kinds of questions I'm interested in and I will give them an idea of what questions I'm going to ask. I have never ever had someone say no. In fact they seem thrilled to talk about their company. The person I spent three hours with asked me what questions I was going to ask and when I told him, he said, 'Fine.' It's always especially interesting when I'm talking with someone in sales training because they know what I'm doing. But in some regards, as a salesperson, I really appreciate it when I see someone doing their craft well. I'm more willing to give time to someone who is competent than someone who isn't."

In order to remember the information gathered through these long customer interviews, Basinger takes notes. "I take copious notes," she explains. "I take notes on Franklin Day Planner pages and put it right into my client files. If the client seems to be disturbed about the note-taking, I will say, 'You know it really is helpful to me to take a few notes on the points you are mentioning so I can make sure that I understand your situation. Do you have any problem with that?' Most people don't seem to care. Of course I'm taking notes on the day planner so they also see my product. As I am going through the sales call, I will go back and do clarifications using the notes that I have made. That gets them more involved with the process and lets them know that I am really listening.

"One call I made recently was to a sales manager. I had been warned that he would be noncommunicative, and initially he was. As I asked questions, he would say things like 'Doesn't every company have that issue?' I would say 'Some do and for some it's more of an issue than for others. I would like to have a better idea of where you fall on the continuum.' Finally, he shared with me what his issues were and then I went back through with a summary and said, 'So, if I could recommend a program to you that would take care of (blank), would that be what you're looking for in this program?' And he said, 'Yes,' and looked over at his associate and laughed. He said, 'You obviously have your questioning and listening skills down well.' He looked at his associate again and said, 'You know the session on questioning and listening skills we're developing? What you just saw done is what our salespeople need to do to be more effective.' "

The one best question

If you could only ask a prospect one question, what would it be? Clark Johnson, CEO, Pier 1 Imports, Inc., had a quick answer for *Success Magazine* (May 1991). Johnson, who started his career selling wholesale lumber in South Dakota, became CEO of Pier 1 in 1985. Since then he has doubled the number of stores and quadrupled sales. His choice for a number-one question is this one: "What can I do to become your most important supplier?" That one question buys you an awful lot of information about what the customer wants and what his or her hot buttons are.

Razzouk's 5-percent rule

Whom you listen to and ask questions of may be as important as what you listen to. This realization led Bill Razzouk of Federal Express to his 5-percent rule, which states: While department heads know 95 percent of what is important in their own departments, they know less than 5 percent of what is important in any other

department. You cannot hope to learn all you need to know about a company's business needs from only one contact. Each person in an organization tends to think they understand the organization, so we have to talk to many people in the organization to get an overall picture.

The importance of talking to people throughout an organization was emphasized repeatedly by star salespeople. Vince Espada with Konica states, "The biggest mistake salespeople make is that they just talk to the dealer/principal. I talk to everyone. I want to know what their problems are. I talk to the warehouseman, the service manager, everyone. Too often the dealer/principal loses touch with others within the dealership. I gather all the information and then I can sit down with the dealer/principal and we can talk about what inventory to carry and what will move and how to make the inventory move.

"The worst thing you can do to a dealer is put a product in his inventory that is not going to move. Sometimes we have a product that we are phasing out and we have a special on it. In order to take advantage of the special, a dealer has to order 50 units. If I look at a dealership and can't see that he can move 50 units within a three-month period, I don't even present the program to him. I don't want him to look at me and say 'I can't buy your new stuff because I still have your old stuff.'

"I am the middleman between the manufacturer and the dealer. I explain my philosophy to my management. I have people tell me that I am one of the first salespeople they've met that thinks about their business rather than just trying to move a product. I try to be a partner in his business because if I do that, I gain his trust. And, when I call, he takes my phone call and when I show up he sees me."

Question words

The words we use in questions direct how they will be answered. Here is a brief list of words that lead the customer into revealing more about their needs and problems:

Open probes	Closed probes
Who	Is/are
What	Could
Where	Do/does
When	Should
Share with me ...	Would
Why	Will
How	Can/may
Tell me ...	Which
	Either
	Has/have

Problem probes

What concerns do you have with/about...?

Does X present a difficulty?

What difficulties are you having with X process?

What dissatisfaction do you have with X?

What do you like about X?

Is X causing any inconvenience?

What inconveniences are caused by X?

What would you like to improve about X?

What worries you about X?

What impact does X have?

What is the effect of X?

What are the consequences of X trend?

What are the ramifications of X problem?

What are the repercussions of doing X?

What are the results of X?

Value probes

How would it help you if...?

How useful would it be to...?

What benefits do you see in overcoming this...?

How would it benefit you if...?

In what ways would it be useful to...?

What advantages would...?

What would it mean if...?

What would be the impact of...?

Example questions:

In what ways would it be useful to speed up distribution between offices?

What would it mean to your operation if you could eliminate overtime?

What impact would eliminating overtime have on your budget?

If you could continually and reliably meet all your deadlines, how would it benefit your department?

If there is a magic key to the kingdom of sales success, it is the simple question. Asking the right questions at the right time unlocks the door to the customer's inner needs, wants, desires and problems. Once that door is open, you can find ways to match your products and services to your customer's needs.

"My great strength as a consultant is to be ignorant and ask a few questions."
—*Peter Drucker, management guru*

```
┌─────────────────────────┐
│     Two Ideas:          │
└─────────────────────────┘
```

What two ideas did you get from this chapter?

_____

_____

I dare you to find a way to use one of these ideas to improve your ability to discover your customer's needs.

Action Plan

```
Research Sources
```

There are many sources of information that salespeople use to find out background information before calling on a prospect. They research the industry as well as the company. Here are just a few sources. Develop a list of five questions you would like to answer before calling on your next prospect and see which one of these reference sources will help you. Research those questions and see what impact that research has on your call.

Annual Reports/SEC Filings. Buy a share of stock so that you will be on the mailing list for all corporate financial information. Look for financial history, a statement of mission or goals—especially in the letter from the chairman—read all of the footnotes which often talk about potential problems, look for corporate structure, lists of officers (and often pictures) and directors of the board.

Hoover's Handbook 1991. Gives a one-page snapshot of the top 500 companies. Includes corporate background, key competitors, the financial position over the past two to three years, trends, significant acquisitions, mergers and so on.

Dun & Bradstreet, Value Line, U.S. Industrial Outlook. All three publications give excellent information on the industry as well as the company. Industry reports will give you what's hot, what the trends are, and who the major players are.

Trade Association Directory. This valuable guide gives you the information on the trade associations appropriate to your prospect. The association can provide you with valuable information about the industry and can also tell you what industry publications are appropriate. Good business school libraries will have most trade publications and back issues. A quick scan through the past 18 months of a trade publication can give you an idea of what's going on in the industry and what your competition is doing. The advertising is as informative as the articles. Look for blurbs about people changing jobs, new products, or programs and contract information.

Directories & Who's Who. Most research libraries will have volumes of different directories on companies, industries, and specific professions. Ellen Manzo, AT&T Computer Systems, uses a directory that lists chief information officers—it not only gives her company names, key executive names, addresses and telephone numbers, it tells her vital information about the installed base. Who's Who directories give a lot of information about the background of the prospect—family, college, interests and accomplishments.

Clipping services. For a relatively minor fee, clipping services (see your yellow pages under "Clipping Bureaus") can keep you up-to-date on new activity with the account. The service can make its search as broad or as narrow as you specify.

Chamber of Commerce directories. For a small fee, you can purchase a directory from the local chamber. It generally tells you the number of employees and gives a contact name.

Contacts Influential. A good source for getting information on smaller companies. It lists key officers, number of employees and SIC codes.

Local business journals. Almost every area will have a business journal that reports on the activities of that business market. Often, these journals have special industry reports where they list the largest players in the area and give vital information about contacts, business trends, and so on.

Customers, service personnel. Talk to people who have contact with your prospect. Sometimes the informal information you can pick up through these sources and through your network are more important than information contained in printed resources.

This list is just a start—contact your local reference librarian and he or she will help you find the right resource for your need.

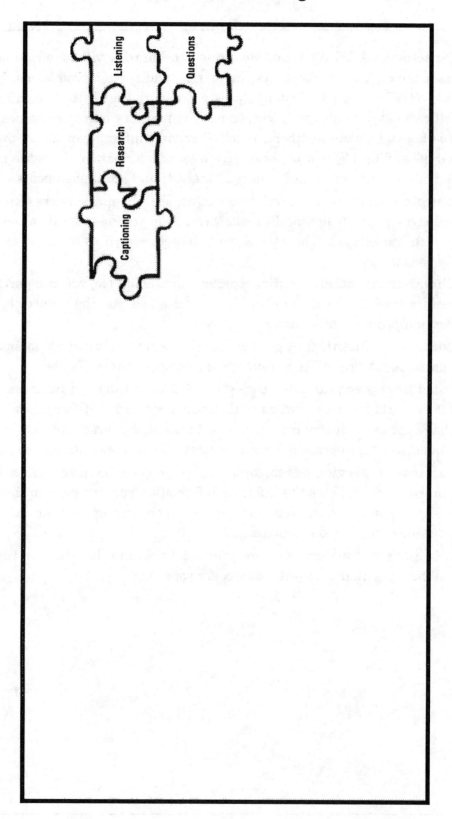

Chapter 7

Walk on the other side

"If our customers' priorities aren't our priorities, then we are operating without priorities."

—Roger Dow, vice president of sales, Marriott Hotels & Resorts

Coming attractions:

♦ Listening strategies

♦ "Customer run" meetings

♦ Do the customer's job

♦ Customer Bill of Rights

In 1982, the publishing industry received a shock. An unlikely business book became a best-selling phenomenon and rocketed its co-authors into guru status. *In Search of Excellence* hit such a nerve with business managers, employees, students, philosophers, politicians and others that its sales reached a level generally reserved for the likes of Stephen King or Jackie Collins. Almost a decade later, co-author Tom Peters, in an interview with *Personal Selling Power,* states that the one thing he is most proud of was that it had a chapter devoted to customers. While working on his second book, he discovered that out of the top 25 business school management texts, *In Search of Excellence* was the only one that had a chapter devoted to customers. The language of business was changed forever when Peters and Waterman urged companies to "get close to the customer."

Suddenly, the spotlight was on customers and how to get close to them. There was a vision of thousands of salespeople across the country nodding their heads, sighing and saying, "It's about time." Finally, management was waking up to what top salespeople had known forever—nothing happens until something is sold...to a customer.

Managers who had assumed that what they were doing was what the customer wanted, were told to test their assumptions. When they tried to do that, they realized how far they had drifted from the closest customer. There were layers of management, supervision and procedures between them and the customer. Closing that gap has created an upheaval in American business, eliminating layers of management, empowering front-line employees and liposuctioning off tons of bureaucratic procedures.

139

AT&T Consumer Products eliminated two full layers of middle management. Jan Carlzon at SAS identified 50 million "moments of truth"—customer contact points—that determined the customer's image of the company. Realizing that those moments of truth are controlled by front-line employees, not management, Carlzon gave the front-line employees the authority and the responsibility for making those contacts customer satisfaction points. Richard Hecht, zone manager with AT&T Consumer Products, states, "We threw away the 87 binders we had in the stores, which told you how to do things. Now we must try to operate on our 10 principles." Its number-one principle states, "Customers are always right, and always come first."

Larry Frank with Comdoc Office Systems says, "What distinguishes the true winners is the ability to analyze customer's needs, to walk in the other person's shoes and treat them the way they wish to be treated. Too often, salespeople say they lost a sale because of price. You only lose because of price if everything else is equal. If you have not distinguished yourself from the competition, if you have not distinguished your product, you aren't meeting the customer's true needs."

But how do companies, and salespeople, find out what it is that the customer wants? Across corporate America, there is a frenzy of customer research—phone surveys, questionnaires, buying-pattern monitoring and statistical analysis. But some companies are simply sitting down with their customers and asking them.

Listening strategies

Steven Hamerslag, president and CEO of Micro Technology Inc., an $85 million company that protects classified data, developed an adopt-a-customer strategy. Each engineer working on a project keeps in touch with two customers, continually bouncing ideas off them. The company also holds what it calls the Knights of the Roundtable sessions twice a year. The sessions are made up of a cross-section of customers who hear confidential presentations about what the company is working on, and make suggestions of their own. Hamerslag also spends about 35 percent of his time visiting customers, and he says, "Listening starts from the top."

When we think of companies being responsive to customer needs or being innovative, we often think of young, entrepreneurial, companies like Micro Technology. However, one of the major recent innovations in the insurance field came from a company that is more than 100 years old and has over 100,000 employees. The champion of this innovation is Ron Barbaro, 15th president of The Prudential Insurance Company of America.

Barbaro, who has been in the insurance industry 35 years, was doing volunteer work at a hospice. The terminally ill people he was working with told him they needed money to ease the financial stress of dying. They needed money for bills, money to make their final months more comfortable, money for a last trip, money to put their affairs in order so that they could die with dignity. Barbaro listened and it led to Prudential's Living Needs Benefit Program, which allows terminally ill policyholders to claim their life insurance proceeds while they are still alive. Howard Richman, director of field education for the Prudential states, "We provide this benefit for anyone who has a terminal illness, anyone permanently confined to a nursing home or anyone who needs a major organ transplant. The full amount of their benefit is available to them. This is a service that the company felt was necessary in today's environment. We added value to our offering and provided a solution for a worry held by many of our customers."

Kieran Quinn, vice president of marketing and sales support with Prudential, has been instrumental in rolling out the program to the existing and prospective policyholders. "We made this benefit available to over 3 million current policyholders at no additional premium. The Living Needs Benefit has been hailed as a revolutionary innovation that will help people live out their lives with dignity. As a result, we have received a lot of positive publicity—from *USA Today* to local newspapers and wire services."

Listening to the needs of its customers has paid big dividends for Prudential. In addition to the policyholder goodwill and positive publicity, it provided a rallying point for the Prudential sales force—an added indicator of the importance of insurance. Jim Temple, vice president of education and development for Prudential, understands how important it is for agents to sincerely believe in the product they are delivering. He brings a unique perspective to his sales training since he has personally tested almost every policy the company offers. "I had a severe auto accident and wound up spending eight months in the hospital and two years away from work. While I was in the hospital my house was robbed and burned, so I've tested every policy we offered...except one, of course. I saw the benefits of our products from the other side and wanted to help our agents understand how important our products are."

Another big company that listens well and tries to understand the customer side is Marriott. J. W. Marriott, Sr., started paying fanatical attention to customer satisfaction cards decades ago, so listening is an ingrained habit at Marriott. However, room guests are only one segment of Marriott's customers—meeting planners represent another very powerful block of clients. Marriott realized that it needed a mechanism for listening to their needs and wants, so it implemented its Customer Advisory Forums. Senior meeting planners and senior Marriott executives meet once a month at properties across the country to discuss what's good and what's bad about Marriott service. Mike Lupfer, director of national sales for Marriott, says, "We can only be successful if we listen to the customer. The Customer Advisory Forum gives us a chance to listen. We tell them not to hold back and we've gotten a lot of ideas out of the forums. We have a corporate executive chair for the forum, and notes from the meeting go straight to our executive committee."

Several major changes have come from the forums. Meeting planners wanted to be able to deal with just one salesperson rather than getting calls from properties all across the country. They also wanted help with all of their meetings—not just the big ones. Out of these concerns came a major restructuring of Marriott's national sales department. Lupfer explains, "Now we have more experienced people in our national sales department—people the meeting planner can deal with for little meetings as well as major events. Also, the tour for the national sales executive is now three to five years rather than the 18 months that it once was. This gives the national salesperson a chance to really get to know the meeting planners—even down to the in-room amenities that they like. They begin to know their customers well enough to give them the personalized touch. They book all of their business

and actually travel with them on site selection trips. Marriott is now known for having the best national sales office in the business."

A recent forum identified the meeting planner's need for fast service during a meeting. Out of this has come a hotline—the meeting planner dials a one-digit number and a phone rings in three places. Three people are immediately ready to solve any problem the planner has with the meeting.

Another program Marriott uses to stay close to the meeting planners is Partnerships in Excellence. This is a training program where the meeting planners spend two days getting to know Marriott's back-of-the house operations, including participating in the preparation of their own lunch! So, as the planners are wearing their chef hats and painting plates with chocolate sauce, they are also learning more about the capabilities and limitations of the hotel. Lupfer states, "We all know that one of the easiest ways to get closer to our customers is to make their job easier, and to make it easier for them to do business with us. Both of those goals can be met when we educate them. This program is a real home run and develops a great deal of loyalty among our customers."

Marriott conducts each of these national programs once a month and averages 10 attendees at each meeting. In addition, each hotel is charged with doing at least two programs a year with local meeting planners.

Lupfer calculates, "Twelve national programs with 20 people and 200 hotels doing even one of each program means having a tremendous impact on over 4,000 of our top customers!"

Marriott's ability to get in touch with what the customers want helps make life easier for the salespeople. Susan Morris, director of national accounts, states, "One of the nice things about Marriott is they really listen and they take action. One idea that came out of a Customer Forum was for a new arrangement of the invoice. Meeting planners develop their budgets in a certain format but when they got our invoice, it was very difficult for them to reconcile the bill to their budgets. So we worked with a lot of customers to come up with a format that would make it easy to track and reconcile. We now hear stories about people taking our invoices into other hotel chains and asking why they can't invoice in the same format.

"Another side benefit," adds Morris, "was that we wondered why it was taking so long for us to get paid. Now we know that it was because the invoice package was so large and hard to reconcile, that the meeting planner would put it aside until they had time to analyze it. Now it's so easy to review, that it makes it easier for them to process the bill for payment."

Listening to customers always pays off, but National Cash Register (NCR) shows us that listening in the extreme can pay off in the extreme. In 1980, James Adamson took over an old NCR plant in Scotland. His task was to turn around the 40-year-old plant and its demoralized workers. Adamson focused on the automatic teller machine (ATM) business where NCR was running a slow ninth in the market. Adamson knew the key was developing the kind of system customers wanted. He developed an intense customer listening strategy, traveling all over the world to talk to customers. He also brought a different customer to the plant *every working day of the year* to be interviewed by marketers, engineers and executives. The listening paid off. NCR is now number-one in the ATM market with an installed base that almost equals the total of the two nearest competitors.

"Customer-run" meetings

A formalized method of listening to customers that can be used by companies of any size is "customer-run" meetings. The following is an example of one such meeting, which was designed to help train salespeople:

Archie McGill was looking for a way to help his sales staff improve their sales skills and become more customer focused. McGill, CEO of Tara, a large computer retailer, had built his company by focusing on customer service and support. He wanted his sales training program to reinforce that customer orientation while at the same time build skills that would help his salespeople be more successful.

McGill and Don Demchik, marketing manager for Tara, decided to implement a series of "customer-run" meetings. They determined the objectives for their initial meeting and decided to invite two customers from one of their major accounts. "We invited Sue Maskin and Sharon Quinlan from Chicopee," Demchik explained, "because they are a large account using a wide range of our services and because we have an outstanding relationship with them. We wanted our salespeople to see what it takes to develop large accounts...from identification to closing and servicing the account."

Both customers invited to the meeting were experienced buyers interested in participating and sharing their ideas and suggestions for improving vendor service. Sometimes companies are reluctant to ask a customer to spend time in this type of meeting. However, most customers have been very willing to share their information and experience once the purpose of the meeting is explained. The meeting can't be a disguised sales presentation or the customer will be turned off.

"Customer-run" meetings are a powerful technique for finding out how customers feel about your service and support. Most meetings generate new information that can turn into action plans for improvements. Customers are doubly impressed by the meetings when they see something they said turn into an action. Hearing what customers like and dislike about the sales process has more impact on salespeople than hearing similar or identical comments from sales trainers or managers. "The sales reps," Demchik says "got a lot of information from our meeting. We've all been through various types of sales training—the nice thing about this type of meeting is that, rather than hearing from a sales trainer, you get it straight from the customer. You hear exactly what they expect and what a salesperson should do and should not do."

The customers at Tara's meeting were two people who perform the same function for two different parts of Chicopee. Their views and expectations of the sales process, however, were very different. "What that taught everybody here," Demchik explains, "is that everyone is an individual and you have to treat them as such. There are no global rules in selling and managing an account. You have to be in-tune with the individual. If only one customer had been at the meeting, we would have gotten a slanted view. We are going to continue with this program once a month so we gather more and more perspectives and ideas."

The relaxed, open, round-table atmosphere of the customer-run meetings generates information that might not come out in the standard sales process. Demchik found out that his customers sometimes felt at a loss when they called and he wasn't in. To remedy this situation, he assigned a backup salesperson to the account and took him out to meet the customers and to see the site. The backup salesperson has all the necessary information to service the account in Demchik's absence. "They (the customers) had never mentioned that concern to me in all the time I had spent with them. It took this meeting to bring it out," Demchik comments.

While the meetings allow the sales reps to ask questions about the sales process, they also allow them to see a successful sales relationship with a major account. They can see how much the buyers depend on the service and support offered by the salesperson and how critical the other company functions are as part of that support.

Most companies provide some token of appreciation to the customers who participate in these meetings. This often includes lunch, a certificate of recognition or company-logo items such as T-shirts, mugs or pens. Frequently, companies end the meeting with a tour of the facilities, which can include brief descriptions of new products.

Most companies that implement customer-run meetings report positive benefits beyond the information generated at the meeting. Although the purpose of the meeting cannot be sales, often customers open up new possibilities for sales or actively refer the vendor to others. When the customers described their experience with Tara to their manager, he was so impressed that he certified Tara as an approved vendor. Both Tara and Chicopee felt they had developed a stronger relationship as a result of the meeting. Demchik says, "As a result of this meeting, another division of the parent company contacted me to discuss the possibilities of doing business with them. On my first visit to this division, I received a purchase order for four new computer systems."

Guidelines for customer-run meetings

Here are guidelines for maximizing benefits from your customer-run meetings.

1. Develop objectives.
2. Select the right customers.
3. Develop good questions.
4. Establish a warm, open environment.
5. Follow up with a staff debriefing.
6. Develop an action plan.

Develop objectives

Successful customer-run meetings depend upon careful planning. It is not enough to just stick some customers and salespeople in a room and hope for the best. You generally invite some of your best customers to participate in these meetings and you want the meeting to enhance your relationship as well as give your staff valuable information. The customer should feel that this is a very important meeting and that you take the information and advice seriously.

You should have a clear idea of what information you would like to gain from the meeting. Organizations that have been successful with their customer-run meetings held a pre-meeting where they discussed possible objectives with all of the staff members who would be attending the meeting. Each person should be encouraged to suggest and discuss objectives. Once a salesperson starts to think about information that might be obtained from the meeting, he or she will be more likely to buy-in to the process. Often, salespeople will be hesitant about having a customer meeting because they talk to customers all the time and they think they know what the customers will say. However, the customer-run meeting offers a safe environment for salespeople and customers to talk about the process of selling. Unique information and perspectives often result.

Select the right customers

Once you have the objectives in focus, you can select two or three customers for the meeting. If you select customers from the same account, you will get an in-depth view of how you are perceived by that account. If you select customers from different accounts, you will get a broader view of your service and products. You may want to experiment with both types to see which is more effective for you.

Customers should be selected on the basis of their experience with the sales process and their understanding of the area you would like more information on. If you wanted to be more successful with large, institutional buyers, you would want to invite buyers from large, institutional organizations. The people invited to these meetings do not have to be current customers. Camadon, an office equipment dealer, invited a buyer from a large company that was not a customer. The sales trainer had known the buyer when she was with another office products company and the buyer was assured that he was not attending a sales presentation in disguise. As it turned out, the buyer was so impressed with the meeting and the company's dedication to become more customer focused, that he invited them to bid on a new series of equipment.

You should invite your customer in person and then follow up with a letter confirming the time and place and outlining the objectives of the meeting. This will give the participants a chance to think about the material prior to the meeting.

Develop good questions

The benefits you receive from your customer meeting depend largely on how well you develop and structure your questions. After you develop your objectives, you can then tailor a set of questions that will lead to meeting those objectives. You should have a clear idea of what you really want to learn from this customer.

Developing good questions for your meeting is similar to the process of probing with your customers. You want to establish rapport, display empathy and ask questions that will cause the customer to open up. Most customers will not want to give you negative comments because they are flattered at being invited to your meeting. You need to put the customer at ease and encourage them to be frank. Questions should move from easy, safe queries such as "What's important to you in service (or training or the sales process)?" or "What does a sales rep do to make a good first impression on you?" to harder probes requiring more candor such as "How would you rate our service on a scale of 1 to 5?" and "What could we do to make our service better?" Questions can be framed as scenarios to give the customer and the client a safe distance from the answers.

Areas for questioning include how to approach the customer, how to find out more about the customer's business, how to deal with objections, how to deal with budget restrictions, how to develop a winning proposal, how to find out who the decision-makers are and what services the customer expects.

Develop a warm, open environment

Most meetings take place in the conference room of the company hosting the meeting. This is the ideal location as it allows the customer to see your facility and makes an after-meeting tour logical. Particular attention should be paid to the appearance of the room. Is it neat and clean? Do the pictures, graphs, etc., on the walls visually tell the story you would like told? Are the chairs comfortable? Does the seating arrangement allow you to talk easily and informally?

Notepads and pencils or pens encourage active listening and note-taking. An easel pad or white board makes it easy to highlight suggestions. Coffee, tea or soft drinks should be available.

Follow up with a staff debriefing

You can maximize the benefits of your customer-run meeting by holding a staff debriefing soon after the customer meeting. At this debriefing, each person has a chance to recap what was said and what they learned. Information gained from the customer should be summarized on an easel pad. Ideas for improving the sales process or customer service can be brainstormed and recorded.

Develop an action plan

After ideas for improvement have been brainstormed, an action plan should be developed. This would be a program for implementing the ideas suggested by the customer and the ideas developed in the brainstorming session. Part of the action plan should be planning for future customer meetings. Each meeting represents the voices of just a few customers—sometimes just one. To continue to grow and understand the needs of your entire customer base, customer meetings should be scheduled at least once a quarter.

Each meeting should be recapped by a one-page report that would include the following:

Objectives. List the objectives that were selected by the group in the pre-meeting.

Customer. Identify the customer and the criteria used to select the customer representative. Why was it important to hear from this particular customer?

Summary of customer comments. This should be the five or six points made by the customer that are the most important.

Customer reaction to meeting. How the customer felt about being invited and about the meeting process.

Staff reaction to meeting. Comments by staff including benefits and ways to improve future meetings.

Action plan. Specific ideas that were developed from the meeting.

If customer-run meetings are implemented on a regular basis, these reports can become a sales tool. When a salesperson is talking to a prospective new client, he or she can talk about the meetings as part of the normal process your company uses to stay in touch with its customers. He or she can include the one-page meeting reports as part of the referral portfolio and show the prospective client how previous meetings have been used to help develop a better service program.

Typical questions

Here are some questions and scenarios that have worked well in previous customer-run meetings:

♦ What are some of the characteristics you look for in an effective sales representative?

♦ What characteristics or actions of a sales rep turn you off?

♦ What does a sales rep do to make a good first impression on you?

♦ What is the best way for a new salesperson to approach you?

♦ What should a sales rep ask you if he or she wants to know more about your business and your needs?

♦ What have sales reps (from any company) done that really impressed you or made a difference in the sales process?

♦ What could a sales rep do to demonstrate his or her company's outstanding service philosophy?

- What would you like to see in the way of references or demonstration sites?

- If you had to rate our company on responsiveness with 1 being poor and 5 being excellent, how would you rate us? (Discuss reasons for any rating below 5.)

- What could we do to make life easier for you?

- When does a salesperson cross the line from being persistent to being obnoxious?

- If a salesperson thinks he or she has a solution that fits your needs but isn't sure whether you have the budget for it, how should he or she find out?

- If a salesperson called you out of the blue and seemed like a valid person and was representing an important product, but you already had a vendor for this product, what would you do?

- If you were running our company, what would you do differently?

What does the customer want?

Customers have a few basic needs that are often ignored by salespeople. They include:

- to never feel like they have been "sold"

- the benefit of the salesperson's expertise

- to feel good about the purchase

Top sales stars have found ways to meet those basic needs. They seem to understand the needs and problems of the customer better than the customer does. Top salespeople have discovered that while a customer may want to buy your product or service, he or she never wants to be sold.

Rick Dyer is the director of sales operations for Apple Computer's southern region. He has also received the Golden Apple, the top sales award for Apple. In less than three years he took the last place (out of six areas) and lead it to the number-two spot. Dyer laughs, "We were second by only about one-half percent and I say I was out-shipped, not outsold, because our area had a bigger backlog.

"My view," Dyer states, "is that, particularly on large system installations, what the customer is really doing is establishing a relationship with us, not just buying equipment. What we try to do is develop a partnership kind of relationship that will be ongoing over the years and not just a one-shot exercise."

Dyer knows how critical it is for his customers to know that he understands their business and their needs. He establishes himself as a consultant to his customers and his job is to help them make their business better. "My attitude and approach has always been to be a consultant. That involves a whole variety of things. First and foremost is an understanding and in-depth knowledge of what the customers are trying to do with the equipment. I want to know everything that is going on in their business. Who are the involved parties—the influencers, the decision-makers, the financial people? What are the political ramifications of going with Apple as opposed to another manufacturer? What we try to develop is a partnership that will be ongoing over several years.

"The key to success in sales," he continues, "is to make the customer feel good about the purchase, about his decision. One of the easiest ways to do that is to ask him what he wants. You would be amazed at how many people don't do that. They think they are there to sell something. My view is that the customer is going to help me sell him by telling me what he wants. All you have to do is ask him, 'What do you want this to do for you? What is it that you expect from your vendor? What do you expect from the equipment you are purchasing?' Then I just try to match that up.

"The relationship is a summation of hundreds of individual transactions from phone conversations to installations of equipment. There aren't any secrets other than doing the job as well as you possibly can and involving the customer in the solution and being straightforward with what we can do and what the ramifications of the decision will be and what impact that will have. Most of sales success is common sense and maintaining a high degree of empathy for the customer. A

salesperson needs to be able to put himself in his customer's shoes."

Learn the customer's job

Richard Waller, vice president and director of manpower development for TeleRep, wants his salespeople to be able to do more than walk in the customer's shoes. He wants them to be able to do the customer's job and he spends six months training them to do so. TeleRep represents television stations and sells time to media buyers at advertising agencies. It is the largest rep firm in the industry with sales of more than a billion dollars. Waller explains his training program, "We teach our salespeople to do the things that we know a customer will normally do. The people that we call on at advertising agencies are time buyers. We want our salespeople to understand what the buyer has to do to do a great job; what the buyers have to do to look good to their bosses; what they have to do to be successful. By being a buyer and understanding the buyer's perspective, we can do a better job for the time buyer and for our stations. The key to good sales performance is to anticipate what the buyer's needs are. By understanding their viewpoint, we can anticipate what their needs might be. So we have our salespeople study each television market and actually make a buy. They consider our station, everything the competition would offer and everything else that a buyer would take into consideration.

"After they have learned how to go through all the research and know all the basic aspects of each television station including price and performance history of each program, we have them sit down and evaluate various television programs and stations and determine what they would select if they were buyers. Then we go through an extensive discussion of that decision. This is normally done in a group situation of four to six people where each person is working on the same market situation. They discuss their reasons for making their selection. In one instance someone might ignore a trend but someone else might use the trend. Someone might balance off one aspect of the demographics with a higher price.

"These are the types of things that buyers do all the time. By getting into a discussion of how a buyer might approach a situation such as this, the sales reps begin to determine what makes up a good buy and what the buyer's decision points might be. Consequently, they develop the ability to deal with each buyer by emphasizing the points that are most important to the buyer. While we know what buyers are going to do on a general basis, we don't know what they are going to do on an individual basis. This training prepares our salespeople to deal with any contingencies."

New salespeople with TeleRep spend three months in the classroom, often running from 7 a.m. to 7 p.m. and some weekends. "In a way, it's something like boot camp," says Waller. "The remaining three months, they work with experienced salespeople on a half-day basis and then come back into class and talk about what happened. It's a long process, but when they hit the street, they're running. We have over a 90-percent success rate with our training program." Because of the expense of this lengthy training program, TeleRep is extremely careful in its sales rep selection process and each new person goes through at least seven interviews.

Chuck Naylor, senior account executive with AT&T Computer Systems, focuses on only one account, Pizza Hut. But, he understands how important it is to be in tune with people from all levels of that organization. Naylor explains how he manages his efforts on one large account, "I realized that the key to success was what I call the multiple effect—working with those customers that had large numbers of locations. Pizza Hut stood out because it had more than 5,000 distribution points. I started working hard with them to identify where their big projects would be.

"I identified a key, strategic project where they wanted to build a competitive advantage in the home delivery of pizza. Most of my competition was focusing on Pizza Hut's traditional restaurant business where the opportunity was apparent and just laying there. No one was paying much attention to other strategic directions. I limited my activities to this strategic process rather than the obvious opportunities. I focused on the champion of this project and helped him with whatever he needed to get it up on the AT&T equipment. I spent all of my time on this project and became more of a strategic partner."

In order to develop the role as a strategic partner, Naylor's group offered to conduct an information study. "We met with the key managers in several areas that had to do with this upcoming project to find out where they were, where they wanted to be in the future, how they planned on getting there, and what obstacles they foresaw. This was a five-month process and preparing the study report itself took two weeks. We had a select team of people who worked on this project.

"We never mentioned technology during this phase—we were focused strictly on Pizza Hut's business objectives. We had about four interviews a day and our team would meet and provide feedback on how well we were listening. We suggested the study but, in order to be fair, Pizza Hut allowed the same access to two other vendors but one declined to participate.

"For our presentation of the report, we wanted to demonstrate that we understood the business, and that we had a recommendation for Pizza Hut. We put the recommendation into a mock-up of a live Pizza Hut environment. When we presented our findings, we put on a production (not a lot of money but a lot of time) recreating a Pizza Hut environment. Our main competition was IBM—it did the information study also and then whisked the customer's senior management off to Boca Raton for two days of golf and presentations.

"I made the decision (since I did not have that kind of budget or manpower) to do something totally different and to do it in Wichita near Pizza Hut headquarters so it would be very convenient for its representatives to attend. They could walk across the street to the Marriott where we were holding the presentation. That morning, we held an open house so we could show everyone what we were going to be presenting to the executives in the afternoon. We rented round tables and got a bunch of Pizza Hut decorations and stuff and recreated a Pizza Hut environment—it was like we were in the front of a restaurant. We had a professional photographer go out and take snapshots of all the different Pizza Hut environments. We had about 75 Pizza Hut pictures all over the room. When we demonstrated our solutions and the specific applications, it felt like they were already installed in the restaurants. The pictures helped the customers visualize how the solutions would work in their environments.

"The general feedback was that we really understood their business. I spent 18 months on the project but we wound up with a $16 million deal over three years, which was an increase from about $500,000 per year." Not a bad return for being able to put yourself in the customer's shoes.

Customer-defined quality

Richard McGinn started out as an account executive and is now the president of AT&T Computer Systems. He spends about 30 percent of his time on customer contacts and customer-related issues. "There are a number of reasons," he explains, "why it is imperative to spend time with the customers. First they are the people who know best what they need. The absence of their input puts you in a position where you have to make assumptions. You have to listen to what they have to say about their business. It is also the best way to find out about the competition. The customers can also tell you about your business because of the way they experience you through your logistics efforts, your operations, your selling efforts and your service and support activities. All of that adds up to a quality definition as seen by the customers, which is more accurate than any internal measurements.

"The successful people I have seen in selling," McGinn continues, "have a logical diagnostic thought process. They try to understand the root cause of the problem before they apply a solution. Without that you have a solution that is not responsive to the customer's needs. The environment is constantly changing—the marketplace, the competition, the internal staffing and opinions. It doesn't require brilliance as much as it does insight into people and the willingness to test your presumptions. It is essential for salespeople to be at a high level of mental readiness. Every single word the customer says has value. You can only have success if you can determine what the customer is thinking about."

Louis Slawetsky, president of Industry Analysts, Inc., consultants to the office equipment industry, was once brought up short when he didn't understand what his customer's concerns were. While Slawetsky was a sales rep at Xerox, the company wanted to replace an old series of machines with a new series that was twice as fast. In order to get the old machines out of the field, Xerox was pricing the new machine the same as the old, and offering a significant commission for the salesperson. "It was a no-brainer for the customers," Slawetsky states. "All they had to do was authorize the delivery, and a machine with twice the speed at exactly the same price showed up." One of his accounts was a maximum security state prison. He went to the prison and explained the exchange program to the person in charge of the copier equipment, confidently expecting another easy commission. He was shocked when he was told, "I don't want it." Thinking the customer didn't understand, he tried to explain it thoroughly but the answer was still, "no." Finally he asked the customer,

"Why?" and got this answer: "We've got people here who are doing a minimum of 20 years. Making copies is part of the work they do while they're here. What am I going to do with them if I save half their time?"

"This is my most memorable non-sale," states Slawetsky. "It taught me a valuable lesson. This particular customer had no interest in productivity—if he could have slowed the machine down, he would have. It taught me to really understand what my prospect needs."

The customer's personal adviser

The American Council of Life Insurance recently conducted a study to discover what insurance policyholders needed and wanted. Recognizing that the "baby bust" was going to have a drastic influence on the industry, the ACLI wanted to help insurance companies prepare for it. The prime age bracket for buying life insurance is 25 to 35, and in the next 10 years, as the baby boomers age, that group will lose 7 million people, a drop of 16 percent. At the same time, the spending power of that group will drop by $38 million.

The results of this research was specific to the life insurance industry, but can easily be applied to other industries. A remarkable revelation was how many policyholders had no regular agent. Only 29 percent of the people had a personal insurance agent. That group was the most positive about insurance.

The ACLI study identified several "hot spots" with policyholders. While the ACLI study relates only to insurance, we believe their findings can be applied to all sales situations. Here are the "hot spots" they identified:

Identify needs. Policyholders want an agent to listen to their situation and honestly assess their needs. They want the agent to be an adviser, an expert. They want the policy to match their needs, not maximize the agent's commission.

Clear explanation. Policyholders want the agent to explain to them the benefits of the policy in a way that makes sense to them. They want straightforward answers, good and bad, about what the policy means to them.

Post-sale contact. Policyholders want to hear from the agent after the sale. They need reassurance to relieve their apprehension. Many complain that they have never seen their agent since the sale—the only contact they have is when they pay their bills.

Information. Policyholders want more information about other insurance products; they want an annual review of their needs.

Throughout the study, the common theme was service—more contact, more information, more advice, more of a relationship. The conclusion of the ACLI study was that the service relationship is and will continue to be the major factor in attracting and keeping customers. As the demographics change, it will be critical to generate sales from current customers. Establishing a service relationship provides trust and respect that makes the customer willing to consider additional products and services.

The customer's Bill of Rights

Here are eight customer rights culled from our interviews with sales stars:

♦ The customer has the right to be told the truth.

♦ The customer has the right to expect the salesperson to have expert knowledge.

♦ The customer has the right to expect that all promises and commitments will be kept.

♦ The customer has the right to be treated with dignity and respect.

♦ The customer has the right to expect satisfaction from the product or service.

♦ The customer has the right to a breakdown of costs and fees.

♦ The customer has the right to service and support.

♦ The customer has the right to have calls returned promptly even when he or she may be calling with a problem or to complain.

While Section I of this book focused on the salesperson and the qualities needed for success, this section has focused on customers: how to build relationships, how to find out their needs and objectives, how to develop listening strategies and how to walk in their shoes. The next section explores the environment surrounding the salesperson and the customer: the product or service, the company and the industry. This environment is the playing field where the customer and the salesperson meet.

"As a rule . . . he (or she) who has the most information will have the greatest success in life."
—*Benjamin Disraeli, prime minister of England in the 1800's.*

```
┌ ─ ─ ─ ─ ─ ─ ─ ─ ─ ─ ─ ─ ─ ┐
        Two Ideas:
└ ─ ─ ─ ─ ─ ─ ─ ─ ─ ─ ─ ─ ─ ┘
```

What two ideas did you get from this chapter?

_____

_____

I dare you to find a way to use one of these ideas to get closer to your customers.

Action Plan

> Listening Strategy

What is your customer listening strategy? What formal processes do you have to listen to what your customer likes about your product, your service, your sales process? Here are some questions to help you develop your process:

- What information would I like to know from my customers?
- How many customers would I have to talk to in order to get a good cross-section of opinions?
- Are there different segments of my customers that I need to have different strategies for?
- How often do I need to listen?
- How could I enlist the assistance of my customers to help make our products and services better?
- Why would my customers want to participate in this process? How could I help them want to participate? What could I give back to them, such as information, insight into our operation, tokens of appreciation?

Customer-run meeting planner

Here is a logistics check list for planning your customer-run meetings:

PRE-MEETING

Decide on meeting objectives _____
Customer selection _____
Decide on staff attendees _____
Develop questions _____
Develop agenda _____
Select time and place _____
Issue invitation to customer (oral and written) _____
Other _____
_____
_____

MEETING

Introduction of attendees _____
Statement of meeting objectives _____
Introductory statement by customer _____
Questions _____
Closing remarks _____
Appreciation of customer _____
    Certificate _____
    Gift _____
Tour, lunch or final activity _____
Other _____
_____
_____

POST-MEETING

Debriefing meeting _____
    What was said? _____
    What are areas for improvement?_____
Action plan _____
"Thank you" letter to customer _____
Meeting report (one page) _____
Other _____
_____
_____

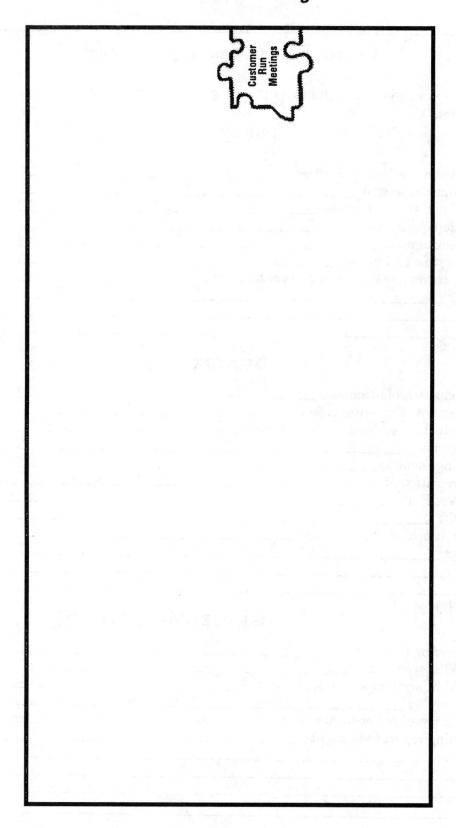

Customer Run Meetings

Section III

Product environment strategies

"There's no such thing as failure if you are always learning."
—*Jeff Herman, literary agent*

Selling is often compared to a game. We talk about winning, coaching, doing end-runs, making a play and lots of other sports terminology. The comparison works fairly well on the individual level. Salespeople have to have a winning attitude and perfect their craft, just as the finest athlete does. But as an overall metaphor, sport is too adversarial, too competitive, too prone to a win-lose situation. The sales stars operate on a different metaphor, and the one that fits most closely harkens back to an earlier age...barter.

In the barter economy, a farmer who needed a new plow might trade a cow to another farmer who had two plows but needed milk for his children. Both parties got what they wanted and needed. The only trick was to find someone who had two plows and needed milk. A farmer might have to talk to several neighbors before he found one who had a plow he didn't want, as well as a need for milk. That farmer making his cow-for-plow trade was the ancestor of today's salesperson.

While today's sales process seems a lot more complicated than that early barter, all of the elements were there. Both traders needed the benefits of the products being offered. They could see and touch the goods. One trader could talk about the fine steel of the plow and the other could talk about milk-producing capabilities of the cow, and both had a high level of confidence in their understanding of what they were getting and giving. They also trusted each other. Living close by, they knew that if the cow got sick or the plow broke, they could get satisfaction from their neighbor.

The focus of Section I was the farmer with the cow (the salesperson); the focus of Section II was the farmer with the plow (the customer) and the relationship between the two neighbors; and the focus of Section III is the

159

cow and the plow and the promises behind them. Even with our neighbor barterers, knowing the capabilities of the plow and how much milk the cow would give probably had some impact on the outcome of the trade. Promising to make good if the cow died or the plow broke or offering to throw in the milk pail and some extra feed would have facilitated the deal.

While the cow and the plow were the focal point of the deal, the trade actually rested as much on the unseen factors of trust, promises and beliefs as on the physical characteristics of the cow and the plow.

Today, it takes a lot more effort and study to understand the cow and the plow. Breakthrough companies perfect their promises of satisfaction and extras (service and performance guarantees). Star salespeople devote their careers to becoming experts on their version of the cow (the product or service). Both the star companies and star salespeople commit themselves to continuously learning about their product and service, their industry and how to provide the extraordinary, uncommon service that sets them apart from the competition.

The product as mission

Don Wallace, senior editor of *Success* magazine (and author of the novel *Hot Water*) has observed sales stars for years. He says, "The one quality I've noticed in people who are absolute aces in selling is their calmness, a certain unflappability, which I believe stems from being able to get behind their product without reservation. They know in their hearts that it's a good deal for the prospect, and this helps them to project a quality of sincerity that can't be faked. Of course, to have that kind of belief means that they work to make it so—they're obsessed to the point of making the product their mission."

When a salesperson catches the vision of his product or service, when he or she believes that selling the product is a mission, then that salesperson breaks through normal levels of achievement into the ranks of the sales stars. This section gives you more strategies for translating your product/service benefits into customer solutions and for building loyal customer relationships through extraordinary service. Developing the philosophies, strategies and skills discussed in this chapter will help you develop your mission and catapult you to a new success level.

"Men give me some credit for genius. All the genius I have lies in this: When I have a subject in hand, I study it profoundly. Day and night it is before me. I explore it in all its bearings. My mind becomes pervaded with it. Then the effort which I make, people are

pleased to call the fruit of genius. It is the fruit of labor and thought."
    —Alexander Hamilton, first U.S. Secretary of the Treasury

Chapter 8: The #1 sales strategy for the '90s: customer service

Companies that focus on customer service build an environment that makes it easy for salespeople to sell. Studies show that providing an exceptional level of customer service and quality is the only strategy that guarantees success. But this simple-sounding strategy is not so easy to implement.

Sales stars provide their customers with an extraordinary level of service and support. They are their customer's advocate and partner. In this chapter, you will learn how to get your customers involved in your sales process.

Learn how to develop a service strategy that sets you apart from your competition.

Chapter 8's Action Plan will help you make it easier for customers to buy from you and harder for them to leave.

Chapter 9: Inside-out product knowledge strategies

Customers expect expert knowledge and sales stars deliver it. They go to extremes to learn their product or service inside-out. Learn how the best in the business of sales find unique ways to get inside their product and service.

The Action Plan will help you develop a tool that will help you maintain your expertise on your product and service.

Chapter 8

The #1 sales strategy for the '90s: customer service

"In all industries, when competitors are roughly matched, those that stress customer service will win."
—*William H. Davidow and Bro Uttal in Total Customer Service, The Ultimate Weapon*

Coming attractions:

♦ The paradox principles of customer service

♦ Six foundation blocks for a winning strategy

♦ Customer surveys

In the Dark Ages, there was a back room filled with phones and overworked, underpaid women with big policy manuals. On the door was a sign: Customer Service Department. The salespeople never ventured into this room but often grumbled about the sales they lost because customer service had fouled up the order. Returned product was subject to policy #7-A4, and cash refunds simply were not allowed.

By the Middle Ages, the salespeople had found the back room and went there occasionally to yell about the incompetence. Policy manuals were bigger but all the people were new—the old people burned out and management hired younger women and taught them how to smile as they told the customer about policy #7-A4.

The awakening

Then came the Awakening. One morning Stew Leonard, of the legendary Stew Leonard's Dairy Store, woke up and said, "Every time I'm not nice to a customer, $50,000 walks out the door." L.L.Bean said, "A happy customer comes back. From now on all of our products are guaranteed to give 100-percent satisfaction in every way." Nordstrom decided to "coddle their customers, big and small." J. Willard Marriott, Sr. started asking customers what they thought about Marriott service and spent almost 60 years reading every single response card. And a small pizza company with an odd name decided that if they could guarantee a hot pizza delivered in 30 minutes or less, people might be interested. They were.

These are just a few of the companies who have awakened to the customer service strategy. And, what they realized was that customer service wasn't a secondary function just to keep people placated. It was the backbone of success. People Express discovered this when its growth rate outpaced its ability to provide service. The "no frills" airline zoomed to "no frills, no service" and then plunged to "no frills, no service, no customers, no airline." People Express pursued a strategy of low price—and it worked until service levels dropped below the tolerance level. People were willing to give up free food, but weren't willing to give up having their plane show up on time, or at all.

Warren Blanding, chairman and CEO of the Customer Service Institute, states that studies show that every unhappy customer tells 11 people about his or her experience. When all of the unhappy People Express (by then, often called People Distress) customers told their 11 people, dissatisfaction grew until it flattened the airline.

Common strategic thinking says that if you can't compete on price, you need to be either technology-driven or marketing-driven. Technology-driven companies depend on innovation, new products, new features; being the first on the market with the newest development. Marketing-driven companies have generic products and depend on advertising, name recognition, market share and sales expertise.

However, in our brave new world, virtually all products are generic. Copiers copy, cars run and look pretty much the same and our word-processing software has at least 100 features we've never used. So the technology strategy often results in massive outlays for R&D to develop a new feature that joins the other unused bells and whistles.

And advertising noise is so high that it is becoming increasingly difficult, and prohibitively expensive, to tell the customer about the product. Anyway, how many new ways are there to tell people the benefits of a home computer or the latest, improved version of dish soap?

Price, technology and marketing are key ingredients to corporate success, but the signs are that they are no longer the best sales strategies. Increasingly, the best strategy appears to be customer service. One of the reasons corporate America has been so slow to adopt this strategy is that it is the hardest to implement and maintain. It's thrilling to turn a room full of engineers loose to come up with a revolutionary product like the Macintosh or the Ford Taurus; it's exciting and glamorous to see your award-winning ad splashed across the television screen, but it is dull, mundane and often boring to try to keep every single customer happy every single day.

Another reason we have resisted this strategy so strongly is the way we look at our profit and loss statements.

Technology is part of the cost of the product and we want the best product possible; it's a given. Marketing, advertising and sales are also automatic. We know we have to have a product and we know we have to sell it, and then comes the other stuff like accounting, legal and support. Until recently, we didn't think about customer service as part of the formula. It came later and we thought of it as a reduction of the bottom line. It was an added cost that needed to be minimized to keep profit margins up.

Lynn Robbins, vice president of customer service for Franklin International Institute, looks at customer service differently. "Customer service is our very best form of advertising. A GE study analyzed and tracked dollars spent on advertising, and dollars spent in the customer service department. Often they couldn't recoup the advertising dollar but the customer service investment generated much toward the bottom line." Franklin is a rapidly growing company that produces time management seminars for about 20,000 participants per month and a mail-order catalog that goes out to more than a million customers. Robbins maintains that companies that have adopted the principle of 100-percent satisfaction have had incredible growth rates. "It is the competitive advantage of the '90s."

In order to make this strategy successful, it is important to understand that good customer service is transparent. If you receive an L.L.Bean catalog and order a ski jacket that you like and a week later you get the jacket and it's just what you thought it would be, that's good customer service. But, do you call and say thank-you? No, because it gave you what you expected—the good customer service was transparent.

Because it is transparent, we are not talking about good customer service being the competitive advantage of the '90s. To be a competitive advantage, you have to do more than satisfy the customer—you have to delight the customer. You have to surprise him or her with your exceptional service. Back to your ski jacket—you go skiing several times during the winter and as the ski season is ending, you notice the cuffs are a little frayed and you don't think they should be. You call L.L.Bean and tell a representative about the jacket, feeling nervous since you've had it so long. The representative immediately tells you to send it back and you'll receive your money back or a replacement. You are relieved, thrilled and delighted. You also have no hesitation about ordering from L.L.Bean in the future because you know that it will take care of you. That is a strategy of competitive advantage.

Three paradox principles

A major obstacle to the implementation of the customer service strategy is that it is built on what Robbins calls paradox principles. These principles look like they would destroy the organization but they actually save it. Here is a basic overview of three of the principles:

1. Ignore the bottom line

As part of Franklin's new-employee orientation, Robbins tells employees that the customer is always right—even when he is wrong, he is always right. Stew Leonard realized this when he questioned a customer's judgment that a quart of eggnog was sour. Even though he gave her a new quart of eggnog, she left saying she would never shop there again because he had questioned her judgment. Leonard realized that he had lost potentially $50,000 in that one customer ($100 per week times 50 weeks times 10 years). He immediately wrote his customer service rules on a granite stone that sits outside his store: "1. The customer is always right."

2. If the customer is ever wrong, read rule #1

Operating on this principle makes companies do what seems like crazy things. Nordstrom gives refunds "no questions asked" to the point that it sometimes offers refunds on things that were not purchased at Nordstrom. Why? Because the customer thought they were purchased there. Franklin gives a new day planner system to people who have had theirs stolen or who have left them on the top of their cars and had them smashed in freeway traffic. Why? Because the day planner becomes a person's brain and that individual is heartsick when it's lost. Franklin considers it a golden opportunity to show the customer that its employees care.

Do customers ever take advantage of companies with this strategy? According to Trine Lyman, director of customer service for Franklin, "Not often. We believe in letting the customer define his needs," Lyman explains. "Once we receive a call, we ask 'How can I help you?' The customer tells us what she wants and we say, 'I can do that.' The customer determines what I need to do to satisfy her." Franklin's catalog customer service department handles 30,000 to 40,000 calls per month and Lyman only remembers one caller who couldn't be satisfied. "He asked for a Mercedes and I had to say I couldn't do that. But, it is not my place to try to determine if the customer is honest or being realistic. It is my place to make him happy. That is the job of each of our customer service reps—to make sure that at the end of the call, the customer is happy."

Companies often implement extensive policies to avoid being taken advantage of by a few dishonest or unrealistic people. Unfortunately, these policies too often alienate the good customers. To develop truly exceptional service, companies have to make decisions based on the value of the customer, not on the bottom line. They have to do whatever it takes to keep the customer and they must understand that the bottom line will take care of itself.

3. Problems are golden

Since good customer service is transparent, often only when a problem occurs can a company demonstrate its exceptional service. John Hall is one of Upjohn Company's top pharmaceutical reps, winner of the Upjohn Academy award six times and recent winner of the highest award given at Upjohn. Hall believes that it is service that sets him apart, "Service has made the difference many times between getting the business and not getting the business. I make regular calls even when I'm not trying to sell something so the customer will know that I'm always there and will come to rely on me. I try to make my customer feel comfortable about calling me any time—even at my home. I tell them not to worry...whenever they need me, they are to call."

Not long ago a hospital client called him at 8 p.m. on a Sunday evening and said he would be out of a critical drug by midnight. Hall got on the phone, tracked down a shipment, picked it up at 10 p.m. and delivered it to the hospital. Hall commented, "I just consider that kind of service part of my job."

Recently a litigation attorney dropped his Franklin day planner on the tarmac of an airport and the rings popped open allowing his important papers to fly all over the runway. He called Franklin, highly irate and threatening to sue. When the customer service rep told him his system would be replaced, free of charge, with a new leather binder with a zipper, he was surprised and de-lighted—and decided to only sue the ring manufacturer.

Responses like these are examples of extraordinary service that customers talk about. Can a company afford that kind of service? When you think of the 11 people that every unhappy customer speaks to and their potential value, can you afford not to give that kind of service? Warren Blanding of the Customer Service Institute says that every time a problem is handled in an exceptional way, that customer becomes a better customer, spends more money with the company and tells his or her friends.

The United States Office of Consumer Affairs has conducted research about faulty products and slipshod service and how consumers handle these problems. Their findings state:

♦ One purchase in four causes a problem.

♦ Seventy percent of consumers do not complain because they don't know where to call, don't think it's worth the effort or don't think the companies will respond.

♦ Eighteen percent throw away defective products and pay erroneous bills without complaining.

♦ Of the customers who do not complain, 63 percent switch brands. Of those who do complain and receive a satisfactory response, 70 percent become the company's most loyal customers.

There will always be problems—the companies that become customer service legends use those problems to build closer ties with their customers.

Front-line power

One of the hardest principles for managers to come to terms with is the empowerment of their front-line people. Most managers get where they are because of their ability to make decisions and establish control.

Turning responsibility and authority over to customer service reps feels like a loss of control and a diminishing of status. It leaves a manager feeling uncertain. How do you maintain control if someone else makes the decisions? Franklin's customer service reps are empowered to do whatever it takes to make the customer happy.

Trine Lyman with Franklin states, "We believe that service is an art form—this means that we will do things that are out of the ordinary. Sometimes this may just mean writing a personal note but it may also mean giving the customer a lagniappe (a small gift presented to a customer...something extra or unexpected), like a book or pen or flowers or even a new day planner system." Control of this system comes from hiring people who can make good decisions, giving them extensive training, and having a clear understanding of the values and principles of the company. Lyman explains the selection process, "We look for life experience as well as college; we also look for a good ethical background, good integrity, and the ability to make good decisions. We teach them correct principles and then they govern themselves. That's our philosophy."

Control also comes from monitoring the results. Franklin keeps detailed records of the calls each rep takes and their results. Although a decision is never changed, if a specific rep's results are consistently outside of the norm, that rep is coached on other possibilities.

Roger Dow, vice president of sales for Marriott Hotels & Resorts, started with Marriott as a summer lifeguard manager and worked his way through housekeeping and into sales. He believes that promoting from within is a key to keeping employees committed and quality-conscious. Another key is communication. "We have 100,000 employees, so communication is difficult but I just finished a 15-city tour. We went to every region and pulled all of our salespeople together and spent a day with about 100 people in each region. We had videotaped customers prior to the meeting and had them talk about their expectations, what the ideal sales person was and what frustrates them. That was valuable because people could hear real customers.

"We also talked a lot about risk-taking. We want our people to be more empowered and able to take risks for the customers. We try to talk about people who have taken risks and bombed. We even have a special recognition award for people who took risks that didn't work.

"We are trying to empower our people to put the customer first and take risks for them. We had a bellman in Newton, Massachusetts,—a customer was checking out of a hotel recently, and the bellman asked him how his stay was.

The customer said, 'Terrific, except for one thing. Room service was kind of slow this morning and by the time I got my breakfast 45 minutes later, it was cold.' The bellman said, 'Well I don't think you should pay for it—do you have a moment?' He walked up to the front desk and said, 'This is Mr. So-and-So and he just checked out. His breakfast was cold and late this morning and I don't think he should pay for it—do you?' The desk clerk agreed and they took it off his bill. We found out about it because the customer wrote to the hotel general manager and to Bill Marriott, amazed that people would take the responsibility to do that.

"The nice thing is that the hotel had a staff meeting to give the bellman a plaque and celebrate him for doing that. The bellman said, 'I want you to know, I was never so scared in my life because I didn't know if I could do this, and I was afraid that the desk clerk would say no or tell me to go to accounting.' We want our employees to know that this is something they can do. We want them to take the risk."

AT&T Consumer Products has made an intense commitment to having an empowered front line. Richard Hecht says, "Our sales associates are empowered to take care of the customer. Because we have eliminated several layers of management, the only way we can operate successfully is to allow each person in the organization to be fully empowered. The bottom line is that I'm not out there selling; the success or failure of the business depends on the associates. They consider themselves owners of the business and they make decisions as if it were their own business. People will know you by the actions you take and if you want to keep your customers forever, you need to satisfy their needs.

"The determination of what their needs are depends on each situation. Some customers might jump for joy if you give them a free telephone cord; others might need to have their entire purchase price refunded. If associates really want to know how to make their customers happy, they have to ask. It doesn't make sense for the associates to make assumptions for the customers. The bottom line is for the associate to ask, 'What can I do to make you happy?'

"We have to divorce ourselves from the emotion of the circumstance and from the financial implication of the situation. You can't make your decision based on the bottom line; you have to make it on what will keep that customer happy over the long term. There are a lot of companies paying lip service to this philosophy, but we do it and we talk about it constantly. It is embodied and woven into the fabric of everything we do.

"We have a pyramid of shared values bordered by owners, customers and people. Within the pyramid, caring, trust, love, integrity and respect form the base. These are the things we live by. We need to think about those values in regard to everything we do. When people ask, 'How do I function?' I just tell them to continue to act in accordance with those values. Every time there is an issue they are wrestling with, they should go back to the principles and shared values. Associates may make mistakes but if they are going to err, we want them to err in favor of the customer.

AT&T pyramid of shared values

CUSTOMERS

"We have what we call commendations and appeals. Our goal is to have zero appeals. Some people think this is unreasonable because someone is always going to be unhappy and make an appeal. But, by making zero appeals our goal, we will always be working on it. It is paramount to our organization. We eat it and breathe it every single day. It isn't just lip service. Of course, for it to work, it has to start at the top and work down and everyone has to believe it."

To have an empowered front line, an organization must have an environment of trust and teamwork. Hecht describes how AT&T consumer products kicked off their cultural transformation. "It started with 'Project Miracles.' Everyone in consumer products participated in the

program. It helped us get in line with the personal issues of our lives and then we could bridge off of that into business teams. We did a lot of self-challenging things and it gave us a chance to jump out of our comfort zone. For some people, it was a breakthrough experience. The responses we've had have been incredibly positive. People were truly astounded that we would give them an opportunity like this.

"Of course you have to keep reinforcing these experiences. So every year we have a program. The last one was called 'Common Learning Experience: Shaping a Decade,' and it encompassed the philosophies and strategies we need to survive and excel in the upcoming decade. Everyone participates in this program.

"Another thing we do every year is an attitude survey of our people. Each August, we mail out questionnaires to every person in consumer products and it covers pay, benefits, empowerment and all the issues that are important to the success of the business and our people. We publish the results and take action on what the people say. Most of the major changes we have implemented have come from the people themselves. We have an absolute commitment to act on the data. This has been a turnaround business and we have been very successful with it. Several years ago it was questioned whether this division would continue to exist and we have pulled it out and made it very successful. A primary factor in that turnaround has been the empowerment of our associates."

Bill Razzouk, senior vice president of sales for Federal Express, says, "Part of our company mission is taking care of customers at the point of ownership (the person taking the call or talking to the customer). This is an ongoing philosophy that we try to constantly encourage. Most of the things that make companies successful are pretty much common sense. One of the simple things we do is to treat people the way we want to be treated—the Golden Rule."

The way Federal Express treats its employees creates an enormous commitment to the company and to its customers. Stories of incredible feats by couriers abound. An example comes from Dave Poznak, president of Vision Products, who had watched his courier for several days. Every day he parked his truck, leaped out the door, jumped over the bannister and ran to the door of the office with his deliveries. Finally Dave asked him why he ran to make that delivery every day and the courier replied, out of breath, "Just doing my job, Sir. Just doing my job."

Razzouk comments, "There are 30,000 couriers in Federal Express and the vast majority of them are just like that guy. I would love to say that there is a magic formula, but there isn't. Our job as managers is to build an environment where people can be motivated. We have almost 90,000 in a company where normally the employees would be represented by a union. There are no unions at Federal Express. One of our overriding objectives is that people are treated fairly and with respect."

Companies must have an empowered front line for a strategy based on excellent customer service. You can't get superb customer service from an uncommitted, unempowered employee. Here are six foundation blocks of a winning customer service strategy:

1. Customer segmentation

The key to a winning customer service strategy is managing customer expectations. Companies who can exceed expectations without destroying the profit margins build a solid foundation of customer loyalty. The trick is to segment the market by customer expectations and then establish service levels that exceed each segment's expectations. Budget travelers' expectations are completely different from those of the first-class traveler. The airline that provides free champagne to everyone in coach not only irritates the first-class traveler, but also raises expectations that will unnecessarily damage the bottom line.

Marriott's Honored Guest program started by Roger Dow is an excellent example of segmentation. Marriott depends on its business travelers for much of its business. To build loyalty with this important segment, it implemented its Honored Guest program. Marriott was the first upscale hotel chain to offer this program, which is similar to a "frequent flyer" program. Points are given to the more than three million members for each night they stay at a Marriott facility and for each dollar spent on food and beverages or in the shops. Points can be redeemed for travel or for gifts available from a special catalog.

2. 100-percent guarantee

The guarantee must be real and not be awash with fine print. "Absolutely, positively overnight." "Satisfaction guaranteed." "No questions asked." Harvey Mackay stunned the book business with his full, money-back guarantee on his bestselling book *Swim With the Sharks Without Being Eaten Alive*. How many were returned? According to *Personal Selling Power*, fewer than a dozen of the more than 600,000 that were sold. But, how many more copies were sold because of that guarantee?

AT&T Consumer Products Phone Stores posts this return policy in all of its stores: "Our Return Policy: You will be so delighted with our products, services, and visit to our store that you will want to return." A delightful play on words but one that lets the customer know that he or she will be taken care of.

3. Feedback strategy

Every company should have a plan for getting feedback from the customer. Studies show that simply listening to complaints reduces customer frustration. Xerox surveys 40,000 customers per month and receives about 10,000 responses. Less ambitious programs can be as simple as having meetings with customers. Listening to your front-line—

the sales reps, customer service reps and order takers—is cheap and effective. If you act interested, they will overwhelm you with good ideas.

One strategy for feedback is the use of toll-free service numbers. In the past 10 years, calls made to AT&T's 800-line network have grown from 1.3 billion to more than 8 billion. The GE Answer Center, winner of several awards and considered the best of the networks by consumer experts, receives 65,000 calls per week. The network helps callers with complaints, questions on how to operate appliances, pre-purchase inquiries and service questions. About 25 percent of the calls are pre-purchase questions, making up about 750,000 selling opportunities per year. *Business Week*, in an issue dedicated to "Corporate Renewal" called GE's Answer Center, "the most remarkable example of listening."

The center's computer system provides answers on 120 consumer product lines and a mind-boggling 8,500 different models. While the computer system is the guts of the center, the heart is its 250 service reps. N. Powell Taylor, manager and developer of the center, studied the methods of Disney University to find out how Disney makes people happy. He describes the training of the service reps, "We train them to be Disney World-perfect people. We teach them about interpersonal skills and how to satisfy people and have empathy and take control of the conversation and to identify opportunities for selling." Hiring requirements for the service reps are high: college degree plus two to four years of sales experience. "Customer service," explains Taylor, "is selling. The reps go through a need/benefit program and know the benefits of all the products. Customer service is the way to differentiate companies from their competition. Customers are sophisticated, and just telling them you care about them is meaningless—you have to prove it. One of the ways we prove it is by being here 24 hours a day, 365 days a year."

"We also get early warning signals on products that are then fed back to operations so that they can improve the products," states Taylor. When the center started receiving numerous calls from mothers complaining that the end-of-cycle buzzer on clothes dryers disturbed their napping babies, the company responded quickly. Customers can now turn the signal on or off.

Although the initial purpose for the center was to improve customer relations, GE calculates that the level of incremental sales from center calls is more than twice the annual operating budget of $10 million. Phillip Crosby states that "Quality is free." GE finds that service is not only free, it pays big dividends.

4. Customization

Part of giving the customers what they want is giving them exactly what they want. Stave Puzzles is a small company in Vermont that makes fine, crafted, wooden jigsaw puzzles. The puzzles cost up to several thousand dollars but the company can hardly keep up with the demand. Each puzzle is tailored to the customer's specifications. Special pieces are cut with names, dates, or silhouettes representing hobbies, pets or any other symbol the customer wants as part of the puzzle. The puzzles are ingenious and sometimes fiendishly difficult to put together, but the customer and the puzzle-cutter become a team to maximize the customer's puzzle delight. Tom Peters says that customization will become the basis for competitiveness—"customizing darn near everything for darn near everyone."

5. Customer service, not a customer service department

In the '80s we discovered that quality could not be inspected into a product. Quality had to be something that the entire organization did. This is just as true for customer service. Jan Carlzon at SAS talks about "moments of truth"—the interactions with the customer that define a company. To a customer, Marriott is not its annual reports or even the lovely hotel room as much as it is the clerk who greets you with a smile and handles your check-in quickly and efficiently. Federal Express isn't a mammoth hub in Memphis that handles over 750,000 packages five nights a week with a 99.5-percent on-time record. It's the courier who picks up your package every day with a cheerful greeting and who comes back again when you don't have your package ready even though you know he really doesn't have the time.

Every person in the organization has to be part of the customer service team or there is no customer service strategy. The accounts payable clerk who is rude to a vendor doesn't understand that the vendor supplies a valuable piece of the puzzle that becomes the product or service delivered to the customer. Customer service has to be a philosophy, a part of the culture that pervades an organization—service to internal customers and stakeholders as well as to external customers.

6. Measurement

All companies with a customer service strategy measure their service. Federal Express recently became the first service company to win the Malcolm Baldridge Quality Award. Quality measurements are everywhere at Federal. When employees walk in the door in the morning, they see the week's package volume and on-time percentages. Their in-house television station gives them a detailed breakdown of what happened yesterday and any potential problems for the day.

Federal Express has a Service Quality Index (SQI) that measures, each week, such factors as on-time deliveries, complaints, lost packages and invoice adjustments. Its service goal is "100 percent failure-free performance," and management bonuses are based in part on the performance monitored by this index. Federal uses the information produced on this report to identify areas of improvement and to find the root causes of failures and implement solutions.

The Fairfield Inn, a subsidiary of Marriott, has developed a computerized check-out questionnaire that asks each guest three basic questions about cleanliness and service. Because the responses are linked to specific times and rooms, they can be related back to individual check-in clerks, housekeepers and service staff. The responses provide a basis for providing performance awards based on actual guest evaluations.

The customer service strategy and its impact on sales

Studies show that it is three to five times cheaper to keep a customer than to acquire a new one. And satisfied customers are the most likely to be repeat buyers or to buy new products from the company. The customer service strategy creates an environment that makes it easier for salespeople to sell. When a salesperson from a customer service strategy company talks to a customer about a product or service, he or she can assure the customers that if they are not 100 percent satisfied, they will not pay.

Low entry/high exit barriers

Kevin Hall, Franklin's vice president of sales, works to create "low entry/high exit" barriers. He wants it easy for a customer to say "yes." And, he wants to make it difficult for a customer to leave—not through contractual requirements or entanglements, but through such outstanding, extraordinary service that the customer would never want to leave. One "high exit" strategy is the customization of the Franklin Day Planner to the needs of the individual customer. A company can have its logo, mission statement and values, plus any special forms or information added to each participant's day planner. The day planner becomes a training tool for the company as well as a productivity tool.

Exceptional service creates an emotional credit with the customer. It makes the customer willing to refer other customers. It also builds confidence in the salesperson because he or she knows that the customer will be satisfied. The companies that consistently exceed customer expectations, delighting and surprising them, establish an environment where salespeople can thrive.

Star service

Just as outstanding companies have discovered the importance of a service strategy, star salespeople have used extraordinary service as their "secret weapon." Long before "excellence" and "service and "quality" became buzz words, the star salespeople were providing uncommon service to their customers. The top salespeople are ingenious at finding ways to serve their clients. They build their emotional bank accounts with their clients to the point that the clients are delighted to refer other prospects to them. Here are comments and examples from some of the stars:

Provide information

One way John Hall of Upjohn Company services his clients is with information. "I try to find out the interests of the person early on. What kind of research is he doing? Then I try to figure out how to fit into his program. I might try to find a study that would interest him. Even if it doesn't pertain to my products, it helps me start to build that relationship. It helps me get to know him and what his needs are."

Recently Hall had been trying, fruitlessly, to build a relationship with a busy cardio-thoracic surgeon. He made little progress until he noticed a heart model on the surgeon's shelf and he mentioned that sometime when the surgeon had time he would like to better understand exactly what the surgeon did. Suddenly the busy surgeon had time and he spent 45 minutes explaining his specialty to Hall. "Since I was interested in what he was doing, he wanted to spend time with me," comments Hall.

Solve business problems

Louis Slawetsky, president of Industry Analysts, Inc., started his sales career selling soda fountain syrups (he doubled his territory's sales of chocolate syrup in three years) and transitioned to Xerox in its mid-'60s heyday. Slawetsky's concern for exceeding the expectations of his customers made him a top salesperson for Xerox and has helped him build his company. He comments,

"We have built success in this organization because we are working with two levels of expectations—one is what the client wants and expects and the second level is what we want and what we expect. We often find ourselves working in the middle of the night when we have long since met the client's expectations, but we haven't yet satisfied ourselves. What goes out the door has to satisfy us. That's how we stay excited."

In the early days with Xerox, Slawetsky helped his clients learn how to benefit from the possibilities offered by his equipment. Often that meant doing something that was not beneficial to him in the short run but which paid off over the long term. "In the early days," Slawetsky explains, "the idea of a quick-copy center with an offset press and a couple of low-volume copy machines was really revolutionary. I looked at our first installation and realized that the franchise operator did not understand why that copier was there and how it was to be used and when to use each of the processes in his facility. He was going to fail—the copying bills alone would have dragged him under. The problem was that the Xerox unit ran so quickly, that franchise operators who were paying by the copy were tunnelling a lot of offset work onto the copier. They didn't know why the machine was there and they were not doing things in the most cost effective way.

"So I spent the bulk of my weekends for several months in that store making copies and running the press. I was trying to funnel copy work to the press. Of course, we would have liked for the copier bills to be as high as possible, but that is a short-term view because after a few months the guy would have been out of business. I wanted a long-term relationship. Finally, we got it to the point where the store was a profitable operation. Copying became a profitable activity. After that, all across the county, this franchise would only do business with me. Within a year we had 39 locations open. That probably represented approximately $80,000 a month in business for Xerox. Which came from showing the client how to run fewer rather than more copies."

Another example of the kind of service given by the truly extraordinary salespeople comes from Jim Euwer at Armstrong. Euwer sells flooring products to retailers who sell the products to consumers. Euwer goes out of his way to help his retailers sell, and recently planned a new account program with one of his major accounts. Euwer states, "Any given company can lose 20 percent to 25 percent of its accounts every year just through attrition, so you have to address the problem. My client had a fledgling new account program in the past, but it wasn't greatly successful. They wanted to try again but were a little gun shy. I worked out a program with the manager and, rather than turning it over to the salespeople, we started making the calls ourselves.

"We got names from the usual sources and then we sent them an introductory mailer—just enough information to let them know who we were. Next, we sent them a Federal Express letter indicating that we would be calling them the next day. We found that almost everyone took the call and we were able to get appointments with about 90 percent of the people. At that point, we had very good prospects. They knew why we were coming and they gave us the courtesy and the time to discuss the products and their needs. We sold the first three people we talked to. Our results gave us a solid base to go back and present the program to the sales staff. Then we broke into teams and started making presentations using the same method. My client has kept this program going and it continues to be extremely successful." By making his customers successful, Euwer has propelled himself to the top of the Armstrong sales force.

Providing proof through customer satisfaction surveys

A common challenge faced by salespeople is how to prove to prospects that they will deliver outstanding service. One way to convince prospects that your company, product and service are the best available is to use customer satisfaction surveys. Being able to produce surveys of satisfied customers provides the prospect with tangible proof of your service. Also, the process of surveying customers gives the prospects reassurance that they will have an opportunity to express their opinion. Peter Drucker

has said that there are only two times when you will learn about a customer's opinion of your service—when the service has been bad and the customer tells you and when you ask for his or her opinion. Asking for an opinion not only gives you a chance to hear positive things, it gives you a chance to fix problems.

Even if your company does not do customer surveys, you can begin to implement your own survey process and build a customer case history book that will be priceless. Here's how to start your survey system:

Step 1: Define customer satisfaction

Talk to several of your customers to find out how they define satisfaction with your product, your service and with you. Each product and service will have different requirements for customer satisfaction. You want your survey to reflect the qualities that are important to your customers—and, thus, important to your prospects.

Step 2: Develop your survey

Design your survey to include questions that address the definitions you received in Step 1. For instance, if a major criteria for your satisfied customers is how quickly you responded to a service call, you might ask about the average response time. Ask questions about how the customer feels about your product, your service and about you.

The survey should be one page only. You can include a variety of question types: ratings on a 1 to 5 scale (poor to excellent), multiple choice, fill-in-the-blanks, and some open-ended questions to prompt more complete comments. Ask questions that prompt the customer to talk about how you approached, maintained and followed up with the account before, during and after the sale. You want the survey to show you as the main problem-solver and consultant to your customers.

Step 3: Compile a customer case history

Collect as many completed surveys as possible to develop a case history book. If you've been following up with your present accounts, and they're satisfied, there should be no reason why they wouldn't be happy to fill out a survey. Include the few bad surveys you receive so that you can talk about how you solved the problem. It is very effective if you can also include a later survey that shows that the problem was solved and the customer is happy.

Telling a potential customer that nobody's perfect and every sales rep has a few unhappy customers displays openness and honesty. Being able to show how you turned those unhappy customers into satisfied customers, shows your commitment to service and customer satisfaction.

Step 4: Implement the survey

The following scenario gives you an idea of how to use your customized survey.

Customer: "How do I know that your service is as good as you say it is? How can I be sure you will follow up after the sale? Every salesperson promises me the same thing!"

Sales Rep: "I can understand how you feel. Most of my present customers said the same thing until I showed them this." (Hand the customer a copy of the survey.)

Customer: "A survey? So what's this going to prove?"

Sales Rep: (Hand the customer a self-addressed stamped envelope.) "Please notice that this envelope is addressed to the president of my company. Every 30 days, each of my customers receives this survey. Our company uses these surveys to measure how the sales force handles accounts. If the president receives any bad feedback from one of my accounts, I have to answer to him personally. By giving you this survey now, my evaluation starts today, and I'm going to do everything possible to make sure that you're happy with our company, product, service and most of all, with me."

Customer: "What have some of your customers said?"

Sales Rep: "Let me show you some of the surveys I've received. Here are more than 50 surveys that my customers mailed in." (Take the prospect through the surveys, highlighting important comments or ratings.) "Here's a survey from one customer who had some problems with the product. And here's her next survey after I helped resolve the problem with our customer service department."

Using customer satisfaction surveys helps your customer understand that you are focused on providing uncommon service. The surveys provide the proof that prospects need to feel safe doing business with you.

Providing exceptional service is a corporate success strategy that has been proven effective. A study of 185 U.S. industrial companies with annual sales ranging from $50 million to $8 billion conducted by management consulting firm Shycon Associates, concluded that customer service can affect sales by as much as 1 percent for every 1 percent improvement in service. In other words, a company could improve sales by 25 percent by improving service by 25 percent.

Providing exceptional service is also an individual success strategy that has been proven by many of the top stars you met in this chapter and throughout the book. For the best in the business of selling, stories like Slawetsky spending weekends determining the breakeven points for a copy machine and Euwer developing a new accounts program for a client are the norm rather than the exception.

"The best executive is the one who has sense enough to pick good people to do what he wants done, and self-restraint enough to keep from meddling with them while they do it."
—*Theodore Roosevelt, 26th president of the United States*

> Two Ideas:

What two ideas did you get from this chapter?

_____

_____

I dare you to find a way to use one of these ideas to improve your service to your customers.

Action Plan

> Low Entry/High Exit
> Worksheet

How can you lower the barriers to doing business with you and raise the barriers for leaving you? Here are some questions to help you think through the process.

Low entry

How can you make it easy for the customer to buy?

◆ Eliminate paperwork, allow verbal approval, place orders by computer or telephone

What are the barriers you can eliminate in the purchase process?

◆ Risk-free trials, guarantees, samples, previews
◆ Commitment—eliminate contracts

High exit

What can you do to keep the customer from leaving?

◆ Service on-site, annual maintenance contracts, rapid response
◆ Customization—providing exactly what the customer wants; adding company logos, names, etc., to products
◆ Partnerships—joint ventures, combined efforts
◆ Training—training in the use of your product or service, industry training, meetings or conferences

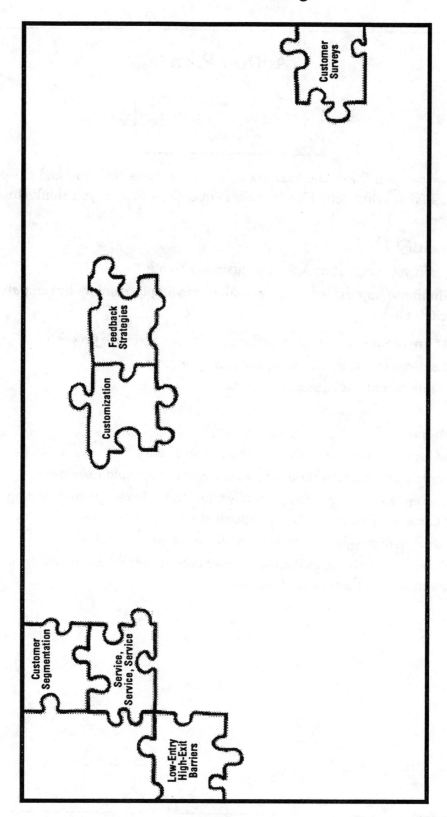

Chapter 9

Inside-out: product knowledge strategies

"We're nuts about product knowledge."

—Roger Turnquist, vice president, Sales & Service Society Corporation

Coming attractions:

- Be the expert
- "Mad dogs"
- Question record

Customers expect salespeople to be experts. The salesperson is the critical link—the one person who understands both the customer's situation and needs and the benefits the product or service offers. If the customer had all the information, there wouldn't be a need for a salesperson.

The sales stars differentiate themselves with their in-depth knowledge of their product and their industry. They specialize in understanding how the product or service benefits can provide solutions to customers.

Marty Rodriquez achieved Century 21's coveted Centurion award when she achieved the level of number-two sales agent out of the more than 90,000 agents in the Century 21 system. Rodriquez, who was number four in the nation the prior year and has now been inducted into the Century 21 Hall of Fame, credits her success to her extraordinary focus on the basics. Hanging above her desk is a sign that states, "Success is the superb execution of the basic fundamentals."

Success for Rodriquez was not automatic. The fourth of 11 children, she was working in an insurance agency when her husband suggested that she study real estate. She liked real estate and thought that selling would be fun, giving her a chance to talk to people and satisfy her natural curiosity.

Rodriquez comments on her success, "People are always telling me that they can tell that I love what I'm doing. They see it in my face and they hear it in my voice. If someone doesn't want to be where they are, then you don't want to do business with them. We motivate people to want to buy or sell by the electricity we generate with our enthusiasm."

Rodriquez also believes strongly in having the best possible product knowledge. "Product knowledge is very important," she explains. "You can have the best sales skills possible, but if you don't sound like you know your business, people will not have confidence in you. My first five years in the business were really important for me. Even though I wasn't producing like I am now, I was building my foundation. I was going on caravans. Going to meetings. Meeting people around town and making it a point to know what was going on in town. I know a lot of people and I know what the city is going to do and what's happening. I know where all the streets are. When people started to call me after I really knew my areas, often I could describe their house and their floorplan...they were really impressed."

One of Rodriquez's secrets is that she works every year like it's her first year in real estate. She still works 12 hour days; she still brings that same fresh enthusiasm to her work; and she still concentrates on the basics. "It is always the basics that make you successful, and too often people forget them," Rodriquez comments. "To me that means doing whatever it takes to get the business—whether it's open houses, mailings, canvassing or whatever. I do a lot of mailings because people will forget you if you don't stay in front of them."

She also has a complete program outlined to show people who list their property with her what she will do differently. This includes advertising in several papers and magazines at her own expense and maintaining a complete follow-up program to provide information to owners. Each Monday, Rodriquez checks every listing, following-up with people who have seen the house, finding out what they liked and what they didn't like. She can give the owners a report that includes information to help them fix problems or show the house to its best advantage.

Rodriquez says she is always selling. "I don't care where I'm at, I'm always selling real estate. I once went to a Christmas party and wound up selling houses to the host and his three daughters. I'm not obnoxious about it—I just allow it to come up in conversation and I let people know what I do. And, I become friends with a lot of my clients because of the way I treat them. Sometimes I set goals just to meet people rather than to try to sell them something," she comments. "If you meet the people and do all the right things, the rest will come. I don't worry about the money because I know it will come."

Rodriquez was recently selected Hispanic Woman Entrepreneur of the Year and she was asked if being a minority and a female had been a hindrance in her career. Her answer tells a lot about her view of life, "Perhaps it was there, but I never saw it. I didn't want to see it.

"It's an excuse people can use. I always wanted to win—I wanted to be the best volleyball player, the best candy seller. We were poor—there were 11 kids and my dad was a barber. But I was a cheerleader even though one of the nuns had to loan me the money to buy my outfit. It is the same now. I want to win."

Training departments at the star sales companies are ingenious at finding ways to help their people develop product knowledge. Roger Turnquist, vice president of sales and service development for Society Bank, says the bank is "nuts" about product knowledge. Turnquist has helped the bank find unique ways to make learning the product fun and effective. At a sales rally, Society sponsored a College Bowl-type contest on product knowledge. Each sales district furnished a team that came in costume and had one minute to introduce themselves with music, color, skits and so on. The winning team won $100 and a traveling trophy. Turnquist's group has also produced a game called "Product Challenge," which is a takeoff on Trivial Pursuit. The game focuses on retail products and can be used at district sales rallies. These fun product-knowledge devices enhance the standard training tools, which include a sophisticated computer based training program.

Federal Express has invested millions of dollars in its computer-based training system, installing more than 1,225 interactive video disk units in 650 locations. With its 25-disc curriculum, the system helps salespeople and customer service personnel stay current in a rapidly changing industry. Salespeople go through a testing process each year to make sure their information is current. By taking these tests, salespeople can determine their areas of weakness and know what coaching or additional information they need.

Gail Gelber outsold her entire sales department in her first six weeks on the job with Terminal Applications Group, Inc. (TAG), selling three computer systems. How? Gelber states, "Knowledge is the key. You have to understand the customer's business and how your products will help him make more money." Gelber had worked in the accounting department of a large corporation processing data on equipment supplied by TAG, so she had a thorough understanding of the TAG system and its benefits.

Gelber was recruited by TAG to teach people how to use the computer, but after six months in that position, she began to lobby for a job on the front lines. TAG systems sell for $25,000 to $3 million, and normally selling such systems is a months-long process. But, when Gelber was finally transferred to sales, she had one major advantage, "I understood the customer's point of view." She also credits persistence and the ability to make very clear presentations. "I reviewed with the customer what I was going to cover, then covered it, then reviewed what I covered, then planned the next step. I was always clear about what I was going to do next. Also, I always follow up and my word is golden. That's how I liked it as a customer, and that's how my customers like it." It must work. Gelber was salesperson of the year three times, sales manager of the year, and is now vice president of sales.

Be the expert

Most sales stars, even when their companies have outstanding training programs, develop their own methods of getting an extra edge on product knowledge. Bill Baril, major account rep with Offtech, acts as his own technical expert and does his own user training. Before joining with five others to form Offtech, Baril was a top sales rep with Xerox. "I was the number-one sales rep in the company," he reports, "and won the President's Club trip every year and was always 200 percent of quota."

"Product knowledge," Baril states, "is often one of the biggest weaknesses of salespeople. I learned the importance of product knowledge very early on. At Xerox when they brought out the 9200, it took weeks and weeks to learn the product and its features before we could ever go out in the field and try to sell it. That taught me that the more you know your product, the better off you are. It's probably the best way to be able to handle an objection."

Baril uses his product knowledge to help him build a close relationship with his customers. By knowing everything about his product, he can find ways to help customers solve their problems. He explains, "The customer doesn't want to be bogged down with all the copier issues and problems. They want someone else to handle them. Handling those problems can be a pain in the neck for a sales rep and most sales reps don't want to do it. I handle problems for them and become the customer's right arm and develop their confidence. They allow me to travel anywhere in the organization—whether it's in the president's office or the treasurer's office—wherever there are copy machines, to take care of the problems. Most major account reps have assistants to do new installation training, but I do my own. It helps me get to know that end user. Because of my product knowledge—I know my equipment inside and out—I can really help them understand how to get the most benefit from their equipment."

Baril gives the following advice to new salesreps: "If I were a new salesperson, I would take every training class offered by the company or manufacturer; I would know, thoroughly, the product manual. I would take my own time at night, or whenever, to work on that particular machine by myself. Also, I would get together with one of the top technicians who really knows the machine inside and out, and I would work with him for hours." Anything you can do to get your hands on your product, to get involved with it, will help you understand it better.

Rick Dyer, formerly director of sales operations for Apple Computer, emphasizes the effectiveness of being your own technical expert. "One of the things I did as a salesperson was to not rely on outside resources to solve technical problems. The key to success is to know where to get the resources to solve the problem. What I liked to do was to be selective about where I used those technical resources. If I was covering an account where I felt knowledge of everything in communications was critical, I tried to be the one bringing that knowledge. I could control my schedule where I couldn't control someone else's. Plus, in talking to a customer, your credibility goes way up if you are able to answer a question on the spot. I found that by not relying on someone else to give me the answers but trying to figure it out for myself, I could use that knowledge and leverage it. There is a tendency among a lot of salespeople to immediately call for help when a technical question arises. I worked a remote territory so maybe I was forced into developing more of a technical knowledge base. But I found that I had the 50 to 60 percent of the knowledge base that applied to 90 percent of the situations."

Dave Poznak, president of Vision Products sells sunglasses, toys and other small items that are sold in toy stores and drug stores. He is so committed to knowing his products that he travels to Taiwan and Hong Kong to see how they are actually made. He states, "My philosophy about sales is that I want to know every aspect about the product I am selling. If you know exactly what kind of plastic is in your product and exactly which plant is producing it, you are able to explain the difference to the buyer. You can explain the level of quality that the buyer is receiving. I know every detail about the product. Information sells your product."

Barbara McClure, sales and operations support manager with GE Jet Engines, shows how far the top sales stars go in getting the product knowledge they need. McClure, with an undergraduate degree in English and an MBA, wound up in an engineering world. She talks about how she compensated for her background. "One thing that has always been important to me is studying the product. Because I wasn't an engineer, I worked very hard to understand the product even if that meant going to a tear-down class. We have a wonderful training school here where we actually go out and tear down an engine and rebuild it. We take the nuts and bolts out and then put it back together. You not only have to understand the theory of jet engines, you have to understand the nuts-and-bolts part of it. My technical strength is on the nuts-and-bolts side."

McClure was the only woman in the class taking jet engines apart and putting them back together. Classes such as these at GE aren't required training for salespeople. But, McClure took weeks out of her sales schedule to build her technological knowledge base.

"Mad dogs"

When McClure was selling repair services, she also spent time with the technicians on the repair line. It was there that she learned a wonderful lesson about "mad dogs." McClure tells the story: "I would sit with the repair people as they actually tore down and repaired, replaced and tested the equipment. This was something I did on my own just to get a better idea of what was going on. We had instruments from a certain airline that the repair people called "mad dogs." I asked the technicians why, and they said it was because they kept showing up over and over...they tested okay when they left the shop but for some reason they kept coming back." McClure recalls that, in order to solve these sorts of problems, she's had to become an ace detective. She'll review all the tear-down reports, lay out all the parts to see if there was some sort of pattern, go back to the customers and investigate their maintenance situation to see if that caused the problem, involve technical experts—whatever it takes to get to the solution.

How often do we see "mad dogs" in our lives? Problems that keep coming back again and again, problems that we are too busy to solve? McClure recognizes a "mad dog" problem, finds the source and uses it as a way to build trust and confidence with her customer. "Mad dogs" show us that something is wrong. Finding the source of the problem leads us to a breakthrough. Whether the problem is in a product, in a customer's system, in our sales process or in our personal life, "mad dogs" offer us an opportunity.

Industry expert

Customers not only expect you to know your products and services, but they expect you to be an expert in the industry. Mary Ellen Blaikie, international account executive with Federal Express has built a striking level of success by her willingness to develop expertise and credibility in a complex industry. Blaikie has been a consistent Hall of Fame winner with Federal Express and was named the International Account Executive of the Year.

Blaikie says, "Customer expectations from the international division of Federal Express are extremely high. Customers expect us to be able to help them with their problems and take a proactive approach. The opportunity to solve a problem for a customer gives you the opportunity to gain credibility. The customer expects us to be a transportation consultant and to understand all the hazards and difficulties of doing business internationally with all the different cultures."

Blaikie has been involved with the industry for more than 10 years and she keeps current by attending government-sponsored meetings and doing as much reading on rules and regulations of international shipping as possible. She recently participated in the federally sponsored "Export Now" conference and in the first videoteleconferencing meeting on the trade deficit. "I was able to bring some of my customers to that conference. That helped me build a high level of credibility with them," she says.

Question record

One exercise that proves useful to many sales people is to list every question customers have ever asked about a product or service and to keep this list updated regularly. Finding the answers to those questions builds a broad knowledge base and, since customers always find new questions, the questions keep you learning.

Sy Gardner with Gardner Carpets says, "If someone asked me a question that I didn't have the answer to, I would go to any length to get it. I read everything that was put out by manufacturers or by the institutes. One of my biggest service items—one of my biggest selling strengths—was that dealers could turn to me for knowledge and information. That made them dependent upon me. In a market where

product and prices are pretty much the same, the only way I could make someone want to buy from me was by helping them, providing information and service. I would often carry brochures of related products that we didn't even sell, but would help the dealers in the installation or handling of their business.

While many salespeople feel that they can't get too technical with their customers, Marc Rosenberg, top commercial real estate salesperson with Cushman & Wakefield, feels that his technical strength has been a critical factor in his success. Rosenberg states, "The average salesperson tries to sell himself based on his track record or qualifications. I try to be a little more financially oriented. I have developed a software package that will analyze a customer's needs and project what they are going to spend over the next five years for moving, phone, utilities, rent and so on. These projections are based on information I get from the client. I try to mix sales techniques with computer research. It helps me deal with the financial people and top management people. It adds a lot of credibility."

Rosenberg gives an example of how his technical knowledge builds his success, "Recently we did a transaction for a large financial company that wanted to lease 200,000 square feet, and wanted us to find some space. After looking into the company, I found out that in the past they had owned a lot of properties. The market in New

Jersey was a little soft right then, so I suggested that we look for a joint venture or an equity participation type of transaction. I took a Lotus spreadsheet and worked with the controller and determined the company's financial position and tax structure. We developed a program that showed how the company could get equity at no cost, depending upon how much space it took. So now the company will share in the proceeds once the property is sold and it has an equity interest if it wants to refinance the property.

"Most brokerage people don't want to get that technical. I found out that if I get a little more technical, I can better serve my clients. It makes the transaction a little more time-consuming and means I can't work on as many deals. I try not to work on more than 6 or 8. By doing that, I have more time for more in-depth research, and my closing ratio is excellent. Any client where I have sat down and explained what I am going to do usually winds up going with me. My ratio is over 90 percent and, in this business, 50 percent is good."

Today's sales emphasis is in building relationships and becoming a partner to the customer. Sometimes it's easy to forget the importance of product knowledge. The keys to building a successful sales relationship, however, are that the customer has to like you, trust you and respect you. The respect is based on your knowledge, your ability to represent your product or service and your industry as an expert.

This section has focused on the product and service environment surrounding you and your customers. In the next section, you'll see how your product expertise and genuine concern for your customer combine with creativity to produce a powerful customer partnership and solution selling.

"Anything will give up its secrets if you love it enough."
—*George Washington Carver, developer of over 150 peanut byproducts*

┌─────────────────────────────┐
│   Two Ideas: │
└─────────────────────────────┘

What two ideas did you get from this chapter?

_____

_____

I dare you to find a way to use one of these ideas to improve your knowledge of your product or your industry.

Action Plan

```
┌─────────────────────────────┐
│      Question Record         │
│        Worksheet             │
└─────────────────────────────┘
```

Keeping a record of all the questions you are asked by customers helps you continue to develop better answers to those questions. You may even want to develop a question-and-answer booklet to give to customers. Sometimes customers have questions they don't ask and sometimes they think of questions when you aren't there to answer them. Such a booklet can help bridge those gaps.

Here is a six-step process to help you develop your record.

1. List every question you can think of that a customer has asked you about your product or service, the sales process and the after-the-sale service process.

2. Talk to other salespeople and service people to find more questions.

3. Talk to several of your customers to ask them what questions they had when they were in the process of considering your product or service.

4. Group the questions into categories—specific areas about the product or maintenance, questions about financing, and so on.

5. Develop your best and most complete answers to those questions. If you need more information, go to a technical person or a senior salesperson.

6. Find a customer who will review the questions and answers with you to make sure they are complete and understandable.

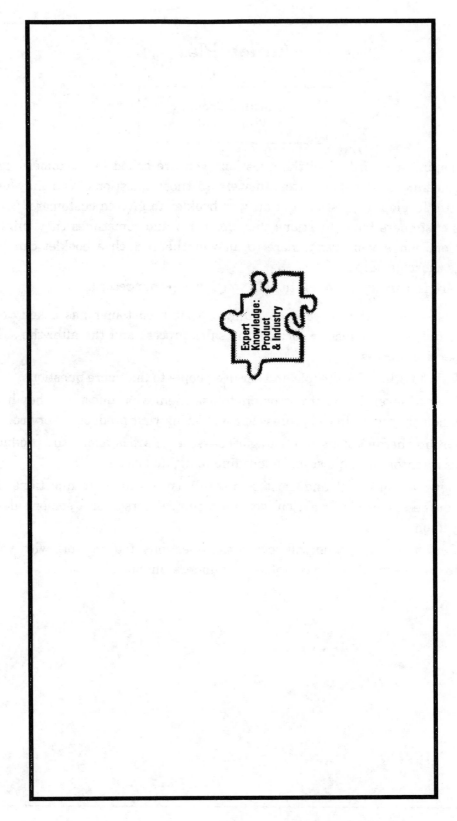

Section IV

Solution strategies

"We have to be an advocate for our customers."

—*Curtis Crawford, vice president, sales, service and support, AT&T Computer Systems*

The easiest sale you will ever make is when you have found a perfect match between your product or service and the needs or problems of your customer. Neil Rackham, author of *SPIN Selling*, in his delightful English accent talks about the prime selling disease. As soon as a customer admits to a need or a problem, the salesperson beats him or her with features and benefits. Salespeople who have become proficient at solution selling, lead the customer into stating all the benefits of having the product or service. At this point, the customer leaps across the desk, rips the contract out of the hands of the salesperson, signs it and demands immediate delivery. Well, almost anyway.

It seemed almost that easy when Texaco delivered a $3.5 million order to Carl Herman, national account sales manager for Oracle USA. However, behind that order was a year and a half of relationship-building and a unique quality program that built the relationship into a strategic partnership.

A popular story at Federal Express involves a fight between a bear and an alligator. The tale is told as a way of showing managers the importance of strategy and providing solutions for customers. The story states that if an alligator and a bear are going to fight, the outcome is determined more by the terrain than by the power or skill of the fighters. If the fight takes place in the swamp, the alligator has the advantage and the bear is in trouble. If the fight takes place on land, the bear has the advantage.

Bill Razzouk, senior vice president of sales at Federal Express, applies the story to a sales situation. "If we start by quoting numbers, we'll be dragged quickly into the swamp. Our mission is to create a satisfied customer at the end of each transaction. To achieve that mission, we need to understand the customer's business, speak his or her language and learn about his or her needs, goals and objectives. Salespeople can avoid swamps by learning how to sell value, not price."

The value that a salesperson brings to a customer is the ability to find solutions that match the customer's problems. The unique perspective of the salesperson is that he or she has the overview both of the customer's business and needs, and all the possibilities of product or service. The salesperson's ability to use that product or service as a problem solving tool, makes him or her an invaluable part of the customer's organization.

Razzouk preaches the philosophy that customer problems are opportunities for salespeople. "What we try to teach our salespeople is that the best sales come from uncovering applications or problems. I'm a vice president of this company, but anybody who can come and help me solve my problems, I've got time for them.

"We spend a tremendous amount of time and money training our sales force...not on answering objections or things like that, but on how to listen and how to probe. We have to be able to find out how the company is organized and what different divisional departments are charged with and what the objectives of the different departments are.

"We are focusing on the whole area of time-based competition. One of the major challenges today is how to shorten the time between the sale and delivery of the product. We recently designed a system to allow a customer to save five hours in the normal delivery cycle. It was worth it to the customer to pay a premium for that because they had high-priced field engineers waiting for the deliveries."

In order to develop a strategic partnership with a client, the salesperson has to do everything possible to try to build the customer's business, to solve problems, to meet needs. Tom Kattmann is a district sales manager for Minolta Corporation. He has been with Minolta for 11 years and when he joined the company, the Florida district was 14th in the country. At the end of his first year, the district was second, and for the past nine years, the district has been the number-one territory. Minolta is running out of awards to give him.

Kattmann's focus is building the business of his dealers. He develops a high level of rapport and confidence with his dealers but he also goes out of his way to help the dealer meet his or her own goals. Kattmann says, "I help the dealer grow. I help them develop a good, solid sales team through training and support. There is a high turnover in dealerships and I try to work with all the training managers to provide them with materials and information to make sure they provide the best training. I also have a lot of patience with the dealers. I always stay in touch and try to see their point of view. Some things are just basic, like I always try to return calls within two hours."

But Kattmann goes out of his way to make sure his dealers are doing well. If he has a dealer who is falling below quota, he sits down with the dealer and tries to figure out the problem. "Florida is growing rapidly," he says, "so if they are below quota there must be a reason. It might be because they are short of salespeople or they need help with sales training." Minolta sponsors open houses to help recruit salespeople for dealerships. Kattmann participates in almost all of the local open houses in order to spot new talent for his dealers. He states, "It's something we do to help the dealers. I've run these open houses for all of my large dealers. I go in like I'm a partner. I want to help the dealer make quota. I think some of these things are so basic that people don't bother with them—they think it's too elementary."

Curtis Crawford, with AT&T Computer Systems, was on the sales team that sold the first multiple purchase of large computer systems. He gives a wry view of the sales relationship. "I was working with a customer to sign the largest order ever placed for mainframe computers—the deal was for over $500 million. We had a meeting set up with the customer and we were sitting in the conference room on one side of the table, waiting for the customer." You can almost see the scene and sense the anticipation as Crawford continues, "The customer walked in and sat down at the table with three or four of his vice presidents. We exchanged pleasantries and so forth.

Finally the customer said, 'I've looked at the contract and we've evaluated it and after serious consideration, here's what we think.' He stood up, tore up the contract and threw it down on the table. My entire life went flat.

"We just sat there and I was groping for words. Finally, I said 'Can you at least tell me what you thought about it?' At that point he laughed, reached into his coat pocket, pulled out the original contract, and signed it!"

Crawford feels that it was an indication of the great rapport they had with the customer that he felt free to indulge in some heart-stopping humor. He works to build intense relationships with his customers, relationships that become partnerships. "Once we were embarking on some major projects involving state-of-the-art technology and I was meeting with the customer. The purpose of my meeting was to ensure them that we would support this very significant project and work with them to make sure we met their needs. During the meeting, the chief administrative officer said to me, 'What's most important to us, Curt, is not that your products are the best of the breed and not that they are the most competitively priced. What is important to us is the fact that we want to build a relationship where we are both working for common ground. While we expect you to have good products at competitive prices, what we are looking for is a partnership.' "

It is an indication of the sophistication of today's customer base that they understand the importance of the strategic partnership. Products have to be good and prices have to be right, but what's really important is the partnership. Crawford says that, often, his purpose is to let the customers know that there is a high level of involvement and commitment in the corporate offices. "I tell them that our objective is not to make them happy, our objective is to delight them with our products and services. We make a commitment to delight them."

In the following chapters you will learn more about how to establish strategic partnerships that delight your customers.

"It isn't that they can't see the solution. It is that they can't see the problem."
—*G.K. Chesterton, British essayist and novelist.*

Chapter 10: Selling beyond the nine dots

Solving customer problems requires the ability to think creatively and look beyond obvious answers. Learn how to focus on your customers' situations and provide solutions that help them grow their business. Learn the key steps in the Breakthrough Pyramid—the numbers game, relationship selling and solution selling. The Action Plan for this chapter is to think creatively and come up with a way to differentiate yourself from others.

Chapter 11: Building leverage

The leap from average performance to star performance requires leverage. Listen to the stars who tell you how to get more results from your sales efforts by getting help from other people, building a positional advantage and licensing a sales network. Learn how to use team selling to break through complex selling situations.

The Action Plan for this chapter will help you build your own leverage.

Chapter 12: Lucky breaks

Sometimes salespeople seem incredibly lucky, accomplishing sales feats that seem impossible. This chapter tells you what's behind some of that luck and how you can put it all together to develop your own luck.

The Action Plan for this chapter is to help you build your own success formula.

Chapter 10

Selling beyond the nine dots

"Discovery consists of looking at the same thing as everyone else and thinking something different."

—Roger von Oech, creativity guru and author

Coming attractions:

♦ We all sell ice cream

♦ Three types of selling

> *The Challenge: See if you can connect the nine dots using only four straight lines without lifting your pencil. Imagine game show music in the background and take a few moments with the puzzle.*

Why am I talking about dots in a sales book? What are the nine dots anyway? The nine-dot puzzle is an exercise in thinking—breaking through our preconceived notions and ideas about how things ought to be. Did you solve the puzzle? If not, it's probably because you set up an artificial barrier for yourself. You probably thought that you had to stay within the box formed by the nine dots. Get rid of your imaginary box and try it again. (If you still don't get it, the answer is at the end of this chapter.) Almost all of us create boundaries that stifle our thinking at least some of the time. We have to break down those boundaries and search for fresh, creative ideas.

The nine-dot puzzle is a metaphor for creative thinking. Sales masters use creative thinking as a tool to break through sales barriers. They use it to find new ways of presenting themselves, new ways of connecting with prospects, new ways to listen and understand their customer's problems and new ways to find solutions. A research project held at the Pecos River Learning Center in 1987 showed a basic difference between "game-changers" as profiled by Larry Wilson's book, *Changing the Game: A New Way to Sell* and the larger group of sales professionals. While both groups emphasized integrity first and relationship-building second, for the game-changers, creativity was the critical third skill. Creativity is the added value that a salesperson brings to the sales process. Creativity is the basis of solution selling, and providing solutions to customer problems is the cement that forms strong partnerships with your customers.

John Covell, vice president of marketing for A-Copy, an office equipment distributor with 200 sales reps and sales of $80 million, tells a perfect "beyond the nine-dots" story. One day Covell was going to Cape Cod to show a copier to an insurance agent. Even if he sold the copier, it was going to be a low-profit call so he decided to challenge himself by taking another copier with him. The dare to himself was that he couldn't leave the Cape until he had sold both copiers.

After Covell made the deal with the insurance agent he was scheduled to meet with, he told him about his challenge to himself and asked him if he knew anyone who might need a copier.

The insurance agent told him about a guy down the street that ran an ice-cream store—he knew they had an old, treated-paper copier so they might need a new one.

Covell explains the situation, "In our industry, virtually every copier rep walks into an office and says the same thing, 'Hi I'm so-and-so from such-and-such.' They ask the same questions about what kind of copier they have,

what the monthly volume is, whether they rent or lease, how long have they've had it and do they like it. Everybody has the same standard set of questions—they are different by industry but everyone in an industry tends to ask the same questions.

"It was now 4 p.m. on Friday afternoon. As I started with the same questions, he started to tell me about his old, treated-paper copier. When I listened to what he was doing with the copier he had and what his needs were, I realized that for him, his copier was absolutely perfect. He didn't care about or need quality and speed. So, I took out a two-by-four and hit myself upside the head and thought, 'I've got to start this conversation all over.'

"So I said, 'Let's pretend the last five minutes didn't take place. Why don't you just tell me a little bit about your business.' He said, 'I sell ice cream. I distribute ice cream to retail stores. I'm also trying to get into specialty ice creams like mud pies and things you see in restaurants on nice dessert menus. There are a lot of restaurants on the Cape and I have a great product with great margins.'

"I asked him how it was going and he said, 'Terrible.' When I asked him why, he said, 'You've got to understand the Cape—90 percent of these restaurants aren't open in the winter. The owners live in Florida. While they're down there, they get their menus set up and all their suppliers set up. They are ready to go by the time they get to the Cape and when I call on them, they don't want to hear from me.'

"I said to him, 'I've got an idea—go to some of these restaurants and pick up some matches or a napkin or anything else that has the logo of the restaurant. Come back and on your fabulous new copier, you make up a menu of your gourmet ice cream desserts and you put the logo on the bottom with a piece of tape and copy it onto some card stock. Now when you make an appointment with the restaurant owner, go through your products and the margins and how wonderful the desserts are. Then tell him that you are willing to put two weeks worth of product in his freezer at no obligation to him, plus you will provide him with these little menu cards to put on all the tables to promote the dessert item. Tell him you've made up some so he can see how they look and show him your sample with his logo. Tell him that at the end of the two weeks, you'll come back and he can make a simple decision as to whether it was a worthwhile test. You will simply charge him for the product he used. If the product has done well, you put him on a routine delivery and continue to provide him with the menus.'

"Well the guy went nuts. Next thing I know, I'm eating mud pie and his mother is making up calligraphy menus. The guy says to me, 'How soon can I have the copier?' Then he also asks, 'How much?' I quote him full list on a lease and he says, 'Is that all?'

"The ice-cream story has become the key to our whole selling strategy and the key to selling in this new era. Regardless of whether you are selling insurance, copiers, advertising, or whatever, you have to get it out of your mind that your product or service is what you sell. Because if the company's business is selling advertising, that is what we sell. If the company's business is selling ice cream, that is what we sell. If the company's business is selling bed springs or providing legal services, then we sell bed springs or legal services."

We all sell ice cream

We all sell ice cream...that thought shatters the box we put around our thinking. It lets us see the solution to the "nine dots." Whenever we start to tell our customers about the wonders of our black box, if we can stop and realize that what we sell is ice cream and that the only thing that's important about our black box is whether it will sell more ice cream to more people, it will bring us back to a solution selling frame of mind.

Earl Nightingale says, "Creative selling is simply the ability to discover problems, get the ideas that will solve them and then put those ideas into action." The first step is to discover the problem. Creative salespeople look for problems that can be solved by their products and services. Once problems are discovered, we can start to partner with our customers to find and implement solutions. Chris McKeever, star national account executive with Federal Express, built his success on his ability to help customers solve problems. One client, a major retailer, was concerned about their ability to have inventory in their stores when the customers wanted it. For example, they carried watches from 22 vendors and each of those vendors were shipping directly to more than 1,500 stores. It was an incredible number of shipments and difficult to control. In working with them, McKeever identified the problem as keeping their customers satisfied by completely eliminating stockouts. Although, in the beginning, the retailer was convinced that ground freight was the only thing that made sense, by focusing on the customer's objectives, McKeever was able to design a program that met their needs.

McKeever explains, "We worked with them to understand their systems, and put together a proposal that showed that we could help them maintain satisfied customers. Their philosophy is that at the end of each transaction they want a satisfied customer, and part of accomplishing that is when the customer goes into their store, the product has to be there. Using ground transportation, the product may not be there when the customer wants it there. With Federal Express, they had more control over when the product arrived at the store and they could also reduce the level of inventory required." As is typical in a solution sale, everyone wins. The retailer has happier customers and better control and Federal Express has a satisfied customer and more business.

Three types of selling

Mike Fields is the president of Oracle USA, known for building software products based on a sophisticated database management system that supports most computers and most operating environments. Fields believes solution selling is the critical key in today's sales environment.

He states, "As I see it, there are three types of selling. There are transaction sales, product sales and solution sales. A transaction sale is not based on a solution or product as much as making a transaction so valuable to the client that whether or not they really need it now, they are going to buy it. A typical example is in the retail market place, if the price is right on a suit, you may buy it even though you don't need it.

"In a product sale, the inherent technology is really something you want. This is the case of a better mouse trap. The customer makes a decision knowing that a product will meet his or her particular criteria. For a solution sale to happen, the seller and the buyer must come to an understanding as to what the product brings to the buyer in terms of solving a problem. That requires a lot more effort than the other two. It takes more time to understand the requirements and the needs of the customer.

"What's happening in our business is that transaction and product sales were relatively easy to do in the '80s. There were a lot of discretionary dollars to spend for good deals or product capabilities. In the '90s there is more interest in solving problems. However, solution selling also includes a good transaction and good product capability. A lot of people call this strategic product sales. I am of the mind that there is no such thing as a strategic product—there are only strategic decisions.

"Salespeople have to understand the specific needs of the client. Solution selling is understanding the client's needs and packaging your solutions, your products, to meet the client's needs and being able to demonstrate the return on investment the client will realize. In our business, we have found that the acquisition costs have to be returned 10 times in 24 to 36 months. If you can't prove that, then you probably won't make a sale."

In solution selling, the salesperson becomes a key player in the customer's business. Fields gives us an example, "We went into an aerospace company recently that was interested in acquiring a technology like ours and they expected to take nine months to make

their decision. We sent in three people to work with them and, within a month, we discovered major holes in the company's inventory management and accounts receivable system. We did an analysis that showed they were losing $2 million to $3 million per month because of these holes. At the end of this study, we told them they could study the situation for the next seven to eight months, and that would cost them $16 million, or they could buy $3 million worth of technology and consulting and fix the problem. They made a decision in five weeks. That is focusing on a solution sale rather than on the technology or product features.

"One of the major changes that has to take place is to elevate the level of the salesperson in relationship to the account. In the technology business we're in, all too often the salesperson gets mired down with the technology trying to prove that we are better than the competition. That generally has little to do with the solution, and the people who are going to make a solution decision don't understand the technology anyway. The salesperson spends a lot of time with the customer's technical people instead of concentrating on the business aspects of the sale.

"Salespeople have to have the broad overview of the objectives of the company. Even when technology acquisitions have been budgeted, they generally require the involvement of capital appropriations committees. In the past we would just go to the MIS director and explain the technology. But now, our competition often isn't another technology vendor, but rather other ways of spending the money that might have a bigger payoff.

"A recent example is an insurance company where we had gotten approval for a $1 million transaction from a CIO of the division. He had done million-dollar transactions in the past with no problem. We booked the forecasted sale, and he came to us later and said that he couldn't get the transaction done. The company had instituted a capital appropriations committee, which was reviewing the transaction with other types of capital expenditures. Originally, he had the budget and the authority, but now he didn't. It had nothing to do with what we were selling. We were able to go in and do a return-on-investment presentation and wound up getting the deal. It just reinforces the fact that we have to focus on understanding and satisfying the requirements of our clients."

The breakthrough pyramid

Another way to look at success in sales is to look at the breakthrough pyramid (shown on page 201). Each level builds on the levels below it and as each step is mastered, the salesperson breaks through to new success:

The numbers game. The first level of all sales is the ability to prospect and make sales presentations. At this level, a copier salesperson cold calls a prospect with a canned presentation that his or her equipment is the fastest, cheapest and best, then ends the pitch with, "Do you want it?" Occasionally someone does so. If the salesperson makes enough calls, he or she will be successful.

Relationship selling. This is the first breakthrough level of success. Salespeople who learn how to make their customers like, trust and respect them by providing extraordinary service, actively listening to their needs and always delivering what they promise, will be propelled to a higher level of success. At this level the copier salesperson finds out what his or her prospects need by listening to them and by having frequent customer-run meetings, building their trust through extraordinary service such as providing service on weekends, getting involved in the training and installation and by developing a regular customer survey program. The salesperson develops friendships and customer loyalty that leads to higher levels of success.

Solution selling. In the next breakthrough level, the salesperson uses his expert knowledge and creativity to solve problems and advance customer goals. When John Covell developed a way for his ice-cream customer to sell to the Cape Cod restaurants, he was selling a solution. The customer

The breakthrough pyramid

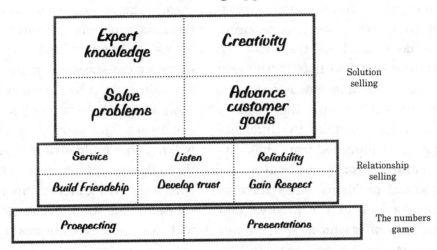

didn't care about the speed or enlarging capabilities of Covell's equipment; he didn't even completely understand Covell's commitment to extraordinary service. But, he did understand that Covell had just shown him a tool that would solve the business problem he had been struggling with. The solution broke through the barriers between prospect and salesperson. Adding the skills of solution selling to a solid base of relationship selling puts the salesperson in the top percentages of sales success.

As customers and prospects become more sophisticated, the tools and techniques salespeople use to gather and process information have to become more sophisticated. John Covell explains, "One of the key things that has changed in our industry is that we have a far more sophisticated buyer. We have a tremendous amount of product parity, and I don't think that's true in just our industry...it's true across many industries. I don't think any company can survive on the basis of price and product superiority alone. The customer is too sophisticated and facing some tough economic times. Tough times make for better business decisions; they buy less on emotion, less on razzle-dazzle. Closing techniques? Forget them. When I first started in the business, I listened to a tape on 400 different ways of closing. Frankly, today, simply closing without good development of customer needs, without understanding customer problems and without presenting good solutions, is not only going to be ineffective, it's going to destroy your chances of success.

"In the old days, you gave salespeople a lot of product training and taught them how to make benefit statements. You gave them some verbal skills and they could muddle through and be okay. Not today...not today," Covell observes. "We have to teach our people in a far more sophisticated way. What we are teaching them to do is think on their feet. To ask questions and to listen. Anybody can make a call and ask a question. Where the rubber hits the road is when they have to take the information they have gathered from that customer and interpret it and understand the potential problems. They have to then take a look at the product and services they offer and say, 'How can my products or services satisfy the needs of that organization?' In my industry, it isn't just understanding their needs for copy services—we have to understand the customer's business. The customers frankly don't care about copiers and fax machines or travel services or insurance—they only care about their business. To the extent

that your products and services can help them achieve the objectives of their business, you'll win their account."

As technology and our business environment become more complex, the value added by salespeople will be their ability to solve problems for their customers. The sales aces of the '90s will not only build strong relationships through uncommon service and support, they will generate breakthrough solutions for their customers. They will use new techniques and technologies to gather information and apply their creativity skills to finding solutions that advance their customers' goals. They will become star solution sellers.

"Imagination begets the event."
—Joe Wilson, president of
Haloid-Xerox, 1946

```
┌ ─ ─ ─ ─ ─ ─ ─ ─ ─ ─ ─ ─ ─ ┐
│          Two Ideas          │
└ ─ ─ ─ ─ ─ ─ ─ ─ ─ ─ ─ ─ ─ ┘
```

What two ideas did you get from this chapter?

_____

_____

I dare you to find a way to use one of these ideas to improve your creativity and problem solving abilities.

Nine-Dot Puzzle Answer

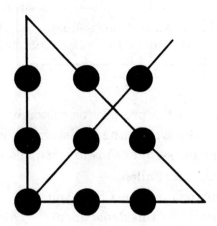

If you would like to pursue this puzzle even further, there are ways to connect the dots with three lines, with two lines and even with one line. James L. Adams, professor at Stanford University and leader in creativity and innovation development, in his book *Conceptual Blockbusting, A Guide to Better Ideas*, gives us several of his favorite answers and tells us that he is constantly getting new answers from people. He complains, "By now, I have received dozens of answers to this puzzle, all exceedingly clever and all depressing in that I had thought of none of them."

Action Plan

```
┌─────────────────────────────┐
│   Move Your Selling         │
│   Outside of the 9 Dot Box  │
└─────────────────────────────┘
```

1. Every time you meet with a prospect or customer, always be thinking, "How can I serve and advance the goals of this individual?" In other words, take the time to ask questions to learn about key needs:
   a. What is your greatest challenge?
   b. What do your customers expect from you?
   c. What are your goals for this department?
   d. What are the three most important criteria you are looking for in a vendor?

2. In business-to-business selling, understand what your *customer's* customer is all about. (i.e., the ice cream story)

3. Do something for your customers that has nothing to do with your product or service. For example, mail a magazine article to your customer on a topic that has to do with their hobbies or interests. Then attach a note that says, "Thought you might enjoy this."

4. Put together your own customer reference portfolio (see Chapter 5) and let your customers sell for you.

5. Start creating instead of competing. Look for ways to differentiate yourself through a unique service.

Selling beyond the 9 dots

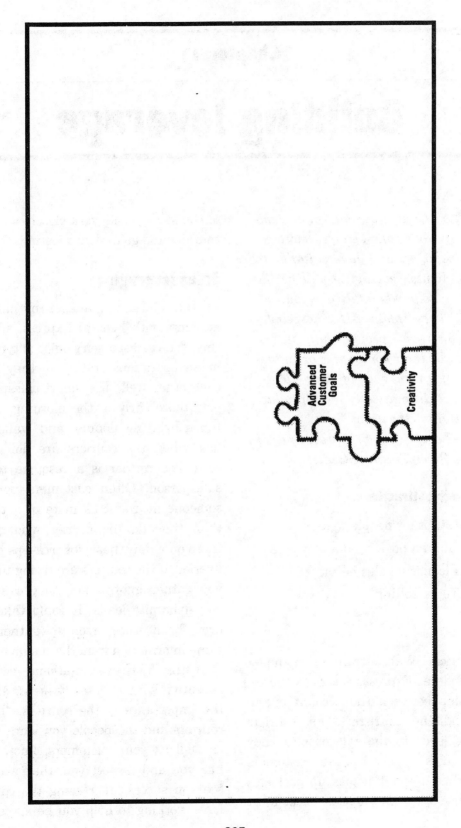

Chapter 11

Building leverage

"As business becomes more complex, as your time becomes more expensive to you and more valuable to your clients, leveraging will be the key to help you multiply your efforts. They (phase III salespeople) see far fewer people than is the norm for their companies or industries. But from each of their clients, they get dramatically more production than is the norm."

—*Larry Wilson, president of Pecos River Training Center*

Coming attractions:

♦ Get other people to help
♦ Build a positional advantage
♦ License a sales network
♦ Team selling

Patricia Walls, training manager with Federal Express, describes the relationship between the account executive and the couriers: "Our couriers provide leads to the salespeople. They make sales suggestions to customers when they drop off or pick up packages and they bring information back. Most of the salespeople work closely with the couriers and go to their meetings."

Sales leverage

Bill McHale, manager of national accounts with Federal Express, adds to this, "The salesperson's office is typically in an operations station so they know each other well. The smart salesperson gets there early in the morning, sometimes bringing donuts, and walks the belt when the couriers are doing the sort. The courier is a resource to the salesperson. Often customers perceive someone in a suit as more of a threat than they do the courier who comes there on a daily basis for pick-ups or deliveries. If the couriers are trying to help you gather information, they can give you dynamite leads. It could take forever for a salesperson to gather the same information from the customer."

Chris McKeever, national account executive with Federal Express, echoes the importance of the couriers, "If the couriers and the people you work with, as well as your customers, know you, like you and respect you, they want to see you successful. Having the courier force working to help you be successful is a real key for the account executive in the field. They will let you know where the business opportunities are, and do whatever they can to see to it that you capitalize on those opportunities. There are different ways to encourage the couriers to bring you leads, such as sales lead contests. But I think the real key is an interpersonal relationship with them. You attend their meetings and you know what they do and how their job works. Whenever possible, you make their jobs easier, because they can certainly make your job easier."

McKeever describes how he builds his relationship with the couriers. "One of the big keys is that you don't become separate and stand apart as the sales entity of the station. The couriers' jobs are intense and you don't want them to think of you as the salesperson who never gets his hands dirty. You have to teach them what constitutes a good sales lead and to focus on the quality of their sales leads versus the quantity."

Most of the top salespeople have found ways to leverage their success. Just as the salespeople at Federal Express enlist the aid of the couriers, salespeople from other industries have found a variety of ways to get the most return from their sales efforts. Most of the methods of developing leverage fall into the following categories:

- Help from other people
- Positional advantage
- Sales network
- Team selling

Getting help from other people

At Federal Express, the salespeople get a lot of help from the couriers. Any organization that has front-line people who spend a lot of time with customers can benefit from having those people become sales-oriented. Top organizations realize that everybody sells. Every person who talks to a customer is part of the sales process. Every accounting clerk who prepares an invoice is part of the sales process. Every warehouse person who goes home and talks to his or her neighbor about how good (or bad) the company is, is part of the sales process.

The top salespeople find ways to get everyone in the organization enlisted in helping them be a success. But they also find people outside their organizations to help them. Charlie Garrison, one of the top 10 agents with Farmers Insurance (out of more than 13,000 agents nationally) leveraged himself by enlisting the help of real estate agents. "Initially when I started," explains Garrison, "I called on realtors because their clients were buying homes and we had a competitive fire coverage policy. I let them know I could deliver that product for them. I developed about 20 to 25 real estate offices that I started dealing with. I would take donuts in and scratch pads and get to know them. I also took some real estate courses—all of the required courses for the broker's exam. I didn't take the exam because I wanted to be a competitor; I wanted to be a communicator and know their language. The classes gave me a chance to rub shoulders with many realtors and I used that as a way to leverage my business."

Garrison also leveraged himself by targeting a niche where his efforts would have the most impact. He developed an expertise in apartment insurance requirements. "We chose to target certain areas," states Garrison, "where we felt we could sell more effectively per client visit. At the time the most competitive product we had was for large apartment complexes. We established certain staff people as experts in that line. They developed expertise in apartment insurance requirements and knew it better than anyone else."

Perhaps the largest group of people you can have helping your sales efforts are your customers. Sometimes this is the hardest group to get help from. You can ask for referrals but to really have leverage working for you, customers need to enthusiastically promote you and your product or service. This is not an easy proposition. But it's the strategy being taken by Saturn Corporation. Saturn, a subsidiary of General Motors, is trying to revolutionize the American auto industry. Today, when only one-fourth of the world's cars come from America, Saturn's mission is: "We're going to build a better American car...however it has to be done."

Saturn has a monumental task—not only building a better car but also to overcome the years of disappointment and disenchantment that cling to the image of American cars. And, if that task isn't big enough, Saturn is also challenging a sales process that is primitive, adversarial, unsavory and often dishonest. If you ask any 10 people if they would rather go car shopping or to the dentist, many would choose the dentist...or at least hesitate. Saturn dedicated a team of 99 people to its development project. This team spent 50,000 hours traveling 2 million miles detailing what it would take to build a successful new car. They weren't about to throw their new car into an old sales process, especially not one that reeked of manipulation and questionable sales tactics.

In order to build a fresh, modern sales process to go with the revolutionary Saturn, it is choosing a new breed of dealer to help build customer enthusiasm. Nanette Wiatr, west coast manager of public relations for Saturn, explains that Saturn wants the entire retail experience of the customer to be different, from the appearance of the facility inside and out to the way the customer is greeted on entering the building. They want the customer to have an exceptional experience—not only when they are buying the vehicle but also when they are bringing it back for routine servicing or repair. To dramatically demonstrate their difference, Saturn developed its test-drive program.

Customers can test-drive a new car for 30 days and if they aren't completely happy, they can return it, no questions asked.

One of the dealers Saturn chose was Charlie McLean, owner of a Buick dealership. McLean had a totally different approach to selling cars, even when he started 27 years ago. For years he only had women salespeople and refused to hire anyone who had ever sold cars before. McLean invites customers to monthly customer meetings where they get a chance to meet everyone in the operation, ask questions and just socialize.

Dan Wade, who was the manager of McLean's Buick dealership, was chosen to manage the new Saturn dealership. He describes their sales environment, "We develop a family atmosphere and people come to the monthly meetings because they're part of the family. We get about 60 people at the monthly meetings, as many as 500 at the quarterly meetings and when we had our 25th anniversary, we had over a 1,000 people there."

At Wade's Saturn dealership, the employees wear T-shirts with their names on the sleeve, and the sales staff is a team with no individual commissions (no sharks lurking on the tarmac waiting for unsuspecting targets). Wade believes that you can't sell anyone anything, you can only help them buy. You can help them buy by understanding what they want and need, and by helping them meet their needs with your product. Bob Chappelle works with Wade as the director of sales and training. He looks for an unusual quality in his sales staff—compassion. He avoids trained car salespeople, preferring to train new people the Saturn way. One new member of his sales staff has a background as a men's counselor.

A challenge for Chappelle is overcoming the preconceived notions that customers have of a car dealership. Chappelle says, "Truth is action. We have to be the change we want to create. People believe the action they see. They see a 30-day trial period with no questions asked if they aren't happy with the car; they see salespeople treating them with respect and dignity, trying to help them rather than sell them; they see everyone at the dealership involved with the sales process; they see a total commitment to service and support."

I say!

But just helping people get what they want doesn't make them go out and talk about you. You have to delight them; you have to make an emotional connection. Wade talks about bonding with the customer and tells us about a unique process called "I Say!" "Even after a sale is done and all the paperwork is complete," explains Wade, "you still don't feel like part of their family. It is still just a business transaction. To really connect you have to celebrate yourselves. It's time to make sure that your customer understands that you are going to be there, no matter what. It's time to have an event that we all share in—all the sales team, all the service team, everyone around here and the customer. It lets them know that we are all responsible for it."

The process that helps them bond reportedly comes from a Navajo ritual. Everyone in the facility comes to the new car as it is being delivered and they stand around the car with the customer and give the following cheer: "I say! I say! I say (customer's name)!" Wade explains that this is their way of celebrating their emotional commitment to the customer. "Unless there is emotion," states Wade, "there is nothing. We've had customers cry at this ceremony. It is that unusual and that powerful. Of course we have to live up to the commitment and responsibility behind that cheer."

Kelly Davis, who recently purchased a new Saturn, practically gushes about the car and the dealership. "Everyone was so friendly; they were like a family. They were willing to answer questions and they weren't pushy. They told me they would take care of everything and if I ever needed to, I could borrow a car. They were really eager to help. When they washed the car and brought it around front, I was really embarrassed because I knew they were going to do the 'I Say!' I turned red but it really felt

good." Davis knew about the "I Say!" because a friend had told her—all of a sudden, people are talking about something that's going on at a car dealership...something good. And, that's leverage—customer leverage.

While it is still too early to make many conclusions about the success of Saturn, Wiatr states that initial customer surveys show that 97 percent of the customers would enthusiastically recommend the purchase of a Saturn to their friends, and 96 percent would enthusiastically recommend that Saturn dealership. Dan Wade sums up the enthusiasm, the commitment and the excitement felt by everyone connected with Saturn by saying, "This is going to be the damnedest thing people have ever seen."

Administrative support

Another way we found the top sales stars get help is in administrative support. Star salespeople know that the activities that build their success are customer activities—building relationships, understanding needs, presenting solutions and providing service. But a lot of other "stuff" goes on in a salesperson's day—reports, paperwork, maintenance. All of this has to be done, but none of it leads to more sales. The average salesperson works very hard to keep up with all the paperwork and administrative requirements, sacrificing some customer time. The super star, however, gets help from someone else—help that leaves him or her free to focus on sales activities.

Too often, the average sales performer has an 'I have to do it myself' attitude, so precious time is spent doing mailings, beating the bushes, scheduling appointments and dotting "i's" and crossing "t's" on reports. The stars spend their time doing the customer activities that count and developing high leverage inside their firm, with key contacts and with customers.

In order to make sure this necessary, but often time-consuming paperwork and administrative detail gets done accurately and quickly, the best salespeople know that it's as important to build that "team" feeling with administrative staff as it is with customers. Top sales stars treat those individuals whose responsibilities are to handle the follow-up with respect, and involve them as much as possible in the sales effort, so that it is as important to them that the customers needs are met effectively.

Build a positional advantage

Once you have built relationships and established an account that recognizes the benefits of your product or service, it becomes much easier to leverage that position to other parts of the company that may need the same product or service. This is a positional advantage.

"Often the way it works," states Rick Dyer with Apple, "is that you find a way to enter into the division or company with a specific application. The first thing you want to do is to make sure that the people are completely happy with that application. That involves committing resources and time to follow-up to be sure that the installation is going very successfully. The next step is to leverage that success across the organization by getting access to other decision-makers and understanding more and more about the business they are in. It just takes brute force labor to go out there and understand more about the customer from as many levels as you possibly can. The road map to an organization is the organization chart and understanding what is going on in each department. You have to know what their prejudices are and what criteria they are using to make decisions."

Carl Herman, national account sales manager with Oracle USA, gives us another slant on how leverage within an organization works. Herman's career includes many awards, and, last year, he was at 300 percent of quota, selling more than $5 million of software services. Herman has one customer—Texaco. However, Texaco has 46 operating units. "What makes me valuable to Texaco is the relationship we have and the understanding and overview we have of its entire business," he states.

"One subsidiary that we worked with," explains Herman, "was having trouble with tracking its properties—it owned more than 14,000 service stations and these were constantly being bought and sold. The company's inability to track these properties accurately was causing problems with property taxes and it was paying more tax than it should. It was developing an Oracle-based *ad valorem* tax system, but it was not going well.

"The manager of the subsidiary was furious with Oracle and believed that it was all our fault. The process of working with this unit and working out the problem was not a matter of waving a wand and making the problem go away. It took a year to get the application right. But by paying attention to the guy and not being afraid to talk to him because he was mad, we started to make progress. We had weekly status meetings—some of them bloody and all of them long—for a year.

"One of the things that is very important in putting together a solution for a client is working with more people than just the client. We wound up working with Texaco's accounting firm, two other developer contractors and the hardware vendor. We worked with all of them to deliver a solution that worked for the client. In the end it did work and has proven to be very beneficial from a cost standpoint—to the tune of $2 million to $3 million per year. The relationship with the project manager wound up being great; he has been offered a promotion and we felt that our project helped that happen. He is now an almost fanatical fan of Oracle and will be taking Oracle applications with him to his new location."

When Herman's client takes Oracle applications to his new location, it is an example of leverage. It may have taken a lot of hard work and effort to get this application right but selling the next application will be easy. The relationship and the trust has been established to make ongoing business automatic.

Develop a sales network

Sometimes you can certify customers to sell your product or service within their organization. The certification process normally includes a special training program in order to represent your product or service. They can then sell the program throughout their organization at a discount from your normal fees. Although the per-unit fee is less, the client has a high level of commitment and ownership in the program. Kim Lundgreen explains how this works for him at Franklin.

"I've leveraged my success," states Lundgreen, "by using our video- and client-facilitated training. We license the client to provide their own training, and I've got 31 people that I've certified in different companies to teach our course. With the 30 companies that have also purchased video licenses, it means I've got about 50 trainers out there training for me. For every person they train, I get a commission. At the highest level of our commission structure, we receive two-

and-a-half times the commission per person trained as at the lowest level. So having all these people training (and in effect selling) for me guarantees me that I'll be at those higher levels. Business comes in automatically now, and the client facilitators can train in ways that are more convenient for their company. My key is to make sure I get the right people certified. Last month about two-thirds of my sales were sold by people I had certified."

Betty Stuart, sales manager with Avon, says that her most successful representatives use leverage. "A lot of the really successful representatives actually have a sales network: people who help them sell. Some of my representatives have "helpers"—individuals who don't want to be representatives but will take a book to work or show it to their family and friends and bring orders back to the rep."

Team selling

Sometimes leverage comes from being able to provide the client with information, skills and services. This can generally only be done by a highly qualified team. Understanding the needs of major accounts is a complex, time-consuming process, demanding a multitude of talents. Carl Herman with Oracle USA has a team of five who spend all of their time finding ways to help Texaco. Federal Express often applies a team of specialists to analyzing the needs and requirements

of a prospective client. Larry Wilson, founder of Pecos River Learning Center, is a pioneer in the field of creating sales teams. Wilson started in sales as an insurance agent in the mid-'50s. He has seen a lot of change since then, and influenced much of that change through his books and consulting.

Wilson describes his early days, "Clearly, the underlying philosophies and values that were taught then were adversarial. It was very much a battle orientation: the customer had my money in his pocket and I had to do everything possible to get it out. All the training was manipulative—trying to talk people into doing things they didn't want to do. What was being passed off as sales training was almost like karate training and based on conflict.

"I was taught all of that and given memorized sales presentations. What I quickly learned was that I knew my lines but the customers didn't always know theirs. So, it didn't work. The orientation was to find someone who fit my presentation. It wasn't until I learned to fit my presentation and my whole being to the person I was with that I began to be successful. I became the youngest lifetime member of the million-dollar roundtable. At that time, that was a real achievement.

"Because of this success," Wilson continues, "I was asked to do a lot of speaking, and one company asked me to develop a sales training program. I didn't really know what good sales training was, so I started looking for a new model. I knew that what I was taught wasn't working. The universe usually comes through when we open our minds to input, and mine came when I was walking by a bookstore at the University of Minnesota. They were having a sale on books and there were tables of books on the sidewalk. I remember I was walking briskly because I was late, but I turned to one of those tables and picked up one book. It was a book of readings on psychology and I opened the book to one of the readings. The article was entitled, 'The Hierarchy of Relative Prepotency.' It was an article by Abraham Maslow, referring to his hierarchy of needs. This was in 1961 and I had never heard of him. As I was reading, it hit me that this was the flashlight I was looking for. I called Maslow and told him what I was trying to do, and he invited me to come see him at Brandeis. As I was waiting for him, he rushed into the ante room, handed me an article and said, 'Read this and you will make a million dollars!' It was called 'Metamotivation or Beyond the Pyramid.'

"We spent an incredible day together," recalls Wilson. "He talked with me as though we were totally equal. As he told me about himself and his philosophy, I realized that counseling was a perfect model for selling. It described what we were doing when we were at our best. It was process-oriented—processes have to happen in order to have success. There has to be trust based on what the counselor's and the client's intentions are. The counselor has to understand the goals, objectives, problems and barriers in order to help the person. The counselor has to understand what is preventing the person from getting what it is they want. There is an information discovery process. The best counselors use a client-centered listening and questioning process. The goal of the counselor is to help the client understand, to help pinpoint what it is that is going on. Mutual discovery is critical as a well-defined problem is more than half-solved.

"Good counselors help the client explore options and possibilities," Wilson explains. "They do not force the client into an option. They develop a mutual criteria and look at options and consequences against that criteria. They also support the client through the process of change. This was a totally new way of looking at the sales process, but one that made sense. People love to buy as long as the barriers of no trust, no need, no help and no hurry are not in their way. As counselors, we are trying to help people do what they love to do. It is a problem-solving approach...a win-win, value-added approach. We introduced this in 1962 and, back then, it was a very hard sell. Eventually, counselor selling became a revolutionary product."

While changing the culture of sales has been like turning a battleship around, Wilson has seen most of the industry come to more of a customer-focused, counselor-selling approach.

Now he is championing sales teams. He gives one example from Kraft, where he was hired by Mike Szymanczyk to help create "the world's greatest sales force." Wilson says, "That got my attention; especially since he had 2,500 salespeople. This is the story of the food industry. Historically, the manufacturers in the food industry had the gun. Their customer is the retailer, and the marketing department of the big food companies were the people with the power. They would market a product using a television blitzkrieg with enormous ad budgets. The sales force would tell the retailers that a huge demand was coming because of the ad blitz. The retailers were at the mercy of this blitzkrieg and they would have to stock the product.

"The salesperson's job was to fill the shelves and get out. What has happened is that the media blitz doesn't work anymore. The three major stations have lost market share and power. While 70 percent of the money was spent on television and 30 percent on promotions, today it is the reverse. Promotions mean you give the retailers money and hope they spend the money to promote your product. The power has shifted to the retailers. When scanning came into being, the retailers acquired precise information that the manufacturer now has to buy from the retailers.

"The sales force that had been effective in the blitzkrieg days was no longer effective. Salespeople discovered that they had to sit down with the customers and find out what they wanted. There were multiple buying influences and Kraft was deploying people to each of these. But the Kraft people weren't talking to each other. They needed a team to call on the various influences, and efforts had to be coordinated. Creating a sales team meant someone had to give up some turf, and the prior way of doing things had to change. A major shift had to take place.

"One of the first things they had to do was create a bonded team. They also had to create a set of skills for their team. We helped them create a program we called partnership selling. The goal was to create a long-term, mutually beneficial customer-focused partnership. The first requirement was to bond the team; the second was to be able to manage information and turn it into opportunities; and the third was to create a plan, which was often done with the customer; and the fourth was to implement the plan.

"These skills turn the salespeople into marketers, but they were all new skills for the sales force. Management also had to change to manage the empowered teams. The transformation has been very profitable for Kraft. It started making its quota, and its future is more assured," Wilson states.

As products and services become more technical and customers demand a strategic partnership, team selling will become a major force. Team selling will revolutionize the way salespeople work together, the way they interact with customers and the way they are compensated. The leverage that comes from team selling is the synergy that happens when the talents and ideas of several people are dedicated to needs of the customer.

What many people call a sales team, however, is just a group of salespeople working together. What does it take to get the leverage that comes from having an effective team? When Carl Herman of Oracle USA was asked how he knew his group was a team, he stated, "Because we have a strategy. We have a plan and we are executing the plan and the plan has a certain task for each person. We have also been very selective about who we have added to the team." Byron Lane, in his book, *Managing People*, gives us some questions to ask to determine whether we have a team:

♦ Do members really listen, trying to understand the points of view, objectives and preferred solutions of others?

♦ Are people being candid—saying what they want to say all of the time rather than being guarded?

♦ To what extent are members trying to find an innovative, mutually acceptable solution rather than fighting for their own individual preference?

♦ How well can each member state the position of another (see the issue from his point of view)?

♦ Are conflicts settled by win-lose confrontation, negotiation and compromise, or creative problem-solving using consensus?

♦ When the going gets rough, do they use a third party to help them find a mutually acceptable solution?

♦ Once a solution is reached, is everybody really buying in, or is there residual hostility that will inhibit its implementation?

♦ Are there power struggles, or is everyone focusing on organizational results?

♦ When decisions are reached, does everyone join in the implementation and follow-through?

Sales has historically been a profession of individualists. The change to more of a team-based approach will require a lot of new talents and ideas. Management will have to come up with new approaches to delegating authority and responsibility. New compensation programs will have to be designed.

The breakthrough pyramid II

Partnership selling—getting customers and others actively involved with the sales process—is the last block of the breakthrough pyramid. The salesperson who reaches this level has a solid basis of relationship skills and provides his or her customers with expert knowledge and creativity. Then he or she goes the next step and finds ways to leverage these efforts.

The breakthrough pyramid II

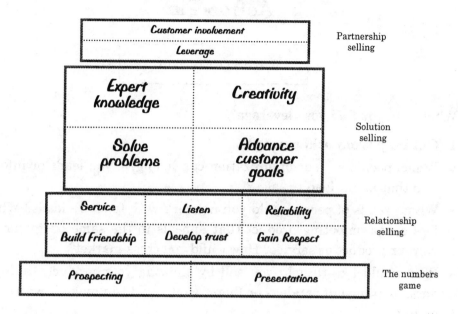

Whether the leverage comes from putting together high-powered sales teams to respond to a wide range of customer needs or getting customers to enthusiastically recommend your product or service, it can magnify your efforts. Sales stars find ways to achieve success that would be impossible by individual efforts alone, just as a lever helps us lift an object that would be too heavy to lift by ourselves.

"Give me a rod long enough and a place to stand and I will move the earth."

—Archimedes, Greek mathematician

Two Ideas:

What two ideas did you get from this chapter?

_____

_____

I dare you to find a way to use one of these ideas to improve your success level.

Action Plan

```
┌─────────────────────────────────────┐
│         Leverage Checklist          │
└─────────────────────────────────────┘
```

Where can you find your leverage?

1. **Get help from other people.**

- Which people in your organization can help give you leads or information that might lead to sales?

- What groups of people could you network with to share leads? Who offers a noncompeting product that appeals to the same customer base as your product or service? How could you cross-market?

- Who would like to help you sell by showing your product, taking orders, handing out catalogs or fliers? How could you make it worth their while?

- How could you make your customers so enthusiastic about your product or service that they would recommend you to all their friends, neighbors and relatives?

- Who could help you with your administrative stuff? What activities could you contract out or hire an assistant for?

- Who could you get referrals from that you're not getting them from now?

2. **Develop positional advantage.**

- What companies do you have an account with that have other departments, divisions or subsidiaries? Who could introduce you to someone in those other areas?

- What other products or services do you offer that your present client base might need?

3. **Build a sales network.**

- How could you build a sales network? How would they be certified? What would be the pay-off to them? What would it cost you?

- Who offers a complementary product who might be interested in carrying yours?

- Who needs your product or service on such a wide basis that it would make sense for them to have internal control?

4. **Develop a customer-focused sales team.**

♦ How can you build a sales team that will be able to meet customer needs more effectively?

♦ What team-building processes will be needed to bond the group into an effective team?

♦ What new skills will the team need?

♦ What new compensation plans will be needed to effectively reward the team efforts?

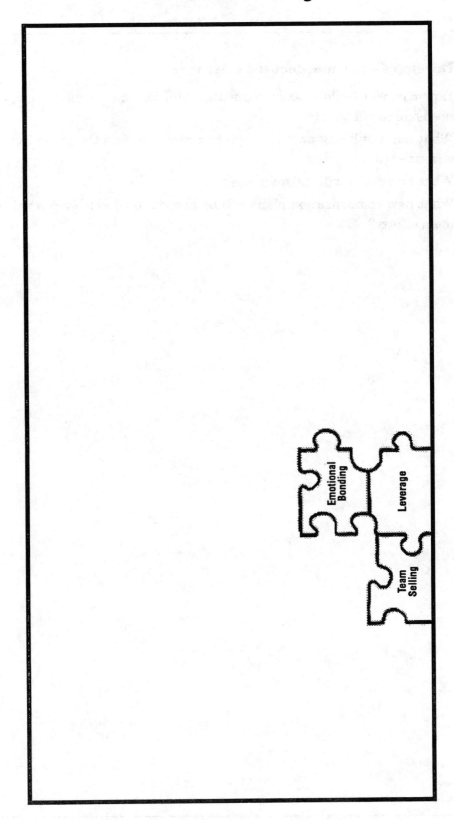

Chapter 12

Lucky breaks

"Luck: When opportunity meets preparation."
—*Bill Wayland, senior vice president, Textron*

Coming attractions:

- Blue darters
- Putting it all together
- I dare you!

When Federal Express landed the account for the second largest chemical company in Germany only months after landing the account with the largest chemical company in Germany, everyone thought they were lucky. However, they had spent three years working on the first account and built such a strong relationship with that client that their way was paved with the second company.

When Marc Roberts signed three Olympic boxing champions, some people thought it was a lucky break. After all, he was up against some of the most experienced, best-known boxing men in the business. However, even though Marc wasn't yet 30 when he signed them, he had been in the boxing business over 10 years.

Literary agent Jeff Herman got lucky early in his career as an agent. "My first big success was selling 165,000 copies of one book to Coors. At the time, I didn't realize what a phenomenal deal it was. But afterward I learned that it was actually almost a record. I felt it was almost an accident. People kept asking me how I did it, and, to be honest, the only thing I did was write a lot of letters. I learned that you have to plant a lot of good seeds. Some of them are going to sprout and it's going to look like you were a genius. But the real smarts was the hard work and doing a lot of things."

Herman sounds modest, and he is, but it took a lot of creativity to connect a book on finding a job to a brewing company. Herman says, "I thought the book was perfect for career-oriented students and would be a great marketing vehicle for companies that wanted to reach them." He looked at book marketing in a different way and found a problem that matched his solution.

Hard work and creativity are paying off for Herman as his agency grows at a lightning clip. He sold more than 90 books in his first three years in business and reached 250 books by 1994. "Even better," says Herman, "is that our book advances are getting bigger." Herman has been extremely successful at attracting authors, primarily because of the promotion work he has done. "I've marketed myself to various networks and individuals," he explains. "I started doing that almost immediately—working to get publicity for myself. I got as many magazine clips as I could in order to start building my credibility." Herman has published his own book, titled *The Insider's Guide to Editors and Publishers*. "It was an idea I had for a long time," Herman explains, "because there is nothing out there for writers telling them who the editors are. The essence of the book is a data base of key editors at the major publishing houses, who they are, what they want and how to win them over. Some people might ask why an agent would give that information away because then maybe a writer wouldn't need an agent. I still think that writers need an agent, but in some cases getting an agent is tougher than finding a publisher. And the book is excellent marketing for me. In order to succeed, you have to build a name.

"I wanted to attract authors because I knew my first priority was to get quality projects. With the right products, I knew I could develop quality relationships. I only accept material that I believe I can sell. I have to reject some good material just because there is no market for it. Less than 1 percent of the American population buys books and, to be a bestseller, you only need to sell 50,000 copies. Publishing has an enormous influence on our culture, but dollar-wise it is one of the smallest industries in the country. I take chances and I go with my hunches, but I have to reject about 98 percent of the material I see."

Sometimes it takes a lot of persistence to make his hunches take off. One book Herman liked went through nineteen rejections before being accepted. "It was *How to Stay Lovers While Raising Your Children* by Anne Mayer," he explains. "The twentieth publisher loved it and bought it. It's going to be their lead title and the Literary Guild has picked it up. You just can't give up." Because he believed in Mayer's project, he persisted until he found the right publisher for it.

Blue darters

In baseball language a blue darter is a zinger with eyes, a hit that finds just the right hole...a lucky hit. Salespeople are often credited with blue darters when what they really have is a success based on a lot of hard work and imagination. Marsha Londe hit a blue darter not long after she started in the advertising speciality business. "It was telephone numbers," Londe laughs. "That's what we call it when it is a really big order." Londe is an extraordinarily successful advertising speciality salesperson with Shadco Advertising Specialties, Inc. Her personal sales level is higher than many of the distributor firms that sell advertising specialities.

Londe differentiates herself from the more than 150 other specialty advertising firms in the Atlanta area with service and creativity. "I tell my clients up front that I may not be the cheapest person they could do business with," Londe explains, "but I'm going to be the most thorough. I'll follow through, and they will have service and attention to detail. I tell them that I will think creatively with them. I try to give them something a little different. Again, that's service." Londe follows through on the basics, tracking orders to their completion, letting her customers know when an order is being shipped and calling to make sure that it arrived and that it was exactly what the customer wanted.

In a business that often goes for the quick order, Londe spends time finding out what the customer really needs. "People tell me that nobody asks as many questions as I do," she explains. "I take notes when they tell me about their business and their needs. I find them creative solutions to their situations, and I am also unfailingly honest."

Her "telephone number" success came from a grocery store account where she had to turn down its first order. "They had an impossible deadline. I did everything I could with the factory to see if we could do it, but it was just impossible. Because I was honest with them, they gave me several additional orders. And, through the regional office, I got wind of a major project—a custom calendar that the home office wanted."

Originally, Londe was told that there was no way she was capable of handling this size order, but she developed an idea, found a factory to help her put together a prototype and developed a proposal. "Selling is a gamble—you've got to take chances," she says. "I called the customer and he said to send him the proposal and he would tell me if it was worth flying up to see him. After he got it, he called and said 'It's time for you to fly up.' The calendar is now in its fifth year. We were the mid-priced bid, but we presented creativity and outstanding service. We were able to be creative because we listened to the customer's needs." Londe was selected as the "Outstanding Salesperson for 1990" by *Counselor Magazine*, the trade publication for the advertising specialty industry.

Carl Herman with Oracle USA was awarded a $3.5 million order in spite of some technical difficulties with the account. While this looks like a lucky break, it actually rests on a unique quality program Oracle implemented with Texaco. Herman describes this unusual vendor-client quality program, "We were having delivery problems, quality problems, shipping problems, order entry problems, a lot of different problems typical of a rapidly growing company. At an internal Texaco meeting where all of the computer users from all over the country attended, we were hearing about these problems. We decided that we needed to do something. At the same time, there was a lot of conversation going on about quality because Texaco is very quality process-oriented and it was interested in applying for the Malcolm Baldridge award."

"We decided what we needed to do was to come up with a quality process to fix the problems that would, at the same time, help Texaco with its quality program. We also felt that while we did have some quality problems, we weren't getting recognition for the things we were doing *right*. We felt that putting together a quality process would give us a way to measure both the things we were doing wrong and the things we were doing right."

Herman describes the process of developing the program, "The account team put together a proposal document for Oracle and Texaco, stating who we thought needed to be on the committee and identified the problems that we knew needed to be addressed. It was lengthy but well-received by both companies. Our president has stated that the '80s was the decade of growth and the '90s will be the decade of quality, so it fit well with what he had in mind. And Jim Metzger, the CEO for Texaco, was saying the same things. Also, when he had his quality audit by the quality management

committee at Texaco, the findings were that his internal quality processes were really good, but one of his weaknesses was that he had little quality involvement with his vendors. The timing was great. Timing is critical—especially in relationships. He thought it was a wonderful proposal and he made sure that it happened.

"Since November I have spent between 20 percent and 30 percent of my time on this project we call QUEST (Quality Ensured Star Enterprise and Texaco). An interesting thing that happened was that Oracle had applied for an industry quality award and one of the things required was a customer mentor. Oracle needed to have a customer that was involved with our quality process. We decided to use Texaco and they sent two of their quality gurus to California to audit Oracle's quality processes. That was good because they were very impressed with what we were doing, and that added to the credibility of the quality program."

Back to the $3.5 million deal that Herman was awarded. "Yesterday, the project manager turned to me and said, 'If we did not have QUEST, I'd be telling you to go jump in a lake and this deal would not happen. But, because I believe in the quality process we're putting in place, I believe that these problems will be resolved and our relationship deserves to be a long-term strategic one. So we will continue with this.'

"What this quality process has really done," explains Herman, "is significantly raise the cost of entry for any competitor in the account. The risk of buying from a competitor now is significantly more than the risk of buying from Oracle now that we have this quality program in place." Oracle has gone from being just another vendor to being almost an internal part of the Texaco organization.

Herman says, "Part of this process was to facilitate better communications between the organizations, and we now have access to each other's electronic mail. That's an amazing change. Now, someone in Texaco's computer department can send a message to someone in Oracle's development department about something he or she would like to see done with the product." It's hard for the competition to compete with that kind of strategic involvement.

Blue darters happen when just the right fit between customer needs and product or service benefits occur. But they can also happen when your competition gets complacent and slacks up on service and support. Kevin Patterson with Marriott is a superb builder of relationships and recognizes the importance of regular face-to-face contacts. One of Kevin's target customers had been a loyal client of a competing hotel chain for over 10 years. Kevin began calling on the customer shortly after the competitor's account rep had retired. The new rep was located at some distance from the customer and was concentrating on other accounts. "I started calling on the customer and told him that I would like to understand his business," explains Kevin. "Over the three to six months that I was calling on the customer, the competitor had still not called on the account. By the time the other rep finally called on him, we had 10 meetings signed for a total of 28,000 roomnights. And, by that time, the first year the customer could discuss business with the competitor was 1999!"

Sometimes, blue darters happen in spite of the opposition all around you. When Haloid (the precursor to Xerox) neared the end of development for its first commercial office copier, the 914, it decided to try to joint-venture with a company that had manufacturing capabilities. It approached IBM, which hired the prestigious, management consulting firm Arthur D. Little to do a study of the potential market. The conclusion of the study was that the machine was far too large and expensive to find a market. The study stated that the nation's total demand, then and in the future, could be satisfied by a maximum of 5,000 machines. The bottom line was that the model 914 had no future in the office copying market. So much for expert opinion.

In Chapter 1, we met Albert (Smitty) Smith with the Marriott Marquis Hotel in Atlanta. Some people think Smitty is lucky since he gets to meet stars from around the world—

the star sports teams from baseball, basketball and football and individual greats from Evander Holyfield and Mohammed Ali to Pearl Bailey and Nelson Mandela. When Atlanta decided to make a bid for the 1996 Summer Olympics, Smitty was chosen to be one of the committee's delegates and he traveled with the committee to Seoul, Tokyo and San Juan. In 1992, he was with the committee at the Olympics in Barcelona, Spain.

It seems like a lucky break for a concierge captain to travel the world with the top movers and shakers from Atlanta. But when you watch Smitty, you understand that he is always selling—himself, the Marriott Marquis, Atlanta. From the first moment you see him in his white gloves, tux and medallion (one of his several Olympic medallions or the very special JW Marriott award) you know he is someone special. Smitty's walk is an energetic, joyful bounce. He doesn't greet guests, he envelopes them—in hugs, concern for their welfare and warmth. He is constantly in motion, juggling a thousand details and yet he has an intense way of focusing on you that makes you feel like you are the only person in the world and the only person he has to think about at that moment. When Atlanta wanted to demonstrate its hospitality, its commitment to service, its attention to detail, it chooses Smitty.

Some may think that Smitty got a lucky break, but they don't see the dedication and energy it takes to juggle the schedules of arriving teams, events and individual needs, or the long hours and meticulous attention to detail that his hospitality program requires. As Bill Wayland said at the beginning of this chapter, lucky breaks come when opportunity meets preparation. We can control our preparation, and the universe gives us opportunities.

Putting it all together

What's the key to sales success? If there is a key to success, it's that the top sales stars differentiate themselves. They find ways to let the customers know that they are different in the way they approach the customer, in the way they work to understand the customer's needs and problems, in the way they find solutions to those problems and the way they provide service. As we have seen in these chapters, differentiation comes in a multitude of different forms—from unusual business cards to an in-depth questioning process, from providing chocolate lobsters to finding a creative way to sell ice cream.

But there really isn't a *key* to success. Success in sales is more like a jigsaw puzzle with a lot of pieces. Differentiation is the center piece, and all the other pieces revolve around it. The more pieces you have in place, the clearer will be the picture (success). With lots of pieces missing, it may be very difficult to see what's going on. So here's a review of some of the critical pieces to the sales success jigsaw puzzle:

Corner pieces. The first pieces we need to put into place to anchor the puzzle are the corner pieces representing the STAR qualities: *service motivation*; *tuned-in, empathetic*; *action bias*; and *rejection tolerance*.

Border pieces. The size of our puzzle is determined by the border pieces. In sales, the size of our success is determined by our ability to build relationships. And relationships depend on our being liked, trusted and respected. Border pieces include honesty, concern for the needs of the customer and integrity. They include your networking abilities, your attitude, your enthusiasm and your vision for your product. They also include your information gathering abilities.

Pattern pieces. The pieces that make up the picture fall into five categories: service, expert knowledge, organization, problem-solving and creativity.

Unlike the puzzle you buy from your local toy store, if a piece is missing from your puzzle, you can create a new one. As they say, "It's not over till the fat lady sings." And, until that final song, we all have the opportunity to fill in the blanks and develop new pieces.

I dare you!

I started this book telling you about William Danforth and his book, *I Dare You!* I told you about how Danforth's life was changed because of a dare issued to him by one of his teachers. Danforth took this dare, grabbed hold of the challenge and developed the life that he wanted to live. He not only created a healthy body and a successful company, he also created a balanced life that brought positive benefits to everyone it touched. I would like to issue a challenge to you...

I dare you to use this book and the ideas in it to break through to new levels of success, to develop the kind of life that you want to lead, to become a positive force in the life of each person you meet.

Please let us hear from you as you break through your barriers.

Write to :

Farber Training Systems, Inc.
250 Ridgedale Avenue, Suite Q5
Florham Park, NJ 07932
Attn.: Gayle Gardner

"I am a great believer in luck, and I find the harder I work the more I have of it."
—*Thomas Jefferson, third President of the United States*

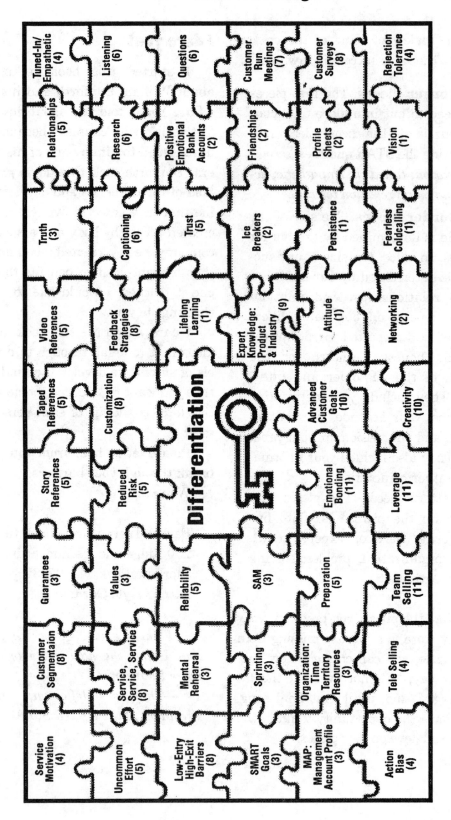

Resources

Chapter 1

I Dare You!, Danforth, William, American Youth Foundation, 1985.

"Everybody Sells," *Success*, DeGarmo, Scott, May 1991.

Perot, Mason, Todd, Dow-Jones Irwin, 1990.

Chapter 2

"Passing Thoughts," Russell, Peter, Volume 1, 1989.

Chapter 3

The Secrets of Subconscious Selling, A Cutting-Edge Approach to Selling Yourself, Your Ideas and Your Product, Corson, Lynea, Ph.D., Hadley, George, Ed.D, Stevens, Carl, CPAE, Berkley Publishing Group, 1991.

Personal Selling Power, "Using Tape Recorded Interviews Can Give You a Competitive Selling Edge," Farber, Barry J., May/June 1988.

Peak Performance: Mental Training Techniques of the World's Greatest Athletes, Garfield, Charles with Bennett, Hal Zina, Warner Books, 1984.

Peak Performers, The New Heroes of American Business, Garfield, Charles, William Morrow and Company, Inc., 1986.

Unlimited Power, Robbins, Anthony, Ballantine Books, New York, 1986.

Chapter 4

Flow, The Psychology of Optimal Experience, Csikszentmihalyi, Mihaly, Harper & Row, Publishers, 1990.

Reseller Management, "Creative Account Management: The Writing's on the Wall!," Farber, Barry J., May 1991.

Sales & Marketing Management, "Sales Force Turnover," Nov. 1989.

Chapter 6

The Little, Brown Book of Anecdotes, Fadiman, Clifton, ed., Little Brown & Company, 1985.

SPIN Selling, Rackham, Neil, McGraw-Hill Book Company, 1988.

Making People Talk, Farber, Barry M., William Morrow & Co., Inc., 1987.

How to Look Things Up and Find Things Out, Quill, Felknor, Bruce L., William Morrow, 1988.

"Everybody Sells," *Success*, DeGarmo, Scott, May 1991.

Chapter 7

Reseller Management, "Customer-Run Sales Training," Farber, Barry J., & Wycoff, Joyce, December 1990.

"Getting Face-to-Face with Customers," *Sales & Marketing Management*, February 1991.

Chapter 8

"How America's Best Companies Get Better," *Business Week*, Sept. 14, 1987.

Total Customer Service: The Ultimate Weapon, Davidow, William H. and Uttal, Bro, Harper & Row Publishers, 1989.

"Customer Surveys—Differentiating Yourself from the Competition," *NOMDA Spokesman*, Farber, Barry J., January 1991.

"Increase Your Sales with Customer Satisfaction Surveys," *Personal Selling Power*, Farber, Barry J., Jan/Feb 1990.

"Surveys that Help You Sell," *Success*, Farber, Barry J., May 1990.

Personal Selling Power, "Harvey Mackay," Gschwandtner, Gerhard, Oct., 1989.

"Twenty Propositions About Service," Speech to the International Customer Service Association, Peters, Tom, Tom Peters Group, 1988.

Chapter 10

Conceptual Blockbusting, A Guide to Better Ideas, Second Edition, Adams, James L., W. W. Norton & Company, 1979.

"The Characterization of the Phase 11 Salesperson from the Viewpoint of Sales Training Executives." Business Dynamics, Inc. Prepared for the Pecos River Learning Center, 1988.

Changing the Game: A New Way to Sell, A Fireside Book, Wilson, Larry, Simon & Schuster, 1987.

Chapter 11

Managing People, Lane, Byron, Oasis Press, 1985.

Chapter 12

The Insiders Guide to Book Editors and Publishers, 1990-1991, Who They Are! What They Want! And How to Win Them Over!, Herman, Jeff, Prima Publishing & Communications, 1990.

Index

About the Author

Barry J. Farber is the president of Farber Training Systems, Inc. Over the past two decades, he has achieved personal success in sales, training and management. He has extensively researched top achievers in a variety of professions. As an author, speaker and entrepreneur, Barry J. Farber educates, inspires and motivates others to success with his own cutting-edge, real-world personal achievement strategies.

Farber attracted national attention with his audiocassette series, *State of the Art Selling*, which has become the top-selling new sales program distributed by Nightingale-Conant Corporation.

Farber regularly motivates audiences as a keynote speaker on the lecture circuit. He also conducts sales training, sales management, train-the-trainer and personal development workshops. Debra Sieckman, director of sales development for Allied Van Lines, says Farber's presentation was "the highest rated program out of over 50 speakers during the past five years." Joe Helms, sales manager of Oasys, comments, "Two words that immediately come to mind to describe the workshop are realistic and useful." Mark Sutherland, vice president of Carolina Ribbon, says Farber's program "will help

us... tomorrow, next month and for years to come."

Farber has shared his insights on personal achievement on CBS, NBC, CNBC, CNN and many other radio and television shows. He has written articles for leading personal development magazines including, Success, Entrepreneur, Training Magazine, and Sales and Marketing Management. As president of Farber Training Systems, Inc., he has been responsible for training thousands of sales people, managers and entrepreneurs. Clients include AT&T, Minolta, Schering-Plough, Val-Pak, Weaver Popcorn, Allied Van Lines and many other Fortune 500 companies.

His soon-to-be released book *Diamond in the Rough*, published by Putnam Berkley Publishing Group, tells how to discover hidden talents and reach peak performance with mind and body. It is an educational and inspirational look at the endless possibilities of the human mind and spirit, plus how to make these possibilities work in real-life.

Barry J. Farber can be reached for keynote speeches, seminars, workshops, audio programs and other materials by calling or writing to the address on the next page.

About the Author

Farber Training Systems, Inc.
250 Ridgedale Avenue
Suite Q5
Florham Park, NJ 07932
Phone: 201-966-6500
Fax: 201-966-6524

For further information please complete this form and mail or fax it to the address above and you will be sent free information regarding Barry J. Farber's products and services.

NAME: _____

TITLE: _____

COMPANY: _____

ADDRESS: _____

CITY, STATE, ZIP: _____

PHONE # _____

FAX #: _____

NOW YOU CAN LISTEN TO
STATE OF THE ART SELLING
ON AUDIOCASSETTES . . . AND SAVE $20!

Barry Farber is a state-of-the-art sales pro. His proven selling tactics are the same effective, tested methods he's used in his own career. And now, if you've enjoyed reading Barry Farber's book, *State Of The Art Selling*, you have the opportunity to reinforce -- again and again -- all of Barry's cutting-edge selling ideas by listening to them on audiocassette in your car, at home or even while exercising!

You'll hear Barry, in his own words and with his dynamic, uplifting voice, detail the techniques and secrets of America's top-producing sales superstars. And with a guidebook and exercises at the end of each audiocassette side, you get the practical tools you need to put the

Six Audiocassettes plus Guidebook
10490A $39.95   (Regular retail price $59.95)

attitudes, attributes and actual skills of these sales giants to work for you -- right away!

Listen as Barry shows that real selling is a natural, non-manipulative act based on relationships, trust -- and most importantly -- offering customers solutions to their problems. And because you've already experienced Barry's insight in his book, we're offering you his audio program for only $39.95 -- that's $20.00 off the regular retail price! With the ideas and insight you'll take away from this high-energy, information-packed audiocassette program, you'll see your sales start rising rapidly!

To Order, Call Toll-Free 1-800-525-9000
or Fax Your Order To (708) 647-7145

NAME_____

COMPANY_____

ADDRESS_____

CITY_____STATE_____ZIP_____

Or send to: Nightingale-Conant Corporation, 7300 North Lehigh Avenue, Niles, Illinois 60714
DHCKFAQ